UNITED COLLEGE LIBRARY
DISCARDED
823.09
W519

The Invisible World

THE INVISIBLE WORLD

A STUDY OF PNEUMATOLOGY IN ELIZABETHAN DRAMA

by

ROBERT HUNTER WEST

UNIVERSITY OF GEORGIA PRESS
ATHENS, GEORGIA

PRINTED IN THE UNITED STATES OF AMERICA

To

O. W. AND S. H. W.

Preface

OF THE MANY possible approaches to Elizabethan drama one of the most favored among scholars in the last ten years has been that which seeks to recover the contemporary attitude toward the plays themselves and toward the things with which the plays deal. Among the latter, sixteenth century spiritualism has been prominent for the attention accorded it by such scholars as Miss Lily Bess Campbell, and Professors J. Dover Wilson and W. C. Curry. They have elucidated the principles and details of Elizabethan spirit doctrine and applied them to interpretation of the play action in a fashion rarely attempted since the publication in 1880 of T. A. Spalding's *Elizabethan Demonology*. Investigators like Herford in his *Literary Relations of England and Germany in the Sixteenth Century* have touched on the history of such subjects as witchcraft, and others like H. W. Herrington and Charles E. Whitmore have dealt with the literary conventions, but the actual doctrine of spirits remained comparatively untouched in the period between Spalding's work and Wilson's first investigations of the nature of Hamlet's ghost.

In his original essay on the ghost in *Hamlet* Professor Wilson intimated in passing that a similar scrutiny of ghosts in the plays of Shakespeare's contemporaries—"saturated with the . . . ghost-lore of the time"—might be worth the effort. Such a scrutiny, though less detailed than Mr. Wilson's of *Hamlet,* I have attempted—not only of the ghosts but of the closely related daemonic figures and of the human pursuits, ceremonial magic and witchcraft, that depended upon them.

My aim has not been to detect sources or check dramaturgical method (though these things I may occasionally seem to do) but simply to uncover the *sense* of the dialogue and action concerned with spirits. For such investigation in a great number of plays exceedingly diverse in kind and separated in time some from others by almost half a century, I have had to adopt a method rather more rigid than comports with the strictest regard for the integrity of the play as such. I have tried, however, to remember that the action of a play can never be taken as though it were action in the outer world.

My assumptions are four:

1) That the most cogent interpretation of pneumatology in a sixteenth century play will be that of the sixteenth century. I do not wish to decry other interpretations. But I am not concerned with them.

2) That the spirit action in a play may legitimately be subjected to interpretation by doctrine much more formal and exact than anything the dramatist need be supposed to have drawn upon directly. I do not attempt to read pneumatology into the plays as of the author's intending, but simply as an understanding of the play action possible or probable to the sixteenth century spectator. My attempt is not to say 'from this pneumatology the play draws,' but 'to this pneumatology the play perhaps appeals.'

3) That play actions may be taken as relating only to one another and to an implicit background with which they compose a world that is distinct from the actual world, yet which by virtue of a certain resemblance is comprehensible in part in terms of the actual world. I do not, however, deny the government of play action by literary convention, a thing not subject to the fiction of the play world nor to any correlation of play world with actual world.

4) That the play world sometimes displays what the actual world never surely does: a certain and consistent adherence to one kind of spirit doctrine. I acknowledge, though, that few plays are to be tagged as of any specific scheme, whether it be Protestant, Catholic, Neo-Platonic, rationalistic, or what not. Professor Curry has demonstrated that two of Shakespeare's plays have recognizable and integrated philosophical patterns. Some plays of Shakespeare's contemporaries are so perfected, in their pneumatology at least; but not many.

If these assumptions seem bold, I can only say that I believe them implicit in the interpretations of many critics who have not thought fit to declare them openly or to proceed on them to what seems to me a logical extent.

In his *History of English Dramatic Literature,* Sir Adolphus W. Ward says that in a consideration of *Faustus* it is as absurd to try to fix Mephistophilis' precise rank in the hierarchy of hell as to try it for his namesake in Goethe. Of this judgment there can be no reasonable question. But it is a sound one not because Marlowe's work and Goethe's are of a kind in their treatment of devils, but because the English play simply does not appeal to so particular an item of daemonology as Mephistophilis' exact rank. Of its quite literal appeal to many general articles of daemonology there can hardly be a doubt. To the value of explicating these articles Professor Ward's annotations of the text sufficiently testify. My aim is to expand such annotations for *Faustus* and other plays and to integrate them with a running analysis of the action.

I do not profess completeness. Shakespeare I treat only in collateral reference. His plays require and have received from Wilson, Curry, Miss Campbell, and others, special and extensive consideration. Nor do I attempt to list, much less to discuss, every daemon and ghost-figure in Elizabethan drama. The exhaustive list may be found in such works as Ankenbrand's *Die Figur des Geistes in Drama die Englischen Renaissance.*

I have been told that spirit lore in the sixteenth century was vestigial, that the attention of the student of the time should be devoted to the new, strong tendencies foreshadowing the future. However this may be, pneumatology in the sixteenth century was not a thing which many people ignored. Some men were incredulous, a few indifferent; but many believed ardently and all had at least a passing acquaintance with its terms and tenets. If pneumatology was an anachronism, it was not more an anachronism than belief today in the universe of Newton. Like Newtonian cosmology today, it was in its time the scheme with which most men were best acquainted and the scheme that seemed reasonable. True, as we can see now, the tide was setting away from the old pneumatology; but in the sixteenth century viewed alone the ebb is slight.

It is fruitless, however, to try to establish just how prominent pneumatology was in sixteenth century England. No one can know, every one has heard surmise, any one may make his own estimate from the body of its literature. It is enough for me that pneumatology was a living element in both the theology and the literature of the time. To apply contemporary theory of spirits to elucidation of the terms and action of spirit scenes in plays may conceivably contribute to our understanding of the plays.

The most searching and accurate use of pneumatological material in Elizabethan drama is probably Shakespeare's. The work of Curry, Wilson, and Miss Campbell proves how close-woven are *Hamlet* and *Macbeth* and *The Tempest* in their treatment of spirits. It may or may not be significant of the inherent worth of such material for sixteenth century drama that also Shakespeare's was the most extensive use of it. He employed it integrally and fully, not ornamentally or incidentally, in three of his greatest plays.

My approach to pneumatology is that of an acknowledged amateur, and to the study of pneumatological doctrine or of its history I make no attempt to contribute. I certainly do not profess to have read exhaustively in sixteenth century pneumatology, a nearly inexhaustible subject. I have sought, however, to have specific, quotable substantiation in source texts for all my major points. I have tried, too, to take account of the varying authority, for my purposes, of works very diverse in time, place, language, and distribution. Particularly I have sought to avoid interpreting any play out of a treatise which it antedated, except when I had positive knowledge that the general doctrine concerned was older than either.

I have, of course, always taken final authority for readings in pneumatological works from sixteenth century editions when these were available to me. I have preferred sixteenth century English translations to the originals of foreign works, otherwise have rated Latin, French, and German contemporary versions in that order. Reliable modern English translations such as those edited by the Rev. Montague Summers I have used extensively—the more that some of them are of books too rare to be otherwise accessible to me.

Perhaps I ought to record here that I am not trying, as Mr. Summers has been accused of trying, to "bring back the witch-panic." Emphatically I am not the advocate of any of the witch doctrines I set forth. On the other hand, there is certainly no reason for me to be here an advocate of rationalism. If I withhold my puny reprimand from the witchmongers and my bit of praise from forward-looking Reginald Scot and John Wier, it is not necessarily because I am of what seem Mr. Summers' opinions about them, but because my purpose is merely to apply their doctrines to contemporary literature, by no means to evaluate those doctrines in the light of either theology or history.

For assistance in getting materials for this study, I have to thank the staffs of the Vanderbilt University and University of Georgia libraries, and especially Miss Louise Hollingsworth. I owe gratitude also to the staffs of the William Rainy Harper Memorial Library of the University of Chicago, of the John Crerar Library, of the Newberry Library, and of the Folger Shakespeare Library. I am indebted, too, to the Andrew D. White Library of Cornell for the loan of a rare volume.

For their kindness in reading the manuscript and for valuable criticisms, I wish to thank Mr. Donald Davidson of Vanderbilt University, Mr. Thomas J. Stritch of the University of Notre Dame, Dr. Edd Winfield Parks of the University of Georgia, and above all Dr. Walter Clyde Curry of Vanderbilt, who to his many suggestions and an indispensable encouragement added the loan of copious notes on Patristic and medieval demonology.

July 23, 1939 R. H. W.

Acknowledgments to Publishers

For kind permission to quote various materials as here indicated, I have to thank the following publishers and copyright holders: Mr. John Rodker for extensive quotations from the volumes of The Church and Witchcraft Series, edited by the Rev. Montague Summers; Messrs. Burns Oates and Washbourne, Limited, and the Fathers of the English Dominican Province for quotations from the *Summa Theologica* of St. Thomas Aquinas; the Oxford University Press for material from *The Sources of the Faust Tradition* by P. M. Palmer and R. P. More and from *The Complete Works of John Webster,* edited by F. S. Lucas; the Clarendon Press for lines from a play in *The Shakespeare Apocrypha,* edited by C. F. Tucker Brooke; the Fortune Press for extracts from Taillepied's *A Treatise of Ghosts* as edited and translated by the Rev. Montague Summers; Methuen and Company, Limited, and Mr. F. S. Boas for quotations from Mr. Boas' edition of *Dr. Faustus;* E. P. Dutton and Company, Incorporated, for lines from Dr. T. M. Parrott's edition of George Chapman's *Complete Dramatic Works,* Volume I; and finally Charles Scribner's Sons and Ernest Benn, Limited, for some material from the Mermaid Edition of Dekker's plays.

R. H. W.

Table of Contents

THE LITERATURE AND BACKGROUND OF SIXTEENTH CENTURY PNEUMATOLOGY

PNEUMATOLOGY IN ELIZABETHAN PLAYS

Literature and Background of Sixteenth Century Pneumatology

Chapter I

The Basic Terms and Principal Authors

I

IN THE YEAR 1607, while *Macbeth* was perhaps on the stage in London, the Courts of Assizes of the adjacent county of Essex returned nine indictments for witchcraft, the celebrated occultist Dr. John Dee was still experimenting with his spirit stone, and a daemonologist sat on the throne of England. The learned Ben Jonson owned a manuscript of magical ceremonies, and the yet more learned Francis Bacon had gravely scribbled the margins of a work on how devils deluded old women. It was to be more than a hundred years yet before an academic history of witchcraft, as of a superstition whose time was out, would be written in England, and seventy before the bastions of the witch belief would begin to disintegrate under the pounding of John Webster. The good Sir Thomas Browne, a child of two in 1607, was mature and reputed a wise man when he wrote: "I have ever believed, and do now know, that there are witches. They that doubt of these do not only deny them, but spirits; and are obliquely, and upon consequence, a sort, not of infidels, but atheists." [1]

That Ben Jonson ever seriously performed the rites his manuscript detailed, or that the pious if gullible Dee was guilty of black magic is improbable. That King James, for all his *Daemonologie in Three Books,* was a pedantic monster who stimulated persecution of witches in England has been disproved; and that Shakespeare believed in the spirits he wrote of has been denied. But it cannot be denied that in 1607 Englishmen—even cultivated Englishmen—were seriously aware in a way that we are not of an invisible world about them, and that they spent an appreciable share of their time thinking and writing on spirits and on those affairs of men in which spirits were believed to join.[2] The courtier who in 1606 or 1607 saw *Macbeth* on the stage, or in the same years *The Devil's Charter* or *The Atheist's Tragedy* or *Bussy D'Ambois,* had perhaps a rather detailed understanding of scenes that in themselves are as vague to us now as the sword play in *Hamlet*. It is not likely that King James' courtiers interpreted spirit scenes by childhood impressions from Grimm's fairy tales, as has many a critic in the nineteenth and twentieth centuries. They knew rather more definitely than did editors two hundred years later what such things as *spirits, witches,* and *magicians* were conceived to be. These are terms that have nowadays only figurative or historical signification; but in 1607, as for centuries before and for generations to come, they or their equivalents were part of a universal faith that was, perhaps, as close to the people as technology is to us. There were those who knew little and those who knew much of it; there were those who rejoiced in it and those who fretted against it. But there were few or none whom it did not touch.

A later century was to characterize this faith as *animistic,*[3] for its fundamental article was that behind or within sensible things existed certain supra-sensible living essences which, in the order of God's providence, sometimes wielded the materials of the physical world though distinct and separate from them all. These animating essences, called spirits, were of two kinds: *souls,* which were spirits vitalizing or withdrawn from bodies; and *angels,* otherwise *daemons,*[4] which were spirits unattached, even by history, to vitalized bodies. All unbodied spirits—that is, daemons and souls of the dead—were conceived to inhabit non-spatial realms suitable to their natures, but to apply their powers sometimes also to the corporeal world and even occasionally to be represented by some temporary sensible form.[5] As beings existing in a grade above the elementary, they were believed God's agents for the suspension and redirection or perhaps even the constant control of nature's normal courses, and to them man could address himself by means of magic.

Of magic dealing with spirits Shakespeare's contemporaries made two main divisions: ceremonial magic and witchcraft.[6] Ceremonial magic was, roughly, the manipulation by a proper operator of certain occult and divine properties in things to attract, and perhaps to coerce, unbodied spirits. Of this magic there were—in the intention of the operator, at least—two sorts: white, which tried to identify itself with Christian worship; and black, which frankly made concessions to damned spirits. Distinct from both white and black magic was witchcraft, which was complete abandonment to damned spirits, a deliberate and unreserved worship by bargain of the devil and his demons for worldly ends.[7]

Of these activities and of spirits there were many rationales in Elizabeth's day—some extravagant, some sober, some scoffing. Almost invariably they contained the proposition that to God all things are possible; but tacitly they recognized a qualified actualization in conformity with an eternal plan God had set for Himself to act by. There were no marvels that *a priori* could not occur; this was the ground of credulity. But there was an order to the world; and man's acquaintance with this order through revelation, experience, and reason restricted credulity to the confines of coherent surmise. As regarded unbodied spirits, such surmise touched three broad questions: do they act in the temporal world at all? What is the nature of those that do? What commerce can man have with them?

To these questions Elizabethans made answers of three general kinds: occult, which elaborated the arbitrary powers of spirits in the world and secret means of man's access to them; orthodox, which accepted on authority all spirit wonders not subversive of doctrine; and rationalistic, which tended to find sufficient explanation of every earthly event in a cause of its own category, confined the unbodied spirit to its own sphere.[8]

These interpretations comprised clusters of general ideas that existed in varying focus in the consciousness of men, and which medieval and Renaissance thinkers systematized into bodies of theory which the late seventeenth century was to call *pneumatology*.[9] Ideally, the literature of pneumatology was deliberate rationalization that by checking one datum against another, and all against the more general findings of theology and philosophy, acquired and applied a set of concepts for explaining, testing, and provoking spirit marvels. Actually, of course, the literature of pneumatology was rarely so cool and judicial as the ideal required. Its verdicts, nevertheless, were reasoned and inclusive; it is in their light, perhaps, that the terms and figures of Elizabethan animism take on the full intellectual meaning they could have had for Elizabethans.

It is safe, perhaps, to assume that the Elizabethan plays that use the terms and present the figures of animism draw from common sources with pneumatology—if not from pneumatology itself—and that consequently implicit in the action of such plays, though perhaps not single and consistent, is a pneumatological rationale of one sort or another. Ben Jonson and Francis Bacon, and the judge who sentenced witches, and the courtier who resorted to Dr. Dee or read the *Daemonologie,* and many hundreds besides them, knew the theory of spirits. That they applied it to the action of *Faustus* and *Macbeth* and *The Tempest* there can be hardly a doubt. Nor can there be much doubt that, within degrees proper to works of art, and each in its own way, these plays and others accommodate it.[10]

II

A critic of Professor Dover Wilson's exposition of the ghost scenes in *Hamlet* has expressed doubt as to whether Shakespeare and his contemporaries were sharply aware of the distinctions Professor Wilson makes between the Protestant dogma on ghosts and the Catholic dogma, and between them both and a rationalistic stand.[11] It may be as well questioned, of course, whether these same Englishmen knew any clear difference between occult, orthodox, and rationalistic views on daemons and on magic. The only affirmative answer possible is that whether the average educated Englishman of the sixteenth century did know the difference or not, he might have, for the distinctions between the three schools of thought were clear in many books available to him and in not a few explicit.

It is true that the sixteenth century was in possession of pneumatological doctrines bewilderingly diverse, and many vague and contradictory; it is true, too, as Professor Wilson's critic asserts,[12] that to the Elizabethan audience of *Hamlet* conflicting hypotheses might be simultaneously present and the play action force no choice. But there is little in the literature of pneumatology to foster doubt that Elizabethans understood not only specific differences in doctrine, but the significance of those differences for a rationale of the whole. That the pneumatological rationale in *Hamlet* is less positive than that in a witch tract affords no certainty that Elizabethans missed it, or that Professor Wilson is straining the text to suit an analysis unimagined by Elizabethans.

The evidence for their clear awareness of the distinctions between occult, orthodox, and rationalistic views on spirits lies chiefly in the special pneumatological treatises of their day. The sixteenth century was flood time of this literature whose particular business it was, in part, to make such distinctions, to label according to sect and trend the myriad doctrines of pneumatology.

Needless to say, the authoritative labels were those applied by the established churches. It is in the orthodox treatises that dogmas, both ancient and contemporary, are explicitly stamped as acceptable, or as superstitious or atheistic. The last two appellations occultists and rationalists were, of course, reluctant to apply to their own beliefs. They preferred to herd with the orthodox in name at least. But of the three general orders of spirit doctrine, however called, few could be ignorant who read such works as Le Loyer's *Treatise of Specters*.

If one may judge from this literature, the theory by means of which the Elizabethan Englishman explained animistic phenomena to himself had its evolutionary source in the doctrines of the ancient and medieval world, and was, further, conspicuously supplied by the very substance of those doctrines. Constant appeal to the past for authority of scripture or of the early church or of classical or scholastic authors is characteristic of the period's polemical and expository writings on spirits.[13] An Elizabethan Englishman might have acquaintance with animistic doctrine in any of its historical stages, and he viewed it not historically as a thing evolutionary and conditioned, but flatly—as a thing whose value was absolute, either index to truth or monument to error. Says *Orthodoxus* gravely in an English dialogue on demonic possession: "Antiquity (how gray-headed soeuer) hath no privilege to errour." [14]

It is generally true, perhaps, that despite the importunity of the pagan past almost every serious pneumatological theory in Renaissance Europe had a Christian stamp. But it is equally true that a great body of opinion was so colored by the past as to be highly unorthodox in a time when Christian orthodoxy was both various and rigid. The courtier who dabbled in the occult, or the philosopher who was half scientist and half magician, might derive his convictions as directly from Neo-Platonic theurgists as from Scholastics or their Protestant successors. Such men as Cornelius Agrippa in the sixteenth century and Robert Fludd early in the next were seldom hesitant about diluting the doctrines of Christianity with those of antiquity.

Most ancient writers on whom such occultists relied for theory (as distinct from examples) of spirits' work in the world were Platonists. Plato's doctrine of separable form and his hints in the *Timaeus* at a hierarchy of spiritual forces, were philosophic ground to most of those ideas of daemonic mediators between the Supreme and man which were rife in the Mediterranean world and became dazzlingly attractive to the Renaissance scholar. It is true that in Renaissance literature of spirits, references to Plato himself are comparatively rare; but on his easier and more sensational followers, and on mythical seers like Trismegistus who were one with them in manner and general doctrine, there is no end of reliance. Ficino had translated the Hermetic Books and the Orphic Hymns and the somewhat more reliably attributed works of the Neo-Platonic hierophants, Iamblichus and Proclus, and their tenth century Byzantine commentator Michael Psellus.[15] To them Renaissance daemonologists were indebted for the doctrines of theurgy and for the much assailed but persistent classification of daemons according to the elements. Less fanciful Neo-Platonists, such as Plotinus and Porphyry, contributed much, of course, to that general conception of the universe as organic which made sympathetic magic plausible.

Earlier and somewhat less formidable Platonists than the Alexandreans, but also important to daemonology in the sixteenth century, were Plutarch and Apuleius. Plutarch's *Essays,* translated into English in 1603, included much theorizing which Alexandrean Neo-Platonists and after them Christians were to borrow. Particularly important were the essays *De defectu oraculorum* and *De genio Socratis.* Apuleius, also, has a short work on the daemon of Socrates, in which he sets forth "that doctrine of daemonic beings which lies at the heart of ancient religion . . . from Plutarch onwards." [16] Often cited, too, in the Renaissance were passages from Apuleius' *Apology,* in which he says he thinks with Plato that there are between gods and men powers that preside over the miracles of magicians.

Excepting, however, men like Robert Fludd, to whom the esoteric had a special attraction, it is probably true that English animists were more directly supplied by classical literature's fund of illustrations than by its express doctrines. The orthodox cite Apuleius' famous definition of spirits more often to refute him than to use him. But Apuleius and Plutarch had written not only works on the daemon of Socrates, but also the *Lives* and *The Golden Ass*—narrative stored with tales of magic and of spirits. These stories pneumatologists of all persuasions retailed constantly, twisting interpretation to meet their own needs. Equally levied upon, of course, were Hesiod, Lucan, Pliny, Suetonius, Virgil, and a dozen other literary men of Greece and Rome.

But of course for the sixteenth century the truly universal and irreproachable source of such material was the Bible. Pharoah's magicians, the Witch of Endor, the daemonic possessions in the New Testament—these things, and many like them if less famous, were instances which there was no gainsaying of magic and spirits. The Bible indicated, too—if certain assumptions were made—their explanation: the kingdom of evil whose father was that Adversary that afflicted Job, tempted Adam and Eve as the Serpent, had once been Lucifer, the morning star, flung from heaven. And the Bible gave the law which the sixteenth century so dreadfully interpreted: Thou shalt not suffer a witch to live.

From the accepted books it was but a step to the *Apocrypha* and the story of the demon, Asmodeus, and that of the sons of God who defiled themselves with the daughters of men and begat giants and demons.[17] And beyond this doubtfully scriptural material lay all the marvels of the legend and history of Christianity—Simon Magus, who bargained for the power of the Apostles and was damned; Cyprian, the necromancer who repented and suffered a martyr's death; Theophilus, whom the Virgin released from covenant with Satan. . . .[18]

Each of these tales of magic and spirits required, of course, interpretation in the light of general doctrine. To them all the occultist applied, so far as he dared, the same semi-pagan explanations he put upon similar ethnic fables. The rationalist, on his part, denied what he could, attributed the rest to a special miraculous order of things which God had terminated with Apostolic times. For the orthodox there remained the Patristic and Scholastic close-knit, dogmatic articulation of spirit tales with fundamental doctrine. In the sixteenth century St. Augustine was a basic authority for both Protestants and Catholics, and Aquinas perhaps the most nearly final authority for Catholics.[19] Protestant doctrine varied from Aquinas' only in some special points, not at all on the fundamentals of the reason and method of daemonic action in the world.

III

Probably the most inclusive, and, at the same time, perhaps the most generally known special expositions of pneumatology in the sixteenth century were the polemics on witchcraft and ghosts.[20] In them are collected for confirmation or refutation, sometimes in quotation, more often in simplified restatement and hasty reference, almost all the pertinent tenets of philosophy and religion, illustrated by the tales and fables of literature and folklore. Frequently enough these treatises, even more contentious than compendious, serve hostile authorities poorly in exposition of their views—and often friendly authorities, especially if abstruse, little better. Many of the polemics, on the other hand, were written by men of great learning and ability. If they seem often to over-simplify their doctrine, it is because their primary aim is to make converts, so that they speak in the most direct terms possible.

Related to the polemical works in subject matter, but severed from them in compositional point of view and not so openly disseminated, were treatises and manuals on magic. These were scholarly or professional in tone rather than argumentative. Suspect as to intention and select in audience, they frequently, for the uninitiate, obscure rather than clarify their matter. They render complex what the polemics simplify, are esoteric as the polemics are democratic.

Most of the special sixteenth century literature on pneumatology falls into three general classes: polemic on spectres; theoretical and practical treatments of ceremonial magic; polemic on witchcraft. Of these the last was the most considerable in bulk and the most inclusive in subject.

The witchcraft controversy, so far as it was a thing peculiar to the sixteenth century, may be said to have opened in 1563 with the publication of *De Praestigiis Daemonum et incantationibus ac veneficiis* by the German physician, Johannes Wier. The book was inspired, apparently, by humanitarian motives, but grounded its argument against persecution of witches upon the theological plea that there were no genuine witches. Devils, it contended, performed of their own wills the crimes attributed to witches and contrived to lay the blame upon friendless women and weak persons and even to induce them to believe and confess themselves guilty. Wier's book had considerable currency. Three editions were published before 1564, and there was a French translation in 1569 that included a sixth book added to the previous five.[21]

The principal work in the field when Wier published was the *Malleus Maleficarum* of the Inquisitors, Sprenger and Institor, which had appeared late in the preceding century and heralded the opening of the witch mania.[22] It was the primary authority of the time on witches and their wickedness and apprehension. To its assistance against Wier and his allies came before the end of the sixteenth century dozens of treatises of varying size and importance written by churchmen and doctors and magistrates, some of whom, as they said, had tried and heard confess hundreds of witches. Nicholas Remy and Henri Boguet were prominent French judges who had been on the bench in scores of witch cases. In the last decade of the century they published works exposing witchcraft; their fellow, Pierre de Lancre, did the same in 1610.[23]

Peter Binsfield, suffragan bishop of Treves, was a churchman who had used plenary powers against witches to half depopulate his diocese. His *De Confessionibus maleficorum* is cited by a later English writer as the work on witchcraft most pleasing to Catholics.[24] A continental Protestant authority was Lambert Daneau, whose *Les Sorcières* was translated into English as *A Dialogue of Witches* in 1575, a year after its French publication.[25]

But perhaps most compendious and influential of orthodox works was *La Demonomanie des Sorciers* by the famous jurist, Jean Bodin. Though his work did not appear until 1580, it replied directly to Wier.[26] It iterates learnedly the orthodox views of dozens of authorities, pagan and Christian, and adds for good measure a few views of Bodin's own which the Sorbonne did not swallow with the best grace. It accuses Wier of being himself a witch.

Bodin was answered from England in 1584 by the Kentish squire, Reginald Scot, in his famous *Discoverie of Witchcraft.* The discovery that Scot proffered of witchcraft was that it was imposture. Skillfully using his and England's Protestantism—he says that he writes against the massmonger as well as the witchmonger—to shield himself and his doctrine, he attacks belief in witchcraft and magic at its root by denying altogether the participation of unbodied spirits in the sensible world. To his sixteen books and an appended *Discourse of Devils and Spirits,* King James of Scotland replied briefly in 1597, calling Scot a Sadducee and Wier a witch and setting forth a severely simplified doctrine of demons.[27]

Besides James and Scot there were many less celebrated British writers on witchcraft. Their works, like that of James, are, on the whole, marked by a certain insularity. Though within the general European tradition and expounding a demonology closely related and often indebted to that of the continent, they seem soberer, more homely, than the contemporary French, Teutonic, and Italian authors. Most of them were ministers. George Gifford, an Essex preacher, issued two works, in 1587 and 1593, in which he assumed Wier's position with some modifications.[28] In general opposed was the eminent Cambridge theologian and preacher, William Perkins, whose sermon, *A Discourse of the Damned Art of Witchcraft,* was published posthumously in 1608.[29] It is, perhaps, the clearest and most cogently reasoned of all the English treatises. John Cotta, a physician, also of Cambridge, exerted himself in his *Tryall of Witchcraft* published in 1616, to improve the methods for the identification of witches in order that diseased persons might not be mistakenly prosecuted.[30]

2

It was impossible to write extensively on witchcraft without touching on the kindred subject of ceremonial magic, and almost all the eristics did treat of it. The most considerable work on magic of every sort was the *Disquisitionum Magicarum* of the Jesuit, Martin Delrio. It pushes with a creeping dialectical treatment through a multitudinous array of questions on all kinds of spirit dealing.[31] Delrio and his allies had reason to treat ceremonial magic the more fully because such magic—unlike witchcraft, which was an occupation of the ignorant and the destitute—had a literature of its own, advancing claims and contentions that required answer. This literature was of two not very clearly distinguished sorts: treatises more or less academic, expounding the theory of magic; manuals, not at all academic, detailing the *modus operandi* of magic.

Of the first sort the most celebrated written within the sixteenth century and the most excoriated by the witchmongers was the *De Occulta Philosophia* of the German savant, Henry Cornelius Agrippa von Nettesheim. It was written about 1510, but the second and third of its three books were not published until 1533, although pirated and distorted versions had apparently circulated for some years before this date.[32] It treated of Natural, Mathematical, and Ceremonial magic, of which it made out the last to be the highest and, in its operations, inclusive of the other two. Agrippa recanted and late in life wrote *De Incertitudine et Vanitate Scientiarum et Artium,* published 1532 at Cologne, in which he anathematized magic in a fairly orthodox fashion.[33]

Not so odious as Agrippa to the witchmongers—Bodin refers to him as the greatest philosopher of his age—was Agrippa's stormy contemporary, Paracelsus, who devised and in many treatises expounded, original theories of magic and of spirits.[34] Sometimes accepted, more often denounced, was Agrippa's preceptor, the Abbott Trithemius of Spanheim, who dabbled in all sorts of occult matters and wrote a work on magic called the *Steganographie.*[35] Another preceptor of Agrippa, the great German humanist, Reuchlin, presented an elevated theory of magic as connected with the mystical system of the Jewish Cabala.[36]

All the works on magic of these celebrated men were produced in the early part of the sixteenth century, but persisted as authoritative throughout the century and well into the next. With them belong some of the even earlier works of the Italian mystic, Pico della Mirandola.[37]

Falsely attributed to Agrippa and to others of his notable stamp were the handbooks of practical magic of which many, some new, some survivals, were abroad in the sixteenth century. After Agrippa's death appeared a *Fourth Book of Occult Philosophy* fathered on him despite the objection of his pupil, Wier. It gave instructions for the commanding of good and evil spirits. Like it, but much more circumstantial in its treatment, was the *Heptameron or Magical Elements* ascribed to the fourteenth century pedant, Peter of Abano. Probably forged early in the sixteenth century, it was translated into English in 1600.[38] Also forged, frankly black magic—that is, devil art—was the *Grimoire of Honorius,* "the Constitution of Pope Honorius the Great wherein may be found the Arcane conjurations which must be used against the spirits of darkness."[39] Related to these works were those of the cycle of Solomon, collections of enchantments which, it was claimed, were translated from the Hebrew form in which the wise Solomon had found them efficacious. Chief monuments of this cycle were *Clavicula Salomonis,* the Key of Solomon the King, probably collected in the fourteenth and fifteenth centuries, and the *Lemegeton* or Lesser Key of Solomon. The Solomonic cycle was held to be a part of the "practical" Cabala, wonder working receipts deducible from the esoteric theory of the Cabala.[40]

None of these works on magic directly gainsaid Christian doctrine; most tried to appeal to it as the foundation of their efficacy; yet there was hardly a one but was implicitly inimical to Christianity in its fundamental assumptions.

3

Not so extensive as the special literature on witchcraft and magic was that on ghosts. It was comprised chiefly in two books: the *De Spectris, lemuribus et magnis atque insolitis fragoribus* of Ludvig Lavater, Protestant minister of Tigurine in Switzerland; and the four *Livres des Spectres* of Pierre Le Loyer, a French advocate. Lavater's work appeared in 1570 and an Englishman, R.H., translated it in 1572. Le Loyer published his work in 1586 and the first book was translated into English in 1605 at which time there was also a revised edition of the French.[41] An ally and perhaps a collaborator of Le Loyer's was the Capuchin, Noel Taillepied, who published in 1588 a relatively brief treatise: *Psichologie ou traité de l'apparition des esprits.*

The works on ghosts were more severely denominational than those on witchcraft; for Protestant and Catholic theologians were largely in agreement on witchcraft, but definitely divided on ghosts. Lavater, asserting the Protestant position, denied that the souls of the dead ever returned to the world; they were gone, he said, to either eternal bliss or eternal punishment. Le Loyer and Taillepied reaffirmed the Catholic position that ghosts were sometimes sent to warn or to plead with men or otherwise to minister God's will.

Although the special polemic on this subject was comparatively slight—its slightness was perhaps owing in part to the fact that ghost doctrine was not the occasion of a persecution mania—the question was extensively argued as an incidental point in dogma concerning purgatory and other major tenets.[42] Calvin, and Lavater's father-in-law, Bullinger, and many other Protestant theologians made pronouncements on the ghost question. Most of the witchmongers, both Protestant and Catholic, have digressions on it.

A minor and subsidiary pneumatological controversy which, particularly in England, had a literature of its own was on demonic possession and exorcism. The English church inclined to deny the reality of possession since Biblical times and to condemn ministers who undertook to exorcise persons apparently possessed. In this it joined issue with both Catholics and Puritans. The position of the English church was a most uncertain one, however, for the activity of devils against men it did not deny; therefore some ministers—notably one John Darrel, a Puritan—were undertaking with seeming success to cast out devils. Darrel's pretensions were officially attacked for the Church of England by two preachers, John Deacon and John Walker, who collaborated on two long and weighty works of ten dialogues each, intended to prove Darrel an impostor and to present a proper conception of demonic assaults.[43] Deacon and Walker entered the controversy to the assistance of Samuel Harsnett, who had written in a lighter vein than theirs against Darrel. Harsnett later took part in a similar quarrel against the Jesuit exorcist, Weston.[44]

It is impossible now, of course, to estimate accurately the acquaintance of the populace of Elizabethan England with the special literature of pneumatology, nor does it matter particularly for purposes of this study whether such acquaintance was widespread and thorough or local and slight. That the more general tenets of spirit doctrine were common property is certain; that at least a few educated persons knew some or all of the controversial and esoteric works that refined and integrated the general ideas is equally certain. To such persons the terms and figures of animistic material in the drama might suggest concepts more complete than those of the groundling. To re-establish such concepts now is to relate the spirit episodes of the plays to a definite, if special, phase of that world to which they most naturally refer, the Elizabethan world.

Chapter II

The Controversies on Daemons

I

SIXTEENTH AND SEVENTEENTH century literature of pneumatology is a monument to the last violent strife over what modern authority has come to consider possibly the most misguided theory of the universe ever promulgated—that general, Christianized Platonism of microcosm and macrocosm, of nature and supernature, of body and spirit, matter and intellect, which had perhaps its finest flowering in the Renaissance, withered in the eighteenth century.[1] It is in this vague, elastic, inclusive metaphysics that Elizabethan spirit doctrines—even the orthodox—orient themselves, and it is within its bounds that pneumatological controversies raged. The bounds, though real, were not very confining.

By Queen Elizabeth's time the revival of learning had renewed pagan occultism, the Reformation had split orthodoxy, and a general cracking of dogma and flux of ideas was encouraging that rationalism which acknowledges as little as possible of what is not sensibly verifiable nor, on the face of it, plausible. Further, the witch mania was giving occasion for dispute that in its several phases embraced the whole field of spirit doctrine in a complex, many-sided fray in which the dissensions of orthodox, occult, and rationalistic authorities, Catholic or Protestant or semi-pagan, were numerous and bitter.

The history of western pneumatology after the triumph of

Christianity is part of the history of Catholic doctrine, and records a succession of struggles in which the church toiled powerfully at once to confine the occultist, enlarge the sceptic, and reconcile its own diverse dogmas. Until the Reformation the church was both party and judge to most collisions over pneumatology; even after the Reformation, Catholic doctrine continued the center for contention, and a general Christian orthodoxy remained an arbiter to which all pneumatologists had, nominally at least, to defer. Occult and rationalistic authors ordinarily were voluble in protesting their conformity to Christianity and often even their submission to ecclesiastical authority.[2] Almost as forcibly, too, as the orthodox they felt the need to rest on scripture—though they did not read there what the orthodox did.

This meant, of course, that the battles were fought on the grounds and often even in the style of theological dialectics. It was, perhaps, a barren conflict since it was *in vacuo* and over issues that could not be decided and were presently to die by default. But of the barrenness that was to blight these issues the sixteenth century was unaware; and if it could not decide them, it yet debated them with great energy and sometimes defined them with nice clarity.

On all the data of animism—pagan, Hebraic, and Christian alike—the church had from the earliest times imposed a rigorous exegesis intended to marshal them with fundamental Christian dogma. It had had to block attacks like that of Celsus,[3] and to stifle those paganizing magical practices within the fold which gave Celsus his warrant and menaced the purity of the faith. The Fathers labored to distinguish Christian miracles from pagan magic and to adjust pre-existent ideas of spirits to suit the Christian scheme of creation and providence and salvation. After them most of the theologians of the Middle Ages dealt with much the same problems, and found and restated—with ample acknowledgment and augmented systematization—the solutions of the Fathers.

These solutions were achieved largely by culling and transplanting from a profuse and fluent tangle of pagan and Hebrew ideas. Christian pneumatology's debt to paganism is, of course, unmistakable, and it was this debt that excused Renaissance occultists like Agrippa, who was also a theologian, in their adherence to many Neo-Platonic ideas of spirits. But the drastic paring and regulating of every borrowed tenet was also, after Aquinas, so obvious as to make a sufficiently plain cleavage between orthodox doctrine and occult.

Christian theology was directly concerned with spirits only in their relation to the after life—that is, in the part they bore in man's struggle for heaven. It remodelled to its own special needs borrowed dogmas, both classical and oriental, of the revolt and fall of angels, and of the consequent temptation and fall of man, and the ensuing persecution of man by devils. Christian thinkers from the earliest times wrote on such subjects as the moral responsibility of daemons, the nature of their fall and place of their punishment, the gradations of rank among them, their enlargement from hell to tempt man, and the powers of possession and delusion that were conditions of that temptation.[4] All this daemonology Christianity needed to explain the fundamental dogma of sin.

But Christianity did not need and presently rejected as at best fanciful and superfluous, at worst conducive to false worship, Neo-Platonic ideas about the mortality and materiality of daemons, and about their direction and animation of all nature under otiose deity, and about their classification as seriate gods, and about many another thing important to Proclus and to those who would put Proclus' interpretation on the term *magic*. The daemon remained, of course, in Christian conception as it had been in Neo-Platonic, a supra-sensible personal essence mediate between God and man, and responsive to magic. But the conception of its essence, mediation, and response was new and the emphasis altered. Paganism's emanatory theogonies Christianity translated into terms of God and His angels and man. To this the Renaissance occultist was blind, and of his blindness the orthodox continually complained.

Not quite so evident as the rift between occult and orthodox pneumatology is the break of rationalism with all positive pneumatology, both occult and orthodox. Rationalistic thought about spirits and magic was not new in the sixteenth century; it too had its ancient authorities. But in all times before experimental science shifted the burden of proof from him who denied spirit marvels to him who asserted them, the rationalist could never venture far unless he was willing to become a materialist. This, most ancient doubters had been willing to do; no sixteenth century author could hold their views on spirits without seeming to identify his reasons with theirs. Sixteenth century rationalists often attacked Sadducees, atomists, Sceptics, and even Peripatetics as roundly as did the orthodox, and to the freedom which Lucretius urged preferred a very minor qualification of credulity.[5]

Undoubtedly many Elizabethans had the rationalistic tendency to reject testimony to phenomena that were palpably improbable and undemonstrable, and explanations that ignored natural likelihoods in favor of supernatural hypotheses. But the rationalist could not exercise this tendency much in argument because for his time the limits of natural cause and effect were uncertain, testimony to marvels often unimpeachable, and the existence of the supernatural universally admitted. Most sixteenth century rationalists sought only to abridge the worldly powers credited to spirits, did not deny spirits nor even their occasional entry into temporal affairs. The rationalist's divergence from orthodox pneumatology is not often, therefore, conspicuous enough to approach heresy. The Catholic Church listed John Wier as a dangerous writer, but did not utterly proscribe him; and his English counterpart, George Gifford, was an orthodox minister whose books on witches are kindly spoken of in a rabid witch tract.[6]

The sixteenth century had, nevertheless, a sharp eye for heterodoxy, and undoubtedly it noted the rationalistic bent in men like Wier—even though it did not classify them precisely as do we who know how the next three hundred years was to transform the somewhat feeble doubts they expressed. Wier has been called the first psychiatrist.[7] Elizabethans could not know him as that; but many did know him, as probably they knew Hamlet's friend, Horatio, as a doubter, though never so mild, of spirit phenomena.

II

Disagreement on pneumatology in the sixteenth century usually sprang from interpretation of the four basic phenomena attributed to spirits: phantasmata, prognostics, possession, and prestidigitation. There were five prominent controversies: (1) on how far and under what circumstances spirits could control a man's faculties and reactions; (2) on whether spectres in the likenesses of dead men might be the souls of the men or were always devils counterfeiting them; (3) on whether ceremonial magic in any form was lawful; (4) on whether witches actually participated in and were morally responsible for, the preternatural activities for which the church and state condemned them; (5) on whether unbodied spirits, whether ghosts, angels, or devils, operated at all in the physical world, and if so to what extent and under what license.[8] The ghost issue was raised by Protestant attacks on the doctrines of purgatory and the real presence, and the question of the legitimacy of magic was an ancient one between the church and various schools of esoteric learning and practice—with which the church concurred, however, in affirming against doubters the actuality of human traffic with spirits and the moral responsibility of the human agent. The dispute on the nature and extent of possession raged first between those churches which proclaimed exorcism and those which denied it, and further between the orthodox of all sects and rationalists who, though allowing that the devil could be in men after a fashion, yet qualified the admission too stringently for the popular belief.

A priori to participation in any of the first four controversies was, of course, a stand on the fifth, and it is in preliminary argument that this question of the temporal power of spirits is treated by most of the sixteenth century eristics. Each man moulds to his own polemical ends the time's malleable conception, and the disputants produce so many criss-cross, misallied modifications of doctrine that it is difficult even to name the parties to the controversy.

It may perhaps be said in general that a thorough-going Catholicism entrenched itself with St. Thomas Aquinas and his fellow scholastics in the position that under God's order spirits could and did act overtly in man's world; whereas a somewhat audacious rationalistic Protestantism, grounding on the Reform tendency to deny contemporary miracles,[9] asserted that the activity of unbodied spirits was confined by God to the spiritual realm.

In occupying the latter position Reginald Scot was almost alone among the controversialists. He had support on particular points from the Protestants Gifford, Wier, Deacon and Walker, and even King James. But none of them made Scot's thorough and consistent withdrawal from the Roman dogma. They preferred to acknowledge the continued activity of spirits in the world,though with such reservations as that departed souls were not so active.[10] This reservation in itself seemed to its Protestant defenders to require special insistence on the activity of daemons, for it was as the malignly delusory work of devils or the beneficent representations of angels that phantasms in the likeness of the dead had to be explained if they were accorded any objective existence at all.

It may be said, perhaps, that the question of the participation of spirits in the world hinged first on the conception of the station and function of daemons in God's providence, and that most of the Protestant disputants conformed to the general Catholic doctrine that daemons could and did act corporeally.[11] It was, of course, a difficult matter for empirical demonstration either way. Scot says that spirits are testified to by the weak and fearful who imagine them. But such argument his opponents offset by the equally specious explanation that naturally demons appeared most frequently to those who were receptive, to cowardly or feeble persons who could be easily frightened or tempted. Lavater, confessing that men frequently mistake natural events for work of spirits and that the "melancholike, mad, and fearefull" are most often deceived, yet insists that there is also excellent testimony from the brave and clear-minded to the appearance of spirits.[12]

The testimony which Lavater and his like actually present is for the most part taken from literature, sacred and profane, so that their empirical demonstration is crossed with their demonstration from authority. The dispute on the evidence became simply a matter of interpretation which frequently descended into logomachy. Scot explains that:

> Such as search with the spirit of wisedome and understanding, shall find that spirits, as well good as bad, are in the scriptures diverslie taken: yea they shall well perceive, that the divell is no horned beast. For sometimes in the scriptures, spirits and divels are taken for in-

firmities of the bodie; sometimes for the vices of the mind; sometimes also for the gifts of either of them. Sometimes a man is called a divell, . . . Sometimes a spirit is put for the Gospell; sometimes for the mind or soule of man; sometimes for the will of man, his mind and counsell; sometimes for the teachers and prophets; sometimes for zeale towards God; sometimes for joie in the Holie-ghost, &c.[13]

But these variant and figurative uses were well understood by men who believed that scripture referred also to the temporal activities of superhuman personal beings.[14] Further, the ancients had expressly distinguished between the daemon that was a man's soul or a power of it, and the daemon that was an essential spirit.[15]

The Englishman, John Cotta, makes an attempt to rationalize the problem of empirical demonstration. Man, he says, can come at knowledge of any sort only through experience and reason. Spirits are beyond man's experience except in their works, but their nature and powers can be known by examination of their works and by proper inference from the findings. That a phenomenon is produced by a spirit is clear when it is seen to be "aboue the power and nature of corporall substances." [16]

But Cotta's test fails, of course; for the believer in these works had obviously to assume that they were of spirits before he began to infer from them spirits that could perform them. Preferable, perhaps, is the authoritarian position of the *Malleus Maleficarum,* which says that to assert such works imaginary is "contrary to the true faith which teaches us that certain angels fell from heaven and are now devils, and we are bound to acknowledge that by their very nature they can do many wonderful things which we cannot do." [17]

III

The phenomena ordinarily attributed to spiritual agents were apparitions, transformations, prophecies, omens, premonitions, prestidigital disposition of objects, and incomprehensible ailments and cures. Upon belief in the ability of spirits to occasion such things rested most of the explanation of the wonders of magic and witchcraft; for though it was thought that daemons might act independently, it was also thought that they sometimes acted in conjunction with the will and perhaps at the instigation of human beings.

The powers and functions of daemons were held to vary with daemonic rank and kind—things that were fixed unalterably in the daemonic nature. The simplest and most enduring classification of daemons was that according to moral nature into good and evil spirits.[18] In the sixteenth century, of course, this division appeared usually in a Christian form that separated the two classes not by a diverse original nature, but by a history that included the fall from God's grace and consequent immersion in evil of a part of the heavenly host. This conflicted with the classical pagan division into spirits good and evil by office to which they were eternally assigned, and the peculiar Christian usage of the term *daemon* added to a confusion of concept which survived even to the sixteenth century.

To the philosophers of antiquity δαίμων had signified ordinarily a spirit that, as "a distributor of destiny," [19] might be of a nature either beneficent or malefic. To the fathers, however, daemon ('demon') came to be exclusively an evil, that is fallen, angel, and they inclined to interpret pagan references to daemons according to Christian usage.[20] In the Renaissance, on the other hand, some scholars preferred to apply the pagan meaning to the term, even as employed in Christian works, and to use it so themselves. Cornelius Agrippa, for instance, throughout his *Occult Philosophy* uses the word *daemon* sometimes of good angels, sometimes of devils; consequently leaves it uncertain, in spite of an occasional pious explanation, whether he does not conceive the moral nature of some daemons according to pagan rather than Christian doctrine.[21]

Authors more orthodox than Agrippa found very objectionable this reversion to semi-paganism. Pierre Le Loyer carefully refutes the pagan usage, and Jean Bodin points out that in 1378 the Sorbonne condemned as heretics those who say with the Platonists that there are good daemons; its action, he asserts, was necessary to destroy the excuse of those who invoked devils under the veil of calling them good daemons.[22]

The simple and, it was thought, scripturally apodictic classification into good and evil, fallen and unfallen angels, sufficed most of the witchmongers; but it was vastly elaborated by theologians and philosophers whose opinions the controversialists often mention in passing. It was generally conceded that there was organization of rank among both angels and devils. Boguet, for instance, says simply that theologians are agreed that as among angels there is a hierarchy, so among demons exists a "cacarchy." Remy cites Aquinas as authority that there is rank among demons.[23]

There was a tendency among those treating of magic to arrange the demonic population fancifully into all sorts of kingdoms and courts. Wier, for example, takes, as Robert Burton says, "out of an old book" on magic a complete account of the organization of the court of hell, even down to the station of cup-bearer filled by the demon Behemoth.[24]

But King James rejects the whole idea of rank among demons, saying that they deceive scholars "in imprinting in them the opinion that there are so manie Princes, Dukes, and Kinges amongst them, euerie one commanding fewer or mo legions, and impyring in diuers artes and quarters of the earth." He will not deny, he says, that there was an order among devils before their fall. That it persists no Christian can believe.[25]

He objects as strongly also to the commonly accepted classification of demons according to the elements. The rebellious angels "fel not by weight, as a solid substance" and so into the elements, but "in quality" by loss of the grace of God.[26]

The classification by elements was ordinarily ascribed to the eleventh century Byzantine, Michel Psellos, who had the substance of it from the later Neo-Platonists.[27] The witchmongering Italian priest, Francesco Guazzo, uses it without acknowledgment. There are many kinds of demons, he says, differing among themselves by fixed degree. The first kind is Fiery; "They dwell in the upper air and will never sink to the lower regions until the Day of Judgment and these have no dealings on earth with men." The second kind is Aerial. They live in the air about us, sometimes descend to hell, appear to men, raise tempests. The third sort is Terrestrial and dwells in forests and fields and caverns and sometimes secretly with men. "A fourth sort is of the Water," and they dwell in rivers and seas and cause storms; they usually appear as women. The fifth sort is Subterranean and lives in caves and mines and causes earthquakes. "The sixth sort is called Lucifugous, because they chiefly abhor and detest the light . . . nor can they assume a bodily form except at night." They have no dealings with witches for they kill men with a breath or a touch.[28] Guazzo makes no application whatever of this classification, apparently cites it merely to show off his knowledge. Occultists, who had a use for it, were chary of citing it.

Wier and Scot object to Psellos' classification, Wier on the ground that Psellos was a magician and had his information from an impious and unreliable source, Scot because if "the divell be earthie [of an element] he must needs be palpable," and such he is not since he is spirit.[29]

2

The special nature of daemonic substance was an article of pneumatology frequently cited by all the disputants on daemons, though for diverse ends and usually without much effort to define the substance. Scot insists that as devils are purely spiritual creatures their attacks must be spiritual only, never "temporal." [30] But *Malleus Maleficarum* asserts, on the other hand, that it is precisely because devils are separated spiritual substance that they can work things temporally which are beyond the power of the feebler, earth-encumbered spirit of man.[31]

Most theologians of the sixteenth century, both Protestant and Catholic, were agreed that as to substance daemons were purely spiritual creatures or of a quintessence which was non-material though capable of place, hence in a manner corporeal. The special controversialists on pneumatology usually mention both views, do not always specifically subscribe to either. Bodin, who discusses the matter at greater length than most of his fellows, says that most authorities hold spirits to be pure form, and that as for himself he follows Augustine in accepting the definition of daemons made by the Platonist Apuleius,[32] but with the reservation that the aerial body ascribed to them is a thing "contrary to the nature of spirits, who are pure intelligences." In order to avoid the absurdity of conceiving spirits as corruptible, which they must be if of the elements, Bodin will simply say that demons are of a quintessence as it is said of the sky.[33]

But Bodin and the other witchmongers seemed to feel no need to labor the point of the non-materiality of demons beyond what was necessary to accredit them as possessors of certain superhuman faculties. Remy says that "all theologians are in perfect agreement . . . that after their fall and apostasy, the demons retained their natural qualities intact, which are immortality, power, motion, speed, knowledge, and other such gifts which were theirs from their origin." [34] Remy does not elaborate, but the *power* to which he refers was undoubtedly that to move bodies locally without union; the *motion,* that local motion of the angelic being which Aquinas explains as simply the transfer of the angelic power from one place to another, and by no means a substantial progression through magnitudes; the *speed,* the angelic ability to make such transfer almost instantaneously; and the *knowledge,* the innate acquaintance of angels with the species of all things inferior to them.[35]

By means of these superhuman gifts, it was held, spirits achieved the wonders of their ministry in the world. Their works were of two sorts: (1) those in which the presence of the spirit was manifest and (2) those in which it was latent. Of the first sort were apparitions and preternatural sounds and demonic possession. Of the second were augury and omen, lycanthropy, and invisibly performed wonders of magic.

That spirits could make a manifest answer to the invitation of a devotee was one of the first articles of witchcraft and magic. Remy explains, and his peers agree, that demons might by virtue of "their fluency and rapid dexterity" in manipulation of the elements take bodies of condensed air like clouds, or of fire.[36] Such bodies, says Guazzo, are palpable as though of flesh, "and to these they can impart motion and heat at their will." [37] Boguet explains that from these bodies spirits are able to speak audibly to men by the agitation and vibration of the air after the fashion of an echo.[38]

Of all this Scot is boldly scornful. He repeatedly denies

that an extrinsic spirit, in itself super-sensible, can connect itself with the sensation of an animal being, and he tries to convict his opponents of materialism.

> Some hold opinion, that spirits and soules assume & take unto them bodies at their pleasure, of what shape or substance they list: of which mind all papists and some protestants are, being more grosse than another sort, which hold that such bodies are made to their hands. Howbeit, these do varie in the elements, wherewith these spiritual bodies are composed. For (as I have said) some affirme that they consist of fier, some thinke of air, and some of the starres and other celestial powers. But if they be celestial, then (as Peter Martyr saith) must they follow the circular motion: and if they be elementarie, then must they follow the motions of those elements, of which their bodies consist. Of aier they cannot be: for aier is *Corpus homogenium;* so as everie part of aier is aier, whereof there can be no distinct members made. For an organicall bodie must have bones, sinewes, veines, flesh, &c.: which cannot be made of aier. Neither (as Peter Martyr affirmeth) can airie bodie receive or have either shape or figure. But some ascend up into the clouds, where they find (as they saie) diverse shapes and formes even in the aier. Unto which objection P. Martyr answereth, saieng, and that trulie, that clouds are not altogether aier but have a mixture of other elements mingled with them.[39]

Scot ridicules particularly the widespread doctrine that the devil in his airy body had carnal copulation with human beings. The devil is but a spirit and has no members for copulation with either man or woman, nor any desire for it. Further, "the power of generation consisteth not onlie in members, but chieflie of vitall spirits, and of the hart: which spirits are never in such a bodie as *Incubus* hath, being but a bodie assumed as they themselves saie." [40]

But Boguet retorts that the devil uses his victims so not because he has carnal desire but the better to bind them to him in sin.[41] Further, he explains, following Aquinas as do most of his Catholic fellows, that though the devil has no "vitall spirits" of his own, either properly his or belonging to his airy body, he can steal male semen while acting as a succubus and then as an incubus inject it into the human female to cause conception.[42]

Of the ability of a creature that is wholly spirit to act in this manner *Malleus Maleficarum* explains that "the contact of a devil with a body, either in the way of semen or in any other way, is not a corporeal but a virtual contact." The demon does not abide in his assumed body in the sense that a soul is united with the body it vitalizes, but directs it by his power as a spirit in the required motions. It is not in any sense the being of the demon, merely represents him.[43] If the devil could shape the likeness of a body at all he could undoubtedly shape its particular members and put them through the semblance of their natural paces.[44] Sexual manifestation of a demon to a human being would be not that inconceivable thing, direct stimulation of animal senses by a spirit, but simply stimulation through materials moved by spirit.

On this Scot's argument seems to break down. But more forceful than his argument was his alternative explanation of incubus as only a "bodilie disease . . . although it extend unto the trouble of the mind." [45] This is Wier's attitude. As a physician he explains that such delusions attack the melancholy and phlegmatic, particularly old women, when the stomach is oppressed by too great a quantity of viands hard to digest. Wier agrees with Scot, too, that copulation cannot be of the devil since the devil has not the needed fleshly substance.[46]

King James says, however, that the disease of nightmare which doctors call Incubus and explain as a matter of "thicke fleume, falling into our breasts upon the heart," merely takes its name from the real devilish abuse and is by no means the same thing.[47]

3

Spirits were held to go about their manifest works sometimes in conformity with the invitation of men, sometimes without the consent or against the will of men. Demons, it was thought, allied themselves with whoever would have them, and afflicted all others susceptible to their attack. Either relation the orthodox considered a malignant assault.

The manifest works of demonic assault were of two general sorts, possessive and obsessive. Possession meant, roughly, control by a demon of a man's bodily faculties; the exact extent and fashion of it was a thing prodigiously debated. Scot, of course, denies it *in toto*. He asserts that in the gospels possession of a devil usually signifies lunacy or some other frenetic disease, or else simply that a man is governed by an evil bent in his character. "But we do not meane thereby, that a reall divell is gotten into his guts." [48]

But this was precisely what many of his contemporaries did mean. The simple popular conception was that demons entered the body through its orifices, ordinarily with bewitched or unblessed food,[49] or, if to a devotee, perhaps through the ignoble parts.[50] Perkins, however, explains that a demon "conueys himself into the substance of a creature, without any penetration of dimensions"; [51] and Deacon and Walker go to the greatest dialectical lengths to prove that there is never local entrance, necessary to what they denominate *real* possession, but only *actual* possession, one "by some powerful effecte." [52]

Possession is, perhaps, to be conceived simply as the application of the demon's power to the springs of a man's behavior. It means "afflicting, tormenting and tempting both inwardly and outwardly" [53] and of this, of course, there were many and debatable degrees of manifestation ranging all the way from convulsions and prophetic utterances down to mental promptings which only experts could recognize as of the devil.

By definition hardly distinguishable from possession is obsession, according to Deacon and Walker. Says their interlocutor, Orthodoxus:

> By the diuell his power of obsession: I do heere understand some certaine predeterminate ability, facultie, or inclination of his spirituall nature, for the more powerful enabling of his restless endeuours, and insatiable desires to worke our daily destruction: wherein he eftsoones assaulteth, circumventeth, encloseth, inuironeth and besiegeth the seruants of God afresh, with a purposed mind to deuoure them quite, were they not mightily protected by an inuincible power of the Lord. And this said power of obsession consisteth especially in an outward assaulting and vexing: or in an inward suggesting and tempting at least.

He further explains that he means "all the external allurements, incumbrances, molestations and griefs" wherewith men are troubled, and the "internall allurements which draw them into dissimulation and other sin." [54]

King James has a more lucid distinction than Deacon and Walker's of possession from obsession—though he does not use the latter term. He says that when a demon "followes upon certain persones, and at divers hours troubles them" the assault is one with possession in cause, though there is the simple distinction that the spirit does not "enter within them" but "attacks from without." [55] The difference, however, is only in the seeming; for both possession and obsession are but applications of demonic power to a particular area for the harassment of a person.

Wier explains that demons can apply their power over local motion of things to shift the humors in a man's body in such a manner as to arouse evil appetites and lead thus to sin.[56] By similar manipulation they can induce hallucination, both in respect to vision and to the other senses, causing a man to believe he perceives what is not actually present.[57] From this it is clear the demons were able to perform their manifest works of assault, even the obsessive, entirely through the minds of their victims and without resort to any objective manifestations whatever.

4

Identical with the works of the demons in method were those of the good spirits, who, classified according to their tasks, appear to have been conceived as of two general sorts: (1) special emissaries from God, (2) guardian angels.[58] The former, of course, came to men only on rare occasions to make announcements, deliver warnings, inspire prophets, or perhaps in emergencies to act on behalf of the good. Guardians constantly attended their charges, though customarily their presence was not manifest.[59]

Angels were, of course, thought quite able to assume airy bodies, but ordinarily when they made themselves manifest it was in dreams or visions or in intuitions. Prophetic or premonitory seizures and visions were usually identical in process with demonic hallucination and possession. Lavater says of guardian angels that they:

> . . . appearing in sundrye shapes, haue admonished menne, haue comforted them, defended them, deliuered them from daunger and also punished the wicked. Touching this matter, there are plentiful examples. . . . Sometimes they haue eyther appeared in sleep, or in manner of visions, and sometimes they haue perfourmed their office, by some internall operations: as when a mans mynde foreshoweth him, that a thing shall so happen, and after it happeneth so in deede, which thyng I suppose is doone by God, through the ministrie of Angels. Angels for the most part take upon them the shapes of men, wherein they appeare.[60]

There was, however, a considerable rift of opinion on whether or not good spirits acted at all in the mundane sphere; particularly was the doctrine of special guardianship attacked. The insular Protestants, Scot and King James, have for once a common cause in their rejection of the guardian angel. Both held miracles "ceased"; since the revelation the need for special ministration by angels was passed.[61] Scot says that there is neither authority in scripture nor reason in nature for the Papistical doctrine of the guardian spirit, and that he stands with Calvin in holding it a great "wrong" to refer to one angel the care God hath to everyone.[62] King James contends that it was from the guilefully beneficent attentions of fallen angels that the ancients and Catholics got the superstitious conviction that men are provided with angelic attendants.

But the Swiss Protestant, Lavater, who needs the doctrine of guardianship in his argument against return of souls, says, though in cautious language, that it may be proved by scripture that all Christian men have not only one, but many angels "whome God imployeth to their service." [63]

Highly circumstantial on the subject of guardian angels is the occultist, Cornelius Agrippa, who to a quite orthodox insistence upon the presidency of a hellish and a heavenly angel over every soul,[64] adds the occult elaboration that every man has three guardian daemons—or a three-fold daemon, it is not clear which—who take care for his career. The first guardian is sacred (*sacer,* presumably the good angel who wars for the salvation of the soul) and is assigned to man from supernal realms, descending from God to preside over the rational soul. The second guardian—or aspect of the one guardian—is the daemon of the geniture, descended to a man from the sidereal arrangement that prevailed at his birth, and is the custodian of his life and earthly fortunes. The third daemon is that of profession and comes to a man when his mind has acquired power to judge and choose an occupation congenial to his nature; it brings to him, or it is, awakening talent and aspiration.[65]

Whether Agrippa conceived this triune genius as a being or beings extrinsic to the mind and acting upon it, or merely as its intrinsic processes figuratively denoted is not quite clear.[66] On the face of it, it seems certainly the former; the time's pneumatology was for the most part quite literal. But just how far the genius was one with the soul it guided is uncertain. It is hard not to identify, in terminology at least, the controlling power of a thing with the thing itself, the ruler of a faculty with the faculty. The conception of the relation between genius and soul seems to have been a wavering one even among the orthodox.

5

One of the principal functions of the attendant spirit, whether good or evil, witch's familiar or heavenly guardian, was to disclose the future. Spirits possessed foreknowledge inferior, of course, to God's but far exceeding anything natural to man. Only God could know the future unconditionally; but unbodied spirits and even man could make conjectures which, guided by previous experience of causal sequences in nature, might be accurate.[67] Angels, both good and evil, possessed great insight into and long experience of nature, could check their conjectures far more thoroughly than the weaker and flesh-bound souls of men, consequently excelled men in natural knowledge of the future. Sometimes, too, they had their foreknowledge directly of God. James says that angels look upon God "as in a mirror" and that devils occasionally get knowledge when God employs them to make true prophecies.[68] More often demons looked into the germs of things and read indications to which their experience and penetration gave them the key. Or, being deceiving spirits, they might employ their speed to make mere early announcement of events occurring at a distance, or predict an event and then bring it to pass either by instigating men to it or by direct action. More audaciously yet they might steal prophecies from the Bible. Secret deeds and decisions they discovered by their invisible surveillance of all mundane events.[69]

Sometimes spirits communicated their prognostications to men directly—from airy bodies or by unlocalized sounds, or through the mouths of possessed persons, or in dreams and visions. As often the spirit was a latent rather than an evident participant in the work of forecast. It was generally agreed that in antiquity demons not only had given oracular answers at Delphi and elsewhere, but had invisibly guided the hands of the officiants in all augurific ceremonies, and that they served similar superstitious practices in Christian times.[70]

The chief works, however, which demons performed latently, without specific corporeal representation, were the marvels of prestidigital illusion which they often enacted in conjunction with the commands and ceremonies of a human operator. In discussing these feats the sixteenth century author's first care, usually, was to distinguish them from the miracles of God. Cotta explains that the works of demons are "natural," because though demons can act above and out of some limited natures, they are never out of general nature.

> For nature is nothing els but the ordinary power of God in all things created, among which the Divell, being a creature, is constrained and therefore subiect to the universal power.[71]

Perkins on the same subject says that wonders are (1) miracles, "done by the power of God simply either aboue, or against the power of nature," [*i.e.,* either by extraordinary exercise of an ordinary power, or by an extraordinary power]; (2) lying and deceitful, not above or against nature, but simply out of the usual course of it, [*i.e.,* in a degree above man's nature, infinitely below God's.] [72]

Demons achieved conviction of marvels in two general ways: (1) by manipulation of natural causes to produce true effects, (2) by creating hallucination in the beholders.[73] Of the first, Perkins says that by virtue of his spiritual insight into the ways of things, and supreme agility, a demon might "apply creature to creature, and the causes efficient to the matter, and thereby bring things to passe, that are in common conceit impossible"; and he might "mooue them, not onely according to the ordinarie course, but with much more speed and celerity." [74] Thus, explain Deacon and Walker of the feat of Pharaoh's magicians against Moses, the devil who helped them, though he could not perform a true transformation of rods into serpents, might apply natural causes, actives to passives, to foster the natural though abnormally rapid generation of serpents in the spot. He did this by the use of the natural germs or seeds of things which he could manipulate to energize almost instantly. More likely still, he might, by his control of the local motions of bodies, in a trice remove the rods and substitute a serpent brought from elsewhere.[75]

Of such works it was admitted that there was a true and natural issue and residue, though they were deceitful in method and end. But demons might, if they preferred, deceive men's senses totally, either from within by taking command of the interior senses through the humors, or by acting on the exterior media of sense to distort or prevent perceptions. Remy explains that vision "depends upon the light or dark of the intermediate air" and that demons can control both light and darkness. Guazzo says that the thickening of the vapors of the air may cause things to appear to us other than as they are.[76]

These explanations of devils' power to make things seem transformed, the witchmongers turned largely to the end of elucidating lycanthropy as a demonic work. They are agreed that a veritable metamorphosis of a man into a wolf is a thing which only God can effect; but they hold that Satan may throw about a man a shape that will deceive the beholder and even cause the man to believe himself transformed. Occasionally, it is suggested, the demon may leave the witch asleep somewhere and himself take the wolf form and commit crimes which he subsequently fastens upon her.[77]

Bodin says that recent philosophers have held transmutation of men into beasts certain, though it is only the figure, not the essence, which changes.[78] This Scot derides mightily, concluding that "indeed our bodies are visible, sensitive, and passive, and are indued with many other excellent properties which all the devils in hell are not able to alter." [79] As for the men who, retaining their human aspect, believe themselves beasts, they suffer from a disease proceeding in part from melancholy as physicians recognize. "J. Wierus declareth very learnedly the cause, the circumstance and the cure of this disease." [80]

Wier does indeed ascribe lycanthropy to pathological causes and name remedies and assert that the devil can neither create nor truly transform; [81] but he agrees with the witch-mongers that demons by control of the fantasy might put a man into a trance and cause him to believe that he had become a wolf and done deeds which the demon in wolf form actually committed.[82] Further, Wier says in another place that it is very difficult for a physician to distinguish between a melancholic disease and a state of demonic possession—also a thing which follows upon melancholy.[83] This is equivalent to a confession that the lycanthropy which is a disease of the senses that causes a man to run in forests and stalk children, may be virtually one with the lycanthropy that is a possessed state in which a human being performs these same wolfish acts with a wolf-like fleetness, strength, and guile far transcending the natural.[84] Such confessions were the fundamental weakness of most sixteenth century rationalism on spirits. It could not find a clear issue.

Chapter III

The Controversies on Magic and Ghosts

I

SIXTEENTH CENTURY DAEMONOLOGY was largely incident to theory of ceremonial magic and witchcraft and to the controversy on them. Witchcraft and ceremonial magic had in common that they were wonderworking pursuits relying on spirits; upon the conception of the nature of spirits depended largely the answers to the day's questions about the legitimacy of ceremonial magic and the actuality and guilt of witchcraft. If spirits could act in the temporal world in concert with a man's will, then magic and witchcraft might be real, and perhaps identical in basic method; if, further, a man could have power over spirits, then ceremonial magic might be distinct from witchcraft, and legitimate. On the other hand, if unbodied spirits did not act in the temporal world, then magic and witchcraft were but degrees of imposture or delusion.

The only universally accepted distinction between the magician and the witch was that the former was the more pretentious in his procedure.[1] Scot thought such pretension simply an unusually astute rascality; [2] King James held it a learned rather than an ignorant devil worship; Wier thought it a damnable but effective diabolical art; Agrippa believed it at its best an esoteric phase of religion. Each represents a definitive line of thought in the controversies on magic and witchcraft.

They are agreed on one thing: that the witch, ignorant and destitute, has in herself no real power, however much malignance. Wier and Agrippa concur that the witch has no art, hence cannot control spirits, though magicians may. James follows orthodox theology in his contention that there is no human art that gives arbitrary control over spirits; and Scot, of course, denies any sort of response from spirits. Agrippa does not join except incidentally in the witch controversy,[3] but Scot and Wier, though from diverse positions, plead the witch's lack of real power, however forward her desire and profession of it, as grounds against her condemnation.

Wier rests his defense of witches largely upon a distinction between the black magician (*magus infamis*), a powerful operator who knowingly and cunningly communicates with evil spirits and by various superstitious means brings them to serve his unlawful ends; and the witch (*Lamia* or *sorcière*), a feeble woman whom devils sometimes delude into believing that she serves them and against whom they turn credulous ire of witch persecutors. The magicians Wier calls "slaves" of the devil since they are for their sins doomed to his clutches, though by his aid, ceremonially won, they may assume a great place in the world. No community of calling with these wicked persons, Wier insists, has the witch, for she possesses neither books, exorcisms, nor characters, but is of the inconstant sex, weak in faith, sick with melancholy, sorrowful and despairing, easy prey to the deceptions of demons who take possession of her faculties and lay upon her the horrid illusions of the covenant, the Sabbat, and the other sins for which witches were arraigned.[4] The magician, Wier seems to say, is inexcusably evil; scripture condemns him, against him the church has properly thundered and the law provided its penalties. But it is by a misconception that these dicta and sanctions have been applied to the wretched women accused of witchcraft, for they are merely victims and deserve of true Christians succor rather than enmity.[5]

After exposing the wiles of devils, "deceiving spirits," in the first book, and of their dupes and allies, the magicians, in the second book, Wier begins in the third his explicit defense of witches with an attack on the key doctrine of the pact. He says that even if the devil appears to the witch in some phantasmical shape and actually goes through the forms of a contract with her, it cannot be binding because (1) the demon participates fraudulently since he needs no license from the witch to go about his evil deeds, (2) the senses of the human party to the contract are not under her control, but are swayed by the demon, (3) man has a prior contract with God that annuls any with the devil; it is confirmed by baptism which is a thing we cannot renounce if we would. Further, God fulfills His promises whereas the devil does not.[6]

Wier then talks of those most subject to the delusions of demons. "Tels sont les melancoliques qui peu de perte ou autre choses s'attristent legierement. . . ." [7] Women, because of the weakness of their sex, are especially apt victims.[8] He explains the confessions of witches as caused by a deluded belief in their own guilt induced by the demon in possession of their faculties.[9]

In the fourth book Wier tries to show that the various woes ascribed to the spells of witches are really caused by devils without human coöperation, or are natural calamities which devils attempt to fasten on reputed witches. Thus nightmare—or seizure by an incubus—and lycanthropy are natural diseases of the fantasy; many other afflictions, including demonic possession, are enacted by devils of their own will and power.

In the fifth book, which was the final one of the original edition, he argues that professing or accused witches are often mere poisoners.

Wier's defense of the witch rested on a favorable interpretation of a body of evidence which, for the most part, he did not impugn as fact.[10] Scot is far bolder. Of course there are witches, he says; but can they do marvels? Certainly not, for there are no devils working in the world to aid them, and even witchmongers confess that a hag's muttering and gesticulation and filthy talismans are of no force in themselves. What are witches then? One of three things: persons of diseased imagination, designing impostors, or poisoners.[11] Scot follows Wier in his insistence that many who seem witches are poisoners. He interprets the Hebrew word *Chasaph* (Latin *Veneficium*) to mean poisoner.[12] The Biblical injunction upon which persecution grounds: "Thou shalt not suffer a witch to live," is, Scot insists, directed against poisoners—criminals well worthy of punishment. He adds that if one prefers to translate the word *witch,* it should be considered to mean impostor, and applied to whoever claims to effect wonders possible only to God.[13]

Scot's contentions are summed up in his definition of witchcraft:

> Witchcraft is in truth a cosening art, wherein the name of God is abused, prophaned and blasphemed, and his power attributed to a vile creature. In estimation of the vulgar people, it is a supernatural worke, contrived betweene a corporall old woman, and a spirituall divell. The maner thereof is so secret, mysticall and strange, that to this daie there hath never beene any credible witnes thereof. It is incomprehensible to the wise, learned or faithful; a probable matter to children, fooles, melancholike persons and papists.[14]

This position the witchmongers hardly bothered to attack specifically.[15] Making all the assumptions about devils which Scot so vigorously protests, they exerted themselves to distinguish the witch from other sorts of traffickers with spirits and to affirm her responsibility. Bodin and Perkins say that a witch is one who knowingly and willingly seeks the aid of evil spirits.[16] This soliciting of the devil was thought to take the form of either a tacit or an express compact.[17] Whoever invokes spirits by unsanctified ceremonies or is party to such invocation, or resorts to superstitious practices such as sortilege in which the operation of spirits is latent, has made a tacit compact. Far more culpable, Bodin says, are such as in the presence of the demon explicitly pledge themselves to him in return for certain services in this world.[18]

The witchmongers held that as a moral agent a human being was an adequate party to such compact although the devil always cheated his partner,[19] and connected himself with a witch not because he needed her, but in order to make her accessory to his crimes and so morally responsible for them.[20] They did not agree with Wier that these things purged any of the evil inherent in the contract.[21]

The chief offense of the witch was not *maleficium,* crime

against her neighbors' goods and persons, though this aided to damn her, but her service to the devil in despite of God.[22] It was this service that distinguished the witch from other criminals and that identified her with heretics; it was the feats of spirit magic which the service enabled that identified her also with the ceremonial magician. Bodin expends several chapters [23] in distinguishing the varieties of those who resort to the devil for help, who make with him some order of covenant. All, whether they treat with him expressly or tacitly, invoke him directly or indirectly, are guilty in some degree of deliberate worship of a false god.[24] This is Bodin's criterion of witchcraft. By it he judges witches and magicians to be at bottom one.

With this opinion James is, in general, agreed. The witch and the magician commit in common, he says, the sin against the Holy Ghost, "a falling back from the whole service of God, and a refusal of all his preceptes." [25] James seems to intend this to signify devil worship by express compact, for he goes on to explain that the use of the magician's instruments, such as circles and charms, does not reach the last degree of culpability until the operator, wearying of his tedious ceremonies, casts them aside and makes an explicit contract with the devil. Yet none can use "the circles and arts of *Magie* without committing an horrible defection from God." [26] James mentions the popular distinction between magic and witchcraft—that the magician commands the devil as a master whereas witches are his servants only—but says that the magician's power is but *ex pacto* and by consent of the devil, who so expects to win another soul to hell.

The sum of the orthodox contention as presented by James and Bodin is that a man, be he artful or simple, can have wilful traffic with spirits, but only with evil ones and only by some degree of alliance and to his ultimate damnation.[27]

II

Opposed to the view of James and Bodin and their allies was the occult view of magic, summed up in the magician's contention that he possessed good means by which he could evoke good spirits who served him because of affinity, and evil who obeyed him through constraint of his worthiness. The magicians, however, were definitely on the defensive in their efforts to show that their practices were within the scheme of Christianity. They could ward attacks only by insisting upon an ancient distinction between white and black magic and by enforcing an analogy between magic and Biblical miracles.

It was largely by reference to authorities of pagan antiquity that Agrippa and his peers sought to establish recognition that there was a magic of honorable ancestry and religious worth. Agrippa says in a letter to Trithemius presenting the *Occult Philosophy,* that they have discussed the question:

> Why Magic, whereas it was accounted by all ancient philosophers to be the chiefest science, and by the ancient wise men and priests was always held in great veneration, came at last, after the beginning of the Catholic Church, to be always odious to and suspected by the holy Fathers, and then exploded by Divines, and condemned by sacred Canons, and moreover, by all laws and ordinances forbidden? Now, the cause, as I conceive, is no other than this, viz.: Because, by a certain fatal depravity of times and men, many false philosophers crept in, and these under the name of Magicians, heaping together, through various sorts of errors and factions of false religions, many cursed superstitions and dangerous rites, and many wicked sacrileges, even to the perfection of Nature; and the same set forth in many wicked and unlawful books, to which they have by stealth prefixed the most honest name and title of Magic; hoping, by this sacred title, to gain credit to their cursed and detestable fooleries. Hence it is that this name of Magic, formerly so honorable, is now become most odious to good and honest men, and accounted a capital crime if any one dare profess himself to be a Magician, either in doctrine or works, unless haply some certain old doting woman, dwelling in the country, would be believed to be skillful and have a divine power. . . .[28]

The ancient and incorrupt magic Agrippa hoped to revive.

But Bodin points out repeatedly that this magic which Agrippa sponsors derives principally from the Neo-Platonics, "nouueaux Academiques,"[29] and is un-Christian in its assumptions. Undoubtedly much of Agrippa's doctrine came directly from the famous *Mysteries of the Egyptians, Chaldeans and Assyrians,* attributed to Iamblichus, and in the sixteenth century the most widely known and respected ancient work on the magic of the Neo-Platonists.[30] It makes the distinction upon which Agrippa insists between two kinds of magic—that of the magus or theurgist, and that of the sorcerer or goetist.[31] Both, according to the Platonists, operated by the sympathy that exists between corresponding parts of analogous realms of a universe in which all causality is psychic, and daemons administer things even to the extremities.[32] The sorcerer, however, an operator sunk in the lusts of the flesh, attracted evil spirits by similitude and by mundane and artificial manipulation. His power was slight and worldly since he dealt only with the last fleeting effluxions of things.[33] But the theurgist, an operator initiate and meritorious, aspiring to mystical union with superior natures, attracted good spirits and even gods by exalted life and practices.[34] He identified himself successively with all the ascendant realms of the universe, and was limited only by the Limitless, the supreme impersonal universal from which all existence flowed.

Agrippa, presenting, of course, a modified doctrine, opens his exposition of lawful magic thus:

> Seeing there is a three-fold World—Elementary, Celestial and Intellectual—and every inferior is governed by its superior, and receiveth the influence of the virtues thereof, so that the very Original and Chief Worker of all doth by angels, the heavens, stars, elements, animals, plants, metals, and stones convey from Himself the virtues of His Omnipotency upon us, for whose service He made and created all these things: Wise men conceive it no way irrational that it should be possible for us to ascend by the same degrees through each World, to the same very original World itself, the Maker of all things and First Cause, from whence all things are and proceed; and also to enjoy not only these virtues, which are already in the more excellent kind of things, but also besides these to draw new virtues from above.[35]

Just so the Neo-Platonic theurgist conceived that he might, by elaborate juxtapositions both material and anagogic to which his arcane wisdom directed him, achieve in the plural world of sense any manifestation or clairvoyance whatsoever consistent with the all-inclusive blank unity of the single source.[36] This is to say, he might render apparent to himself any essence of being and participate in its disposition of inferior provinces. Such communion is no doubt better conceived as a transfiguration of the magician than as an evocation of superior intelligences out of their own proper kingdoms. But this gathering up of the temporal into the eternal might be initiated by the human operator.[37]

The procedure of the Christian mage as Agrippa explains it in his *Occult Philosophy* is on the theurgical principle that a ritually purified man, learned in the occult bonds between things, may exert influence in an extra-temporal sphere. Thus Agrippa:

> Magicians teach that celestial gifts may, through inferiors being conformable to superiors, be drawn down by opportune influences of the heavens; and so, also by these celestial gifts, the celestial angels (as they are servants of the stars) may be procured and conveyed to us. Iamblichus, Proclus and Synesius, with the whole school of the Platonists, confirm that not only celestial and vital but also certain intellectual, angelical and divine gifts may be received from above by some certain matters having a natural power of divinity and which have a natural correspondency with the superiors, being rightly received and opportunely gathered together according to the rules of natural philosophy and astronomy . . . for this is the harmony of the world, that things supercelestial be drawn down by the celestial, and the supernatural by those natural, because there is One Operative Virtue that is diffused through all kinds of things; by which virtue, indeed, as manifest things are produced out of occult causes, so a magician doth make use of things manifest to draw forth things that are occult, viz. through the rays of the Stars, through fumes, lights, sounds and [other] natural things which are agreeable to those celestial in which aside from their corporeal qualities, there is also a kind of reason sense and harmony, and incorporeal and divine measures and orders.[38]

This is, of course, verbally a far more elevated conception of spirit traffic than any to be deduced from the formulae in contemporary manuals of magic such as the Solomonic books. But their practice rests upon Agrippa's theory, and his theory reduces to their practice—as orthodox writers insisted and Agrippa himself later confessed.

Agrippa declares repeatedly in the *Occult Philosophy* that

true magic is possible only to a man who because of the purity of his life has received the virtues of religion and has been especially prepared by instruction and experience and finally by ceremonial consecration,[39] for true magic is in conformity and indeed in alliance with religion. Ceremonial magic, he says, has two helps whereby natural means are supplemented and made sure: Religion and Superstition. These are the dynamos that charge the spirit of the operator, either by a true faith or by credulity. Superstitious is every cult foreign to the Christian faith, either in a lack or in an excess of any article or rite. Since all cults partake in some measure of truth, all even the most superstitious, bestow some power upon their devotees. We must take care not to neglect the religious observances that renew our contemplation of the divine; equal care not to estrange God and His angels by excess. We must be certain that the errors of the ancient originators of magic do not stain our practice of it.[40]

But Bodin asserts that these very errors do most foully stain Agrippa's magic—the worse that Agrippa possesses the revelation of the true God—and particularly the error that the spirits that answer magicians are good. Agrippa and his like, Bodin says, derive their whole practice from the doctrine of Proclus, Iamblichus, Porphyry and others that, since the supernal world is joined by sympathy to the terrestrial, man can attain divine power by manipulation of whatever elementary corresponds to divine existences. When the ancients sought by inferior daemons and demigods to attract superior gods and finally the sovereign God, they performed mere idolatry for they did not know true worship; but Christians who duplicate such practices are *Sorciers,* that is, witches, for they knowingly compact the devil.[41]

The doctors of the Sorbonne, he continues, in the year 1318 condemned as impious whoever held that the power and virtue of celestial intelligences flows in the soul and the power of the stars into bodies. It is not possible to attract stars and planets by elementary creatures, and by the stars their daemons and then the angels and lesser celestial gods and *"puis par ce moyen auoir Dieu."* All *"ces beaux mediateurs"* draw only Satan.[42]

For all the spirit-summoning operations of magic Bodin

has a blanket rebuke that amounts to this: Man cannot coerce superior natures, and he can offer persuasion or alliance only by worship; of worship there can be but two willing recipients —God and the Adversary. Ceremonies performed to angels transgress God's express commandment that no service shall be paid to creatures which is owed to Him.[43] Such ceremonies can attract only devils, for as worship of false gods they are practices damnably impious to which Satan eagerly responds.[44]

Bodin's reduction of magic to terms of worship was in conformity with the defense by which the Catholic Church parried the magician's claim that his marvels were like those of the Apostles and saints of the church itself. Its wonders the church contended to be not magical but miraculous, special answers by God to the appeals of His servants. So God helped Moses when he contended with the Egyptians, and so He permitted the Apostles in their ministry to heal the sick and raise the dead. The power, they constantly said, was not theirs but His; ceremony was not needed, simply faith and prayer.[45] God might act in behalf of the appellant directly, that is, in a wholly miraculous manner, or by delegated spirits; in either event the human operator addressed himself directly to the Supreme, and all virtue in the matter came from that source.

The church, it is true, ritualized its miracles; but its ceremony, even that which signalized transubstantiation and exorcism, was to be regarded as, in intent, nothing more wilful than prayer—though certainly prayer with a prerogative. Under the Christian scheme of the universe there could be no other path to spirit marvels, no other magic than this of prayer and faith, but by some sort of alliance with the enemies of God. That such alliance consisted of a contrary prayer and faith, a diabolic, or at best a superstitious, worship was the constant contention of Christian theologians.[46]

In all theory of a magic that bases upon or mingles with one of the higher religions there exists, no doubt, the problem of reconciling the real power of the magician's art with the omnipotence of the deity.[47] The magician extends his will into realms not ordinarily subject to man, bases his operations upon occult principles with whose functioning mankind is little familiar. Under what license does this creature so exceed the usual limitations of his animal kind? Are his "occult principles" really a part of unvarying providence, as certain as the laws of mathematics, or does he have his response merely by the grace and special direction of some being who transcends all laws which any man may know and use?

The Neo-Platonic magician conceived providence as the spontaneous participation of every generated thing in the inclusive Source,[48] so that in this universal plan there was provision for the influence of even a mundane being throughout the entire universe.[49] The soul's descent from superior realms and the possibility of its reascent established for it those sympathies that made the universe a single animal. The theurgist might conceive his enchantments as cosmologically irresistible in the sense that a mathematical verity is so, which in every specific demonstration inevitably draws its terms into a relation that, abstractly, they always occupy.[50] The theurgist realized his ability by conformity to truth and goodness. His operations were a translation of merit into power.

Agrippa undoubtedly had a similar conception; but it was deflected to some extent by the Christian dogma that providence did not include the sensible world nor even the souls of men as eternal, that is, without beginning or end, but as fiat creations in time. In the Christian providence there was no provision for any influence of the mundane upon the supernal world except the dependence of the created on the creator.[51] It was this which necessitated the theological reduction of ceremonial magic to terms of worship, and eliminated from the Christian scheme the conception of such magic as a thing efficacious in itself.

There was room left, however, for the provocation and perhaps the direction if not the mandatory evocation and control of marvels. The Christian magician, preparing himself by an intimation of priestlike living and his instruments by dedicatory ceremonies, was making the basically pagan assumption that special disciplines confer of themselves preternatural powers, that with things subject naturally to human manipulation he could influence an intrinsically separate and superior sphere. But whereas the pagan magician had based on the order of an impersonal universal, the Christian magician based on the *promise* of God or of Satan. The church had assumed to itself in part the promise of Christ to the Apostles that by faith they should do greater miracles than his in his Father's name; the individual priest might feel that he as a consecrated person and the layman that he as a true believer participated individually in this promise.[52]

Christian magicians did not, usually, care to consider themselves witches, workers by the promise of a Satan whom they compensated with worship. Rather they held themselves to work like the church by the word of God whose name and worshippers were loved by angels, hated and feared by devils.

Agrippa says that devils may be controlled by a man who uses worshipful names and signs. He cites the Fathers on some of the names to be used and admonishes that evil spirits may not be handled in a worldly fashion without damnation of the operator.[53] In a subsequent chapter on the three sorts of bonds—elementary, celestial, and divine—by which spirits may be bound he emphasizes as most important the third, the religious bond, which is exercised in the use of divine names, holy water, the sacrament, and other symbols of divinity.

But against such use of holy things Bodin rages, calling it profanation.[54] This, of course, was the view of the church; but the church made no question of the efficacy by God's will of divine symbols as handled by a properly consecrated practitioner for proper ends, to influence spirits. This, with its corollary that on the church alone had God bestowed the consecratory power, seemed to put a premium for magic upon ecclesiastical consecration, and it added to the confusion that existed between the practices of the Christian religion and those of magic. Though the church itself certainly held even its rites of exorcism religious, not magical, and contended that the blasphemous use of holy things for unholy purposes could achieve nothing but the attraction of fiends, many ignorant priests—and, by popular legend at least, some learned ones—relying on their formal investment, oblivious to the unchurchliness of their aims, wrought zealously in magic.[55]

The whole matter of the coercion of spirits came to be a question of winning favor from some exalted spirit who would honor his worshippers with the service of underlings. The church made its appeal to the Most High; but He seemed to the practical magician the least responsive lord of spirits. The church's appeal was unique because it was to the Creator, the Infinite. White magicians such as Agrippa called first upon the median spirits, good angels, and by them controlled evil and inferior spirits. Black magicians, distinguished from Agrippa also in their aims, which were sordid, called first upon superior devils and by them ruled inferiors.

But it is to be emphasized that both white and black magicians relied ultimately upon God—or at least on the truths of the Christian religion as conveyed in its forms—for even the princes of Hell by whom the goetist worked, though they contemned God and truth, had to acknowledge both. Only those spirit workers who from ignorance or disillusion did not observe ceremony but resorted to express devil compact, turned utterly from the Infinite spirit in favor of direct alliance with His adversary, thus, became witches in the ultimate degree.

The Reformation with its insistence on the priesthood in some sort of all believers [56] gave the sixteenth century secular magician a better theological purchase so far as his consecratory powers were concerned than his predecessors had possessed and no doubt stimulated the exercise of magic for awhile.[57] But this was rather the fruit of confusion resulting from conflict between theologies than of express acceptance by any orthodox theology of the claims of magic. Rome, of course, consolidated rather than modified its position, and those who denied that the creeds and observances of Rome constituted true religion were not minded to leave Rome in possession of its special powers. Scot presents the Protestant point of view when he says sarcastically that Papists attack other conjurors lest they get the upper hand of them and draw off the emoluments of the conjuring trade.[58]

Protestants proclaimed magic, whether lay or ecclesiastical, either nonsense or forbidden on the ground that all power was from God and that He dispensed it to men not according to ceremony but solely according to His grace. The Roman church could not, therefore, infallibly endow its ministers with the magical powers of consecration and exorcism. These gifts, Protestants contended, might descend upon any faithful person, be withheld from any priest. This in substance was not, of course, remote from the Catholic view or even from the magician's view; but in practice Protestants inclined to believe that God withheld His grace from Catholics and magicians as ceremonialists and idolaters, granted it to themselves as proper believers. To Protestants, therefore, even churchly magic was nonsense or of the devil.[59] Similarly, Protestant theologians declared, God refrained from granting power to lay magicians. He could, of course, grant such power. Simply He did not.

III

Very similar in method was Protestant dialectic on ghosts. Lewes Lavater puts it simply: God *can* send souls back into the world—but He never does.

As touching the first obiection, that all things are possible unto God, we denie it not. We graunt them that God can bring soules out of heauen or hel, & use their trauaile & seruice to instruct, comfort, admonish & rebuke men. But for that no text or example is found in holy scripture, that euer any soules came from the dead, which did so scoole and warn men: or that the faithful learned or sought to understand any thing of the soules deceassed, we cannot allow the sequele of their reason. For this is a principle holden in scholes, that the reson doth not truly folow, that is fet from the power of doing, to the dead done. For God doth nothing against himself, or his word writen, to warrant their reson: they shold first haue proued, that it was gods wil, that soules shold return into the earth. . . .[60]

For himself, Lavater seeks to establish that there is no known event in which God did so will. Particularly he tries to explain otherwise all the Biblical incidents which Catholics cited as proving return of souls. Thus of the necromantic apparition of Samuel to Saul, he gives the customary Protestant explanation that it was a demon in Samuel's likeness and, not very convincingly, offers equally debatable ethnic tales such as the Erichtho episode from Lucan's *Pharsalia* as parallel occurrences.[61] The appearance of Moses and Elias to Christ and three disciples, Lavater explains as a visitation unique in circumstance since it was to Christ.[62] As for Lazarus, "he came againe both in bodie & soule," not as a soul only.[63]

Aside from thus trying to discredit positive evidence of ghosts, Lavater presents arguments of probability that God does never will souls to return to earth. In the first place if souls could return, the devil would be able to deceive men with his lying apparitions—as, indeed, he does deceive the misguided, such as Catholics—and this advantage over believers God would never give him.[64] Further, souls of the dead can have no mission for which God would return them to earth. It is not conceivable that an unfinished earthly business could draw any of the departed back from the eternal resting places; [65] nor need any bring the word of God or testimony to it, since those things we have in scripture.[66]

This stand necessitated, of course, a discussion of purgatory,[67] and from Lavater's arguments it is clear that Protestant recession from the Roman ghost doctrine was subsidiary to renunciation of the belief in purgatory and in intercession of saints. Lavater's father-in-law, Bullinger, successor to Zwingli at Zurich, had said that Catholics used ghosts "to prop purgatory"; [68] he had attacked the doctrine of purgatory with the assertion that there were no ghosts. Approaching from the other direction, Lavater avers that there is no purgatory, hence are no dead in a state of expiation asking our help to pass their probation.[69] As for the sainted dead whose presence at their shrines Catholics held to prove return of souls, there was no need for them; for men are damned or saved by God's grace, not by influence of supernal patrons.[70]

The Protestant objection to ghosts, as to purgatory and intercession, probably was rooted in part in the reforming effort to halt "the Romeward flow of German gold." To say masses for the dead and to sue to the saints were alike expensive. Protestants practised economy of both doctrine and coin when they dispossessed the guilty dead of purgatory and the saintly dead of worldly audience, and, to bolster these improvements, denied the return of the dead of any sort.[71] The argument to the purse Lavater makes in full. The cupidity of priests, he says, who want masses bought for the dead is at the bottom of many tales of apparitions, and even of the very visitations themselves. He recites many anecdotes of priestly dupery.[72]

For the rest, whatever veritable spectres come to men in the likenesses of dead persons, professing to need aid of masses and candles or to confer the warning and guidance of God, are probably deceitful demons seeking to injure those they visit.[73] But that occasionally it is angels that come Lavater admits, and he makes from the admission argument to show that the Apostles to whom Christ appeared after his bodily death believed they saw not his ghost as Catholics claimed, but a good angel.[74]

Against Lavater, the Catholic champions, Le Loyer and Taillepied, argued vigorously that God not only can but does by special dispensation return disembodied souls to earth in His good service. Such return and any ensuing materialization are, it is true, to be regarded as miraculous, out of the order of nature; [75] but the occurrence is established by testimony of Holy Writ, a true exegesis of which reveals clearly that souls do return. Le Loyer and Taillepied do not deny that demons sometimes cunningly pose as ghosts, so create uncertainty as to the identity of spirit visitors in general; [76] but for one firm in the faith, they say, it is possible to resolve such uncertainty by tests of an apparition's purposes and powers. The whole of Le Loyer's fourth book (in the original edition) treats of such tests. To the Protestant denial of purgatory, Le Loyer of course opposes a flat contradiction that entails review of the whole argument for purgatory. With a summary retort of slander he meets Lavater's assertion that priests advanced the ghost doctrine for profit.[77]

2

Although the sectarian contention that ghosts appear as the Catholic Church says they do supplies the central matter of Le Loyer's book, there is in it much ghost lore not directly pertinent to the controversy with Protestants and, indeed, alien to the controversy and to the Christian providence the controversy posited. Those "accepted historiographers"—mostly pagan—whom even Lavater holds next in authority to scripture and the holy Fathers are the source of this material. Principally classical, it is to sixteenth century pneumatology a fringe unassimilable nevertheless treasured, even by the orthodox, for its antique connections, and it is warrant for every tenet of sixteenth century occultists.

In Le Loyer's work this material is prominent chiefly as he rebuts it or adjusts it to his Catholic conceptions. He cites doctrines like Trismegistus' that the souls of evil livers will seek the body after death, only as preliminary to banishing such error.[78] But to occult authors Trismegistus is nearly gospel. On him and on Pythagoras and Apuleius and Plutarch and a score more of ancients, both legendary and historical, Agrippa, for instance, relies directly and with their lore mingles Christian almost indiscriminately.[79]

There is an important though not always very sharp distinction between the sort of ghosts for which Le Loyer contended against Lavater and the ghosts of pagan conception which inhabit the tales of the "historiographers" and are the lore of occultism. The ghosts for which Le Loyer contended were beneficent beings come from purgatory or heaven,[80] testifying by their divinely licensed presence to the truth of Christianity. Very different were the ghosts of which Cornelius Agrippa as an occult theorist treated. They were usually desolate and terrible vestiges of malignant or lustful personalities not received into heaven and perhaps escaped out of hell, moving in the shadow of their earthly bodies about their still earthly interests. They were but vestiges because they lacked the divine part, which left them at death and returned blameless to God; and they were natural, not miraculous, because they manifested themselves by the astral shapes which even living men wore and which survived awhile the dissolution of the elementary body.[81]

Le Loyer in his chapter on ethnic eschatology[82] labors to disperse a nebulous cloud of notions about souls wandering earth-bound. But these very notions Agrippa, writing "What concerning man after death, diverse opinions," his forty-first chapter of the third book, seems bent on fostering. Presenting the same material as Le Loyer, he does not intersperse it with the repeated disclaimers by which the Frenchman keeps clear the path of orthodoxy, but on the contrary so mingles pagan with Hebrew and Christian doctrines that they form one great mélange.

Scot, who of course stands with Lavater that there are no ghosts, says that though the people reject popish fables of purgatory they incline nevertheless to believe in apparitions of souls out of heaven or hell. "Whereby I gather that if Protestants believe some few lies, the papists believe a great number." [83]

But the truth seems to have been that the apparitions thus popularly credited were not so much conceived to be from the Christian havens for souls as from the more immediate and gruesome charnel house and grave or from some indefinite limbo of the disembodied where they retain the lusts of fleshly life. This idea that the souls of the dead were swayed by earthly passions and frequented the resting places of their bodily organs, or spots which hope of sensual gratification made attractive to them was one that persisted despite the theologians and that was at the heart of occult pneumatology on ghosts. It was essential to theory of necromantic ghosts and treasure-guarding ghosts and revenge ghosts and, indeed, of most ghosts that, as opposed to the drab, candle-begging ghost of Catholic theology, were dramatic in mission and circumstance.

With Le Loyer and others of the orthodox this idea of sensual ghosts was a discredited one. Remy, for instance, digresses from his witchmongering to assert the Romish doctrine that for the dead there are fixed unworldly abodes from which they issue only by miracle, and to criticize as absurd in the light of it the common belief that the souls of the dead linger about tombs.[84]

But Agrippa, though in his customary cautious and evasive way, seems to countenance the ancient doctrine of earth-bound souls. In agreement with the general pneumatology of the time he holds that ghosts, like daemons, take perceptible bodies by condensation of air or other materials,[85] and he seems to add as doctrine what orthodox pneumatologists took no notice of but as pagan superstition: that souls of the wicked after death come from their punishment to take airy bodies and seek worldly aid of their friends and pursue their enemies.[86] Further, the souls of such as greatly love corporeal things may remain on earth in what bodies they can achieve. It is known by experience that souls of those dead by violence stay near the corpse and are subject to the incantations of necromancers, who use them to make dreams and pestilence, awaken discord, and do other things which the spirits have power to do.[87]

It happens, too, says Agrippa, that earth-bound spirits enter the bodies of living creatures, even of men, and that such men partake of the spirit's personality. A profligate spirit will soon wear out a body it enters. Agrippa adds that it is granted sometimes that the spirit of a holy dead man enter into a living man and act as his good angel. So the spirit of Elias came over Elisha.[88]

But ghosts were comparatively little prominent in Agrippa's pneumatology—or, indeed, in the general pneumatology of his time. There is, of course, a vast Christian literature on the soul after death; but very little of it deals with the return of souls to earth and their activities there. Not a quarter so much pneumatology was written of ghostly as of daemonic apparitions; for though association of apparitions with the dead was a natural and vivid one, and one that commended itself to the common people and to imaginative authors, it was an association difficult to make consistent with Christian eschatology except soberly as Le Loyer makes it. Less confined, the conception of the daemon was a more fertile and workable one for the pneumatologist, one which he found easier to adjust at once to the dogma of Christianity and legends of paganism. In daemonology there was at bottom little more difference between Christian Renaissance and pagan antiquity than one of terms; but on ghosts the doctrines were fundamentally irreconcilable. Christianity could not accommodate the classical cycle concept of the soul. Christian doctrine of the after life had little or no sanction for such interesting figures as the revenge ghost and the tomb dweller. The bounds were so firmly set that the occult pneumatologist found them difficult to pass with safety, and the churchman did not, of course, want to pass them.

So circumscribed, ghost lore did not flower into that organization and elaboration that marked daemonology, although it participated in the more general pneumatological conceptions. These in the sixteenth century were basically orthodox; but they appeared often with an occult embroidery which, created by a greed for wonders and easy power, did much to enrich with dramatic detail the bare and abstract concepts of theologians.

Pneumatology in Elizabethan Plays

Chapter IV

The Relation of Pneumatology to the Drama

I

ALTHOUGH ANIMISTIC MATERIAL in Elizabethan drama has a history virtually co-extensive with that drama's, it does not appear in its most characteristic form earlier than the middle years of the 1580's when Marlowe's *Faustus* brought the "practising magician" [1] on the stage for the first time and Kyd's *Spanish Tragedy* began the native tradition in the treatment of ghosts.[2] The "practising magician" was the magician of contemporary actuality as distinguished from the legendary Merlin, a wholly literary figure; and Kyd's shade of Andrea was a departure toward that stage ghost which was stripped of its "Senecan cerements and became a vivid phantom, a thing of terror and awe, a spectre that might stand by the side of any-one of the audience in the lonely watches of the night. . . ." [3] With *Faustus* opened the vogue of plays on the theme of the infernal pact.[4] Such theme entailed the devil and his angels and their works, not in the medieval style of the miracle plays but in a style harmonious with the contemporary invocateur. And after *The Spanish Tragedy* the play ghost ceased to be entirely decoration or apparatus, began to acquire vitality and, inevitably, some relation to living contemporary belief.

The vogue of the "practising magician" in tragedy, for reasons which Mr. Herrington points out,[5] declined rapidly in the Elizabethan age, so that although *Faustus* is the first it is also the best tragedy on the theme and after Barnes' *Devil's Charter,* published in 1607, there is not another tragedy that has a "practising magician" as a central character. Similarly in comedy Greene's *Friar Bacon and Friar Bungay* has no worthier successor than Munday's *John a Kent and John a Cumber.* But the popularity of the related material of witchcraft after *Macbeth* caused a continued serious handling of the diabolical pact, so that as late as 1623 we get *The Witch of Edmonton,* a play which, although its subject matter seems on a very different level from that of *Faustus* and *The Devil's Charter,* yet considered according to the orthodox opinions of the age, is a treatment of another aspect of the same magic with which Marlowe and Barnes deal.[6] In comedy Heywood and Brome's *Lancashire Witches* is yet later.

The daemon, which despite, or perhaps because of, its career in the miracles had little purchase in its own right in tragedy, was preserved on the stage by the witch plays and by a satirical vogue beginning about the turn of the century with Haughton's *Devil and his Dame* and perpetuated in Dekker's *If this be not a good play, the devil is in it* and in Jonson's *The Devil is an Ass.* In tragedy, though there is some miscellaneous appearance of daemonic creatures in by-episodes of various plays and, of course, frequent references to them, there are few plays in which a daemon has any considerable role apart from connection with a conjuror of some sort.[7]

But while the daemon failed in tragedy, the play ghost, which had in Seneca more respected antecedents than the daemon's in the miracles, and in the popular revenge play a more enduring vehicle than the magician play proved for the daemon, recovered from a lapse in popularity during the 1590's and remained in its own right a prominent figure in tragedy through the reign of James. The ghost is rare in comedy, however. One investigator finds only seven ghost-figures in comedy to 1642, and all but one of these is used satirically.[8]

The characteristic Elizabethan dramatic treatment of ghosts and daemons which began with *Faustus* and *The Spanish Tragedy* was largely a matter of escape from literary tradition and of consequent heightened verisimilitude; that is, of increased reference of the play to the actual contemporary world. It was most fully and rapidly realized in the magician plays both because Marlowe's independent genius achieved it at a blow and because the magician plays had the lighter and less tenacious tradition to escape from.[9] After *Faustus,* magic and daemons in tragedies, though sometimes approximate or fanciful in details, conform in general to the notions of their day about the nature of such things in the actual world.

Analogous conformity of the ghosts in the period's plays is much less pronounced. The well established Senecan convention gave way only slowly, and it was the manner rather than the matter of it which Kyd displaced. The dead formality and woodenness of his model he overcame; but he did not annul the convention in so far as it related to the essential conception of the ghost as a ghost. His successors, Marston and Chapman, go further; but their ghosts too have a suggestion of the classical that makes them, perhaps, appeal for interpretation as directly to the barren literary authority of Seneca as to the period's fertile theories of the actual world.

II

The place of animistic material in plays is various. The general observation may be that there are some plays that are *of* the supernatural and others that merely use it. It is the central subject matter of some plays; more present it in passing, as auxiliary action. Of some plays it is the warp and woof; in many it is merely "decorative"; [10] in some simply instrumental, a device to get the action forward.

The instrumental use appears, for instance, in Webster's *White Devil,* where a conjuring scene seems to be inserted solely to convey some necessary information, both to the audience and to a character. The use appears again, with a decorative function added, in the conjuring scene of Chapman's *Bussy D'Ambois,* and similarly in the necromantic episode of Greene's *Alphonsus of Arragon.* Nothing intrinsic to the themes of the plays called for these presentations of the supernatural, but simply the playwrights' whims, minor exigencies of structure, and the public liking for spirit shows.[11]

Very different are those uses of animistic material as integral to the action in plays, such as *Faustus,* that rest upon it by the intrinsic nature of their themes. In tragedy *The Devil's Charter,* and in tragi-comedy *The Witch of Edmonton* and *The Birth of Merlin* are diverse examples. *Bacon and Bungay* and *The Devil is an Ass* are comedies very different from each other in kind, yet alike in that to them both animistic material is integral.

In the ghost plays, the distinction between an integral and a decorative or instrumental occurrence of spirit scenes is less sure than in the daemon plays because the former are for the most part primarily revenge plays and the ghost is present rather by custom than by the inherent obligation of the subject matter. There is an obvious difference, nevertheless, between such active ghosts as that of Andrugio in *Antonio's Revenge* by Marston and the nebulous, brief, and silent apparition of Isabella in Webster's *White Devil. Hamlet,* of course, is the best example of a play of which the ghost is as organic a part as any other, even the protagonist himself.

Presentation of animistic material, whether it be instrumental or integral in place, is of many kinds. Sometimes, as in Rowley's *Birth of Merlin* and even more in Jonson's unfinished pastoral, *The Sad Shepherd,* it is romantic. Again, as in *The Devil is an Ass,* it is satirical. Often it is conventional as in the Senecan revenge tragedies; sometimes as in the conjuring scenes of Chapman's *Bussy D'Ambois* and Greene's *Alphonsus,* it is basically fantastic, that is, drawn at the author's caprice to suit a scheme of things that finds no certain authority either in previous dramas or in the world. Sometimes, as in *The Spanish Tragedy,* the presentation is explicit; sometimes, as in *The Duchess of Malfi,* indefinite and enigmatic. Sometimes it is circumstantial, as in *The Late Lancashire Witches,* sometimes momentary as in *The Atheist's Tragedy.* But rarely is it wholly without reference to contemporary doctrine of spirits.

The romantic plays rest directly upon legend or folklore, take their authority from traditional rather than theoretical spirit doctrine. But it was this very literature of legend, this very tradition, that supplied much of the data of theoretical pneumatology, so that the theory was in the opinion of Elizabethans often directly applicable even where there had been originally no thought of it.

Even the satirical treatment did not always part with pneumatology. In fact, the learned Ben Jonson, who took pains to be authentic even with what he apparently scorned, is impeccably faithful to pneumatology—except in spirit—in his *Devil is an Ass*. The satiric attack itself is aimed less at superstition than at London's fantastic vices that overreach hell. Jonson had his tongue in his cheek, of course, as he so carefully observed the details of theory on devils; but the pneumatology is on the whole a pedantic and rather fruitless top dressing on the satire. Haughton's and Dekker's somewhat similar satiric treatments of animistic material are much freer in details.

Perhaps no other plays are so consistent in fidelity to pneumatological authority as *The Devil is an Ass,* but many appeal to it rather more meaningfully. Such plays as *Faustus, The Devil's Charter,* and *The Witch of Edmonton* rest their whole sense upon it—not upon the details, but upon the general scheme that in theology shaped the details into a significant design and really was the thing which determined the acceptability of data which there was no experimental way of testing. That the authors of these plays consciously and deliberately wrote pneumatology into them—as, upon the evidence of his footnotes to the *Masque of Queens,* Jonson unquestionably did into his plays—there is no necessity to believe, though it is perhaps a possibility not to be excluded. But the plays seem to lend themselves in their essential action to interpretation in the light of pneumatology.

Much less satisfactory for such comment, of course, are those plays whose spirit scenes, composed loosely as instrument or decoration, are obviously remote from any but the most general connection with pneumatology. The conjuring scene in *Bussy D'Ambois,* for instance, presents a daemonic feat that has neither a rationalization in formal pneumatology nor a strict analogue in tradition. It must be accepted as peculiar to the world of the play, for it does not correspond to theory of such things in the outside world. This is, of course, not necessarily a reflection on the artistic merit of the scene. But it is a fact which confronts the expositor.

There can scarcely be, nevertheless, a sixteenth century spirit scene that is utterly without reference to pneumatology. The witches in *Macbeth,* once thought to be wholly creatures of Shakespeare's imagination, have been shown by Spalding and even more convincingly by Professor W. C. Curry to have a very specific reference to current doctrine. The reference in *Bussy* seems certainly much less complete; but it exists.[12]

III

A phenomenon of Elizabethan drama's maturity was the tightening of its canons as fiction shown in the rejection of interlude and Plautine practice of addressing speeches and action directly to the audience. [This restriction of action to the stage scene and the fictitious off-stage continuation of it, and of dialogue to the players as fictitious characters, accented the distinction and the artistic barrier between the world that contains the play and the world which the play contains.]

Perhaps a play exists first as a thing of the theater, as a phenomenon that fits into exterior time and events. But it exists also, in a necessary fiction at least, as a cosmos by itself; the world of the play is the play as its events relate only to each other and to their implicit background. The world of the play, although originated and existent within the actual world and largely correlative in plan, is, as itself, separate from the actual world and without cognizance of it. Properly conceived, the play world has no place for any utterance or action addressed to the spectator, although as a total it is addressed to the spectator. It is this fictitious world that is the artistic creation, and to apprehend the relationships that exist within it is surely indispensable to apprehension of the play.

The world of the play must be grasped by the spectator predominantly in terms of the actual world, though partly, perhaps, in terms of the worlds of other plays and partly in terms unique to it. The thing which the interpreter attempts is a rationale of the world of the play, that is to know its principles.

Now, so far as the world of the play is a simulacrum of the actual world the exposition of it must have reference to something known or surmised of the actual world. Such reference of the spirit scenes in Elizabethan plays seems often in part to authority of contemporary pneumatology, for it is pneumatology that offers the readiest and most complete system of principles explaining the action of spirits. Obscuring such reference and hindering the construction of a pneumatological rationale are five impediments: (1) dramatic convention, which has a literary rather than a scientific authority for the traits it gives to spirits; (2) approximate or fanciful presentation, which merely indicates the sphere of the spirit's action, gives no ground for exact interpretation according to pneumatology; (3) existence in the play of matter extrinsic to the play world, as, for instance, prologue figures and speeches addressed to the audience and perhaps coming from the author; (4) anachronisms in the indicated rationale; (5) the possible subjective implication of objective presentations, that is, the possible subjectivity of an existence in the play world which nevertheless appears sensibly on the stage. These things sometimes prevent a consistent rationale according to pneumatology. The play world has for contradictions a certain proper tolerance that sixteenth century pneumatologists did not intentionally allow of the actual world.

For the expositor of the spirit scenes of a play there are four general questions: (1) as to the nature of the spirit figures, that is whether they are essential beings and are objective, or are creations of a character's mind, and so wholly subjective, or are abstractions of some sort and thus symbolic; (2) as to the license of the spirits, that is as to their place and function in the play world's providence; (3) as to the works of the spirits, that is as to the extent and means of their control over earthly things; (4) as to their relation to men, that is, whether they are attracted or coerced by men and if either by what connection, or whether they are sent to men or come of their own will.

Pointing the answers to these questions within the play world are three classes of indices of varying authority: (1) the opinions of the persons of the play world as displayed in speech and action; (2) unquestioned facts of the play world as revealed in its events; (3) the general philosophical and theological cast of the play world as revealed in its historical and religious setting. Of these the second is, of course, most authoritative—in the end solely authoritative. The opinions of the characters often duplicate the dissensions of the actual world,[13] and anachronisms or romanticisms confuse the period and creed of the play world.

In dealing with these indices the method of the expositor must be to detect the terms and concepts of pneumatology, assign them value according to their occurrence, and from them try to construct a rationale which will be consistent with them in the values assigned.

Since all pieces of general literature appeal necessarily first to an ordinary rather than a specialized knowledge, it is not supposed that any profound or esoteric learning was required for a reasonable understanding of Elizabethan plays by the public for which they were produced. Nor is it necessary to think that every playwright who treated of spirits kept in mind the speculations of pneumatologists. That artistic use of daemons and ghosts in plays demands circumstantial pneumatology such as Ben Jonson provided in his *Masque of Queens* and his follower, Shadwell, in *Lancashire Witches and Teague of Divelly* is no part of the thesis here. Elizabethan plays doubtless proffer, nevertheless, various levels for appreciation and can sometimes accommodate a close as well as a wide correlation with contemporary theory of spirits. Certainly, at any rate, many Elizabethan Englishmen had access to the literature of pneumatology and with it must surely have conferred spirit scenes of the plays whether the authors intended it or not. So far as the dramatic action can reasonably bear the pneumatological theory, thus far, surely, the theory may illuminate the action.

Chapter V

Daemonic Names, Places, and Rank

I

WHETHER OR NOT any stage figures of Elizabethan drama were designed to appeal to a spectator's knowledge of pneumatology, one thing is sure: some plays in the presentation of certain figures use many terms and names in common with pneumatology. It may be best to approach interpretation of the figures by means of this certainty.

Such approach is productive, however, only if the daemonic figures be taken, so far as a just dramatic estimate permits, rather as essential beings within the world of the play than as literary abstractions. The metaphysical rather than the metaphorical existence of spirits is the indispensable preliminary to positive pneumatology. Professor Stoll says of the Elizabethan play ghost: "And psychology in the sense of refining and subduing it into a symbol or personification never, so far as I can discover, came into play at all." [1] The same thing seems true of daemonic figures. There is hardly one in Elizabethan drama that may not be taken as objective, that is, in the independent play world substantially existent beyond the minds of the characters.

The generic terms *spirit, angel, daemon, devil, genius, guardian,* are applied to a class of play figures many of which, in addition, are denoted by "proper" names of which the plays have some in common with the literature of daemonology.

Designations of daemonic figures in the plays, then, fall into three classes: (1) the generic, such terms as *devil* or *good angel;* (2) "proper" names that are unknown to daemonology; (3) "proper" names that the plays share with the literature of daemonology. With these can be cross-classified a further group of daemonic names: those which designate daemons who are in the play only verbally as in incantations, not otherwise represented on the stage, though sometimes properly conceivable as of the play world.

Of considerable daemonic figures in Elizabethan tragedy there are more than a score, most of which have "proper" names. The most prominent such names common to the plays and to daemonology are Lucifer, Belzebub, Asterote, Belimoth and Mephistophilis in Marlowe's *Faustus;* Astaroth, Varca, and Lucifer in Barnes' *Devil's Charter;* Behemoth in Chapman's *Bussy D'Ambois;* and Hecate in Rowley's *Birth of Merlin.* Names either unknown to daemonology or relatively obscure are Baliol and Belchar in *Faustus;* Belchar in *The Devil's Charter;* Cartophylax in *Bussy;* Armel and Plesgeth in *The Birth of Merlin;* Harpax and Angelo in Dekker's *Virgin Martyr.* Some of them, Cartophylax and Angelo for example, are evidently adapted etymologically to suit their special dramatic uses. All the plays mentioned except *Bussy* and *The Virgin Martyr* have also anonymous daemons denominated only *angel* or *spirit* or *devil.*

In comedy some devil names known to daemonology are Demogorgon, "master of the Fates," and Belcephon [2] in *Friar Bacon and Friar Bungay;* Satan in *The Devil is an Ass;* Belphegor and Akercocke [3] in Haughton's *Devil and his Dame.* The latter play also has devils with the classical names Pluto, Rhadamanthus, Aeacus and Minos, as has Dekker's *If this be not a good play, the devil is in it.*[4] In the latter play Shackle-soule, Lurchall and Rufman are devils' names which seem to be original with Dekker. But Friar Rush, the name and title which Shackle-soule assumed in his work on earth, is, of course, well known to legend, as is Robin Goodfellow, the name which Akercocke assumed. Pug in *The Devil is an Ass,* and Pug and Mamilion in Heywood and Brome's *Late Lancashire Witches* are, like the 'Tom' of *The Witch of Edmonton,* homely names of the sort which crop up in the English witch trials, were ridiculed by Archbishop Harsnett in the work from which Shakespeare took his devils' names for *Lear*.

These various designations are listed in the *dramatis personae* as though of human characters in that they stand for determinate stage figures, and no doubt the pit took them thus simply in the play itself—that is to say, accepted the name of a daemon as standing for an entity sufficiently realized in the visible figure. Perhaps this anthropomorphic way would be the best, as it is certainly the simplest, way to take daemonic names in plays were it not for two things:

1) To daemonic names which the plays have in common with the literature of daemonology there are connected significations that adhere to the names in the plays as extraneous to, whether or not in agreement with, the dramatic action that occurs under the names. There was no possibility that a figure labelled Astaroth or Lucifer or Behemoth could come on an Elizabethan stage without appealing to a previous knowledge in the minds of at least some of the spectators. That the significations of the names in the plays correspond with any strictness to the significations in daemonology is quite unnecessary dramatically; but there is no escaping correspondence of some sort, slight or great. To know the extent of it may be desirable, and that can be determined only by applying the name in a play as daemonology applied it in the actual world.

2) Not every daemonic stage figure with a name can be comprehended as what it necessarily appears, a discrete personality. According to pneumatology, daemonic names denote scarcely more than do the generic terms *angel* and *devil*. The names make no certain distinction between daemonic beings. They signify the daemonic being generally, as represented to the senses of the audience and sometimes of the characters—that is, usually concretely on the stage though not always concreted in the play world—by figures [5] and action meagerly definitive of some play world personal essence and will which contrives the figure and performs the action but which is not determinate within the temporal world of the play and to which no utterable name can apply personally and immediately. A daemon's essential identity is something with which man's earthly receptors of knowledge give him no contact.

The inadequacies of language and man's constant inclination to anthropomorphism led sixteenth century daemonologists—especially the occult—to speak sometimes of spirits with a circumstantiality not consonant with their knowledge. It is necessary to remember that no matter how named or represented, a daemon is in essence a separated intelligence, a form untouched by matter, hence not subject to human senses. Though the human intellect could conceive the daemon to be form, it could have no grasp of the form of any particular daemon save as an abstraction from his manifest works.[6] Such an abstraction was entirely inadequate to express his essential form. Though daemons possessed personal form and existence, the minds of men had no images of them any more than of abstract good and evil.

Language, of course, applied names to daemons, as to persons, for purposes of identification. But the circumscription of identity could not be nearly so complete for a daemon as for a man since a man informs with individuality his body, which registers upon the senses, whereas the body which a daemon took was but representative, might represent any daemon. A daemon could be known only through his assumed body and his other peculiar works, and daemonic works were not peculiar to single daemons, but at the narrowest to classes.

Names, however, have perhaps two kinds of signification: (1) intrinsic or formal, that which inheres in the name by virtue of etymological or necessary symbolic meaning, (2) extrinsic or arbitrary, that which adheres to the name as a name, *i.e.*, as a word that stands for the essence, with its history, of whatever identity it is assigned to. Daemonic names, according to sixteenth century theory, were unlike human names in two ways: (1) they were deficient in extrinsic signification so far as that signification applied to essence, that is, defined the individual as a being, a thing distinct from his actions; (2) there was customarily some correspondence, though not always a close one, between the intrinsic signification and the extrinsic so far as the latter related to a daemonic history rather than essence. Thus the name Lucifer signifies the brightness that had been its bearer's in heaven. Later daemonologists say that at the fall the name became by antiphrase *Lucifuge* to signify the spirit's recession from God's light.[7]

Agrippa says of the names of spirits:

> . . . the whole virtue of angelical essence cannot be made by any humane voyce, therefore names for the most part are put upon them from their works, signifying some certain office, or effect, which is required by the quire of Spirits. . . .[8]

He adds later that "spirits of divers offices and natures may be noted or marked by one name"; even sometimes fallen and blessed spirits may have names—though never particular works—in common.[9]

The use of names in treatises on pneumatology shows that the formal significations of daemonic names are of general works to which correspond not particular daemons but rather the broad classes of the daemonic being. Thus the name *Beelzebub,* Agrippa says, means "old god" as designating the prince of the first order of evil spirits, those who in pagan days were false gods.[10] But, as is plain from testimony elsewhere in the *Occult Philosophy* and in many other books, this false assumption of godhood was a work general to demons, and any demon engaged in it was, to men, Beelzebub. The name, in its meaning "old god," is obviously intended to signify simply a phase of daemonic works. The formal signification of the name is given otherwise by other authorities. Bodin, explaining that devils were the gods of the pagans, says that of one nation the chief god was called *Bahal,* "c'est à dire en Hebrieu, Seigneur, d'où est venu Bahal-zebub, qui veut dire Maistre mouche, par ce qu'il n'y auoit par une mouche en son temple. . . ." Remy, also, interprets Beelzebub to mean lord of flies,[11] as does *Malleus Maleficarum,* which, discussing how names "indicate what order and rank there is among [devils]," says that in scripture every unclean spirit is named *Diabolus* or *Demon,* and continues:

> . . . He is also called Beelzebub, which means Lord of Flies, that is of the souls of sinners who have left the true faith of Christ. Also Satan, that is the Adversary. . . . Also Behemoth, that is, Beast, because he makes men bestial. . . .[12]

Bodin speaks of "ce grand Satan" that scripture calls Behemoth or Leviathan or Asmodeus. Behemoth is the enemy of man's body and soul. Further, "Il est dit que la force de Behemot est en ses reins, en son ventre, & en sa queuë: qui signifie la cupidité & partie bestiale: &, comme les anciens Hebrieux disoient, que Satan a la puissance des voluptez bestiales." Bodin seems to make no distinction of application between the three names, *Satan* (which he says the Hebrews applied to the being who is "l'ennemy"), and *Behemoth,* and *Diable,* "en Grec Calomniateur." [13]

Agrippa and the *Malleus* and Bodin seem to take the significations of the names cited to be of phases of common demonic nature or of the divisions of demonic labor and rule—divisions so general that particular names are considered mere formal variants of the generic terms, *Diabolos* and *Demon.* Agrippa identifies the name *Astaroth* with the Greek *Diabolos,* Accuser [14]—an indication, with the similar assumptions of Bodin and the *Malleus,* of how little distinction pneumatology made as to terms between "the devil" and any particular devil.

It is well to remember, however, that Bodin speaks of "les diables" as well as of *Le Diable;* neither he nor the others quoted took daemons in any nominalist sense, as unreal personifications of the qualities of the world or providence or the human mind. Devils were real and substantial evil, as real as the souls they persecuted. Simply, because they were remote from man's knowledge, their names were not personal and immediate, but abstractions from their works, and applied to them often collectively. Because of the kind of beings daemons were, the individual denotation of a name faded away into the connotation of a literal translation of the name. Gifford says:

> First consider this that there be multitudes & armies of deuils, as we see in the gospel, that manie deuils wer entred into one man, & Christ saying, What is thy name, answer is made, Legion, for we are manie. Mark 5. Now, although the deuils be manie, yet they be all carried with such hatred against God with such desire to haue him dishonored and blasphemed, and burne with such bloudy malice and

crueltie against men, that they bend their studie all together, one helping and furthering another what they can in their worke: in so much that the Scripture doeth speake of them, as they were but one deuil: . . .[15]

There is a manifest difference in aim between such a broad use of daemonic names as Bodin's and the use in occult works like the *Lemegeton* and *Heptameron* which seem to refer to daemons personally and specifically. Bodin seeks simply to establish the existence of devils as evil beings of certain general characteristics connoted by formally significative names; but the *Heptameron* and the *Lemegeton* are practical manuals for effective treating with whatever beings daemons may be, and are eager to attach to particular names particular services. As practical, they have no concern with the theory of names, seem to apply them in the way that is readiest—that is, as though to human beings. But Agrippa writing on the theory of names for ceremonial use had said that the names bore no essential relation to specific beings; and the *Arbatel of Magic,* a transcendental handbook, says in its aphorisms for magicians that names are effective only temporarily and are not absolute.[16] The *Lemegeton's* explicit comments under each name in its list of Solomon's devils, though perhaps effective guides to conjuration, do not bind the names exclusively to demons with the histories and places there allotted any more than the name *George* is necessarily bound to the actions of any particular English king.[17]

Differing, too, from Bodin's use of daemonic names is the use in such narrative works as the *Faust Book.* For purposes of narrative—not to say fiction—the *Faust Book* localizes demonic being under static and singular symbols, names applied as though to fixed individuals. Yet strictly, no individual is indicated, but simply the existence of certain demonic powers applied by a personal will with which they are one to an area of the sensible world of the narrative.

That this is so in the *Faust Book* is perhaps indicated by a suggested etymology, *Mefaustophiles,* "Bad for Faustus," for the name, *Mephistophilis.*[18] The name seems to have been new to daemonology with the Faust legend, hence was perhaps devised for the place it fills. It signifies a general demonic assault on Faustus, administered, so far as it was manifest, by a single representative figure.

The works of the Mephistophilis of the *Faust Book* belong to a genus: fallen, unbodied intelligence, that is, demon; and to a species: a subordinate order of demon. So much we can infer from them of the being or beings that perform them. It is to these works and the concepts to which they give rise that the name Mephistophilis attaches, and further than this the name cannot particularize Faustus' tormentor to human understanding.

Plays, of course, far more than the *Faust Book,* are impelled by the requirements of fiction to use names anthropomorphically, and they have further the necessity of presenting a concrete, identifiable figure for every character, daemonic or human. This should not, however, obscure the fact that daemonic characters on the Elizabethan stage can in most serious plays profitably be conceived according to the doctrines of daemonology, their names applied in the mode in which daemonology applied them. Such application permits, sometimes, a correlation in sense between play names and identical names in daemonology, or demonstrates that none can be made; and it occasionally explains satisfactorily what seems loose, contradictory usage in the plays.

2

Marlowe's Mephistophilis is known to Faustus and to the audience by name and works. The name attaches to a figure that is, in the play world, only a representational apparition with which are associated certain other daemonic contrivances. The sum of them, uncertainly definitive of a sphere of daemonic application, is all that either Faustus or the audience knows of Mephistophilis as an individual, and all the extrinsic signification the name has. But nothing indicates that Mephistophilis' work in the play world need be thought exhausted by what we can associate with the figure to which a *dramatis personae* would attach the name. It is allowable, both pneumatologically and dramatically, to conceive him one in essence as he is certainly one in purpose with Faustus' anonymous Evil

Angel. Most of the open enticement and compulsion that leads to Faustus' damnation is associated with the figure denominated Mephistophilis; the inner inspiration was the Evil Angel's. But at the end Mephistophilis reveals that long before his initial apparition he had assailed Faustus insensibly, turning the pages of the Bible and leading his eye.[19]

Pneumatologically it is impossible to say with certainty whether Mephistophilis and the Evil Angel are one in essence, and dramatically it probably matters no whit. What may matter dramatically and what is sure pneumatologically is that daemons in plays, though to be conceived substantial and personal, not personificatory, are to the human characters but abstractions from daemonic works and are neither defined nor numbered by their names. One daemon might answer to many names or many to one.

This helps to account for certain inconsistencies in Marlowe's use of demonic names. For instance, Faustus in his invocation of Mephistophilis uses only two names as though of demonic princes and neither name is *Lucifer.* "Orientis princeps, Belzebub, inferni ardentis monarcha, et Demogorgon, propitiamus vos. . . ." But when Mephistophilis materializes and says he is servant to great Lucifer, Faustus asks, "Did not he charge thee to appear to me?" This together with information from the *Faust Book* which calls Lucifer Prince of the East, and the similar address in Faustus' compact, leads to A. E. Taylor's conjecture [20] that the *Orientis princeps* of the incantation is not in apposition with *Belzebub,* but signifies Lucifer, of whom Faustus, as his subsequent questions show, knew as "an angel once," now become "prince of devils." Yet when Mephistophilis tells him that the shortest cut for conjuring is to "pray devoutly to the prince of hell," and Faustus replies that so hath he already done, it is Belzebub whom he says he holds only "chief" and to whom he dedicates himself and to love of whom, he admits later, his appetite inclines him. On the other hand, at the signing of the compact there is no naming of Belzebub, only of Lucifer. Later when Lucifer and Belzebub appear together to chide Faustus, Lucifer asserts there is none but him has interest in Faustus' soul; yet Belzebub says: "We are come to tell thee thou dost injure us." Obviously the names Belzebub and Lucifer here convey no essential distinction, signify merely the sphere of action in the play world of certain temporally indeterminate, though personal, forces of evil.[21]

Indeed, there is hardly more reason to suppose the apparitions labelled Lucifer and Belzebub to be managed by demonic essences distinct from Mephistophilis than to suppose it of the unobjectified Evil Angel. One daemon could appear as many.[22] The names Lucifer and Belzebub have only this distinction from Mephistophilis: the rank associated with them is significant of the order which demons maintained in their war with man.[23] The assault on Faustus is guided and ruled by demonic beings superior to Mephistophilis. It may or may not be that these beings participate directly in Faustus' overthrow. The action cannot indicate—nor, of course, need it indicate to serve dramatic ends.[24] But in reading the sixteenth century play one may, perhaps, well keep in mind how veiled from man's knowledge the sixteenth century conceived such a being as Mephistophilis to be. The critic who forgets this may take Elizabethans as much more naïve in such matters than they were.

The only cleavage that certainly distinguishes one play daemon from another is that between the blessed and the damned. The fallen spirits designated by the names Mephistophilis and Lucifer and Belzebub have no being in common with Faustus' Good Angel. The Angelo of Massinger's *Virgin Martyr* is as distinct as he seems from the loathly Harpax.

II

The abstraction of the daemonic being, erasing as it does for man's understanding the individual identity of the daemon in the world of the play, obviously blocks any very close correlation of the play names with their counterparts in daemonology. Many different names are centers of identical or cognate legends, and many conflicting legends adhere to a single name. It is almost fruitless to refer for understanding of a particular daemonic figure in a play to the extraneous information which adheres to its name in daemonology unless there is a direct debt of the play to a daemonological work, as of *Faustus* to the *English Faust Book,* showing itself not only in identical nomenclature, but in resemblance of action. If such agreement exists the spectator may, perhaps, safely supplement the play with the extraneous information of the source. Thus, for instance, the *Faust Book,* which lists Lucifer as Prince of the East, helps to confirm Mr. Taylor's surmise that the *Orientis princeps* of the incantation is Lucifer.[25] In general daemonology many names besides Lucifer are attributed to the ruler of the east.[26]

If a play has no detectable debt to a specific daemonological work, it is unlikely that any daemonic name it has in common with daemonology can convey more than the most general indication of daemonic nature and place, that is, signify the action of non-human spirit and perhaps indicate whether it is fallen or unfallen. The full extrinsic signification of a daemonic name is as particularized as the lowest common denominator of the conflicting legends surrounding it, and the intrinsic signification is neither certain nor closely binding. All in all, a genuine daemonic name in a play can—without connection with a particular, consistent, and self-sufficient source—convey in itself little if any more than a generic term, good or evil angel.

One play proper name well known to daemonology does not yield even so much, for the extraneous meaning of the name seems largely contradicted by the action in the play. The name *Behemoth* in Chapman's *Bussy D'Ambois* attaches to a figure which, like much else in that play, is oddly enigmatic. The name is a fairly prominent one in daemonology and one which authorities almost universally agree denotes demonic bestiality—that is, the brutish offices of deviltry and a brutish devil or devils.[27] But in *Bussy,* Behemoth is by implication "a good aerial spirit," and he does nothing to prove the term a delusion of the exorcist's. Though at one point in the play Bussy is convinced that Behemoth is indeed "Prince of Lies" as Mother Church calls him, the event proves the spirit truthful.

The motives of Mephistophilis and Lucifer and Belzebub in *Faustus,* and of Astaroth and Varca in *The Devil's Charter* are frankly devilish, and the license under which they act in the world is that which God extends to diabolic agents: to try men with temptation and to punish transgressors.[28] There is no doubt that they are to be conceived limited, as all orthodox theologians held demons to be, by God's permission. But Behemoth is neither tempter nor scourge, shows none of the eagerness proper to a devil to trap souls. He materializes at the Friar's invocation unwillingly and by compulsion, does a detached and non-committal service that, by his profession at least, not restraint imposed of God but a Fate that is perhaps to be taken as Stoic, saddens him by limiting.

All indications—scanty enough—given by the play's action seem, if taken at face value, to contradict the signification of the name Behemoth. If the pneumatological rationale of *Bussy* is orthodox, it is in a tacit fashion very different from the express fashion of *Faustus* and *The Devil's Charter,* which inform the spectator on the place and motives of their daemons almost as explicitly as would a witch tract. The spirit action of the play world in *Bussy* must have been nearly as puzzling to the Elizabethan Englishman as corresponding isolated action in the real world would have been if unlinked to any systematized belief.

Of course, the same sort of trampling rationalization which orthodox daemonology insisted upon for the real world will serve in a way for the play. Starting from the assumption that any daemon that answers invocation is evil and so deceiving, even though he appear as an angel of light, the orthodox daemonologist of the sixteenth century would have interpreted Behemoth's actions as the designing ones of a devil putting upon his invocateurs an elaborate hoax leading to destruction —as those of a fiend pretending submission and service while preparing catastrophe, showing part of the truth in a way that insured total misconstruction. But though the play permits, it does not encourage such an interpretation and a bald imposition of it would have been but theological ax-grinding. Behemoth as presented—not only to the invocateurs but to the audience—is not the filthy, vicious Astaroth of *The Devil's Charter* nor the terrible, feline Mephistophilis of *Faustus.* He is no sin-rotted, cross-willed vehicle of negation; but a vast being of dignity and sorrow, lost in mysterious meditation; emperor, it is granted, of darkness, but of a darkness hiding "deepest truths," a darkness of inscrutable wonders and mysteries, not the darkness of pain and error, deprivation and despair, not the darkness of hell. All this, it must be said, is by the spirit's own showing. But if the audience is to form any other impression of him, there is no hint.

If the rationale of the play's spirit-action is occult, Behemoth may be taken as an evil angel coerced by ceremonies into making a fair appearance and doing honest service. Such were many of the spirits catalogued in the rituals of the Solomonic cycles. Tamyra's terrified plea before the invocation that the spirit be raised in "some beauteous form," and the Friar's adjuration that Behemoth appear "lucente, splendida, amabili" testify to a belief that Behemoth was a spirit who might appear as the diabolic reverse of *amabili,* and this anxiety in the invocateurs links with the common eagerness of the users of the occult rituals to procure of fallen angels amiable manifestation.[29] But if Behemoth is a fallen angel he is so thoroughly mastered by the Friar's power as to give no sign whatever. Though the occult rituals put emphasis rather upon the magnificence and power of evil spirits than upon their hellishness, such spirits ordinarily made their nature clear by recalcitrance if not otherwise. Against the acceptance of such a conception of Behemoth is his uncompelled manifestation to Bussy without the "decent rites of art." But the name and his circumstances as king of darkness seem to preclude equally a conception of him as a good angel. Further, the Friar has promised to raise not an angel, but "any spirit of earth or air," that is, a sublunary spirit. Most authorities would take this to mean a fallen spirit.[30]

It is probable that Behemoth must be understood simply as a dramatic figure which has very little reference, so far as his place and motives are concerned, to any theory of the actual world. No correlation with daemonology can shed much light on his place and motives, and in the rationale of the play world they remain obscure. The daemonic action is instrumental and decorative rather than integral and necessary to the play. Pneumatologically, the presentation of Behemoth is both fanciful and random. Superficially occult, it leaves an uncertainty that cannot be resolved. Dramatically, of course, resolution which squares with pneumatology is necessary only so far as the play requires a pre-fabricated background. But so far as the action leaves uncertain both the pneumatology peculiar to the play world, and its own conformity with the pneumatology of the outside world, the concept in the mind of the spectator must remain incomplete. It can only be said that the figure of Behemoth is at once more fanciful and more noble than orthodoxy allows, draws a dramatic and ornamental value from a vague and general relation to the occult.

2

Another odd, but more explicable, use of a daemonic name occurs in Chapman's unacted tragedy, *Caesar and Pompey*. A devil, Ophioneus, appears with flame and thunder in the form of a dragon to a despairing rascal flying from a region of civil war, and talks to him in the usual language of the fallen angel trying to make a league with a mortal ripe for it. This, of course, is an anachronism in the world of the play since it projects the Patristic doctrine of the fall of angels and the medieval doctrine of the witch pact into the classical setting. There is, however, no fault of name or event in the scene. Ophioneus was a name known, if obscure in Greek mythology, denoting an evil spirit who contended with Zeus, was flung into the abyss.[31] To take such a legend as prefiguring the Christian doctrine of Satan's rebellion was not, to the unhistorical-minded Elizabethan, incompatible with a fiction of Roman time and place.

In the play the devil declares himself:

> *Ophioneus.* Read the old stoic Pherecides that tells thee me truly, and says that I, Ophioneus (for so is my name)—
>
> *Fronto.* Ophioneus? What's that?
>
> *Oph.* Devilish serpent by interpretation—was general captain of that rebellious host of spirits that waged war with heaven.
>
> *Fron.* And so were hurled down into hell.
>
> *Oph.* We were so, and yet have the rule of earth; . . .
>
> (II, i, 57)[32]

For the application of Christian concepts to the tale of "the old Stoic," sixteenth century pneumatology gives full sanction. Bodin, for instance, explaining the opinion that the angels created in grace, fell from it through wilfulness, says: "Et mesme Pherecides est de cest aduis, appellant le Dragon Ophionaeum, chef des Anges rebelles, . . ." Agrippa in a chapter on the order and fall of the evil spirits says: "Pherecydes the Syrian describeth the fall of the Devils and that Ophis, that is, the Devilish serpent, was the head of that rebelling Army. . . ."[33]

Of course the scene in Chapman is largely foolery, and as such needs no license from pneumatology. Nevertheless, to the extent indicated it has license.

Similarly incongruous to the modern ear, but similarly licensed by contemporary pneumatology as well as by literary usage is the occurrence in a scene of Rowley's *Birth of Merlin* of classical names. Merlin's father, an incubus devil, calls on:

> Lucina, Hecate, dreadful Queen of Night,
> Bright Proserpine, (III, iii, 7)[34]

to summon up the Fates and assist at the miraculous birth of his son. Agrippa gives the three names *Proserpine, Lucina, Phoebe* (*i.e., Hecate,* the moon goddess) as of a princess of devils, triform because she has power in three elements—air, water, and earth.[35] The universal Christian dogma that all gods of heathendom, of whatever time or place, were but masquerading devils, made such classical names as acceptable in sixteenth century pneumatology as Biblical ones.[36]

III

Most of the genuine daemonic names in Elizabethan tragedy attach, like the name Behemoth, to beings who in the world of the play are of rank and distinction among their fellows. They wear great titles, are invoked with respect, appear in splendor. They are obviously of higher rank in spiritual hierarchies than those daemons who in the plays are either anonymous or nondescript in designation. Of one group are the great kings of hell and of the regions of the world, spirits by whose names magicians command inferiors; to another group belong daemons of the lower orders: guardians, familiars, incubi and succubi—presented often without any explicit connection with the rulers, active in daemonic works, though not of the grandest.

Dramatically, of course, some of the lesser daemons are as important as any of the greater; the distinction between the two groups is entirely pneumatological and, since the rulers are not different from the lesser daemons in substance or in general daemonic being, is one of station. According to most authorities lesser daemons were less splendid than the greater in original nature and grace, hence inferior in what among men would be called political rank, correspondingly humble in specific function and at the disposal in worldly works of superior daemons.

Mephistophilis may not serve Faustus without the bidding of Lucifer, "Arch-regent and commander of all spirits"; Behemoth is an "Emperor" and rules legions; Bacon mentions "The great arch-ruler, potentate of hell"; and to Alexander at his conjuring enters "a King, with a red face crowned imperiall riding upon a Lyon, or dragon,"—presumably the "King Varca" with his "mace of Iet" "attended with his ministers of state, Andas and Cynaball," whom Alexander seemed to expect. These princes ruled, it is to be assumed, by right of their exalted original stations bestowed by God at creation, and persisting even in the fallen with respect to nature, though dissipated with respect to grace.[37]

In *The Devil's Charter* when Alexander's evil career is approaching its end, three demons meet with no human being present, to gloat and to plan his taking off, for "The date of his damnation is at hand." Of the three devils one has the name Varca—the same name Alexander had applied to a demonic king—and another, Astaroth, the name affixed to Alexander's charter and one often mentioned in daemonology as of a ruler among daemons.[38] With no show of rank the three meet and embrace, and Astaroth cries jubilantly that the Cimmerian ghosts may muster to dance about the lost soul of Alexander. Each fiend then boasts the torments he will inflict on Alexander in hell and Astaroth cries: "Then let us for his sake a horne-pipe treade"; "They dance an anticke."

The demons and their meeting are as bare of the trappings and pomp of demonic rank that go with the apparitions in the earlier conjuring scene as any manifestation of the demon dog, Tom, to his mistress in the earthy *Witch of Edmonton*. To Varca and his associates here attaches only the horror of foulness triumphant, no shred of the red and terrible, if tarnished, grandeur that becomes the demonic princes in *Faustus* and the equivocal Behemoth of *Bussy*.

King James says that there is no rank among devils, who deceive scholars in "imprinting among them the opinion that there are so manie Princes, Dukes, and Kinges amongst them eurie one commanding fewer or mo legions. . . ."[39] The scene of the three devils seems to indicate that Alexander has been so deceived, that Astaroth and his fellows are without pretense of rank when there is no human victim to be deluded. Varca says of Alexander:

> Our firy region voyd of all religion,
> And diuilish order by necessity,
> Compell'd requires his present policy.
> (V, v)

The necessity by which there is no order is, it may be thought, that of their fallen condition; as there is order in that which is good, as among the good angels, so there is none or disorder in evil, and so among evil angels.[40]

To such a rationale, however, can be opposed the explanations of daemonic order which countered King James' thesis. According to the scholastics what is devoid of "diuilish order" is the "firy region," hell; and scholastic theology affirms that in hell there is no natural rank among demons, for they are in hell according to sin and punishment, not according to nature. But in the world they have an order. Thus, from the *Malleus Maleficarum:*

> It can be said that the devils deputed to work are not in Hell, but in the lower mists. And they have here an order among themselves, which they will not have in Hell. From which it may be said that all order ceased among them, as touching the attainment of blessedness, at that time when they fell irrecoverably from such rank.[41]

Now, Varca and his fellows have completed the work of temptation and overthrow of the soul of Alexander and carry him away to hell. Astaroth says:

Be ready then for I the first will beare
As swift as wirl-winde his black soule to Stix.
(V, v)

Perhaps it may legitimately be gathered that in the play world of *The Devil's Charter* there was rank and differential function among demons according to nature when they operated on earth, none save that of God's scheme of retribution when they were in hell.[42] Even the occult rituals substantiate this. The *Lemegeton,* for instance, says in detailing an incantation that if a spirit does not answer, his king being invoked to send him, it is probable that he is in hell bound, and hence not then subject to his king.[43]

The question immediately arises, intensified by certain passages of *Faustus,* as to when demons are to be conceived as in hell. Scholastic theology answers that they are in hell locally whenever they are not working on earth, and in hell virtually at all times. *Malleus Maleficarum* says that demons belong by sin to hell, by duty to the "clouds of the air"; nevertheless, "bear hell always about them." [44]

Mephistophilis to Faustus' unbelief replies:

Why this is hell, nor am I out of it:
Think'st thou that I, that saw the
face of God,
And tasted the eternal joys of heaven,
Am not tormented with ten thousand hells,
In being depriv'd of everlasting bliss?
(I, iii, 78)

His suffering is the *poena damni,* the virtual hell.[45] It is the moral state of fallen spirits, the pain of recession from grace, and is a constant aspect of the demonic being, persisting even when a demon's exertion of his natural powers over material things has, in a sense, localized him in the "lower mists" with regard to his duty, his worldly work. But though in the gradation of their pains demons are without natural rank, in the performance of their temporal duties the rule of the superior over his natural inferior endures. They fight, says the *Malleus Maleficarum,* in an orderly manner, since so they fight most effectively.[46]

Lucifer, then, "Arch-regent and commander of all spirits," with whom Mephistophilis is damned in hell rules his demons in their earthly works. That such works are simultaneous with a state of sin and punishment which recognizes no innate priority of one devil over another is simply an accident of time, presents a contradiction only in the phenomenal world, none in the intelligible. For the spectator of the play it is simply a matter of emphasis. While the emphasis is on the work of temptation and overthrow of a soul, there is rank among the assaulting devils; with the removal to hell, the entering of the soul into a state of damnation, the rank dissolves. Thus as there is no indication of rank among Astaroth, Varca, and Belchar, so at the end there is none among Mephistophilis, Lucifer, and Belzebub. It is Mephistophilis who boasts the work of downfall and at the last it is he, to judge from Faustus' exclamation, "Ah, Mephistophilis!" who has gripped the sinner.

2

In the plays the great princes are for the most part background figures and the daemonic action is performed by inferior spirits whose rank is manifest either, as is Mephistophilis', by announced subjection to a greater, or by the lowliness of their works, as is 'Tom's' in *The Witch of Edmonton;* or by both, as is Pug's in *The Devil is an Ass* and Akercocke's in *Grim, the Collier.*

Mephistophilis is a "familiar," that is a spirit who by agreement serves a man without necessity of incantation. The agreement might be, as was Mother Sawyer's with 'Tom,' a direct compact with the serving spirit; or, as was Faustus' with Mephistophilis, it might be by bargain with the spirit's superior. If it was the latter, occultists supposed that the human party to the compact had, through the superior spirit, a sanction over his familiar, hence true power of coercion. The orthodox, of course, believed the whole arrangement a trap set for the soul.

The function of the familiar spirit resembled that of the evil angel—indeed, according to the orthodox was that of the evil angel manifest.[47] In *Faustus* there is little distinction between Mephistophilis and the Evil Angel except that the former has a proper name and acts overtly, whereas the latter is anonymous and never manifest to Faustus. This is not to say, however, that they are necessarily to be identified, conceived as aspects of a single being although perhaps they may be so conceived. It is true the formal signification of Mephistophilis' name may be taken to indicate that he, like the Evil Angel, is a spirit allotted individually to Faustus; but this does not make Mephistophilis one with the Evil Angel, for authorities inclined to allow more than one special spirit to a man. Further, Mephistophilis, the overt actor in the assault upon Faustus, was, so far as the play shows, not assigned to Faustus at birth. But, of course, no decision on the point is necessary. It is enough if the affinity between the figures of Mephistophilis and the Evil Angel be understood.

The spirits who served persons were, in general, of the lower grades and within those grades the dignity of an attendant spirit, whether good or evil, corresponded to the importance of the soul it sought to guide. Faustus' soul was "amiable," full of grace, and to assault it came Mephistophilis, a king himself, the *Faust Book* tells us, though subordinate to Lucifer. Dorothea, the virgin martyr of Dekker's play, won by her piety a special angel direct from God. Mother Sawyer, on the other hand, had the service of a spirit who appeared always in the form of but a dog.

The most ignoble of demonic functions, however, was not that of the familiar or the genius but that of the incubus. Again, of course, there is some combination of function; for the incubus, like the evil genius, acted against those whose weakness and sinfulness invited it to confirm their downfall—thus the incubus in Rowley's play assails Merlin's mother in the hour of her vanity—and the familiar often served as succubus to his master or incubus to his mistress.[48] So in Heywood's *Late Lancashire Witches* the Justice questions an apprehended witch upon the practices of her familiar:

> *Doughty.* And then he lay with thee, did he not sometimes?
>
> *Peg.* Tis folly to dissemble; twice a Weeke he never fail'd me.
>
> *Dough.* Humh—and how? and how a little? was he a good Bedfellow?

Peg. Tis folly to speake worse of him than he is.
Dough. I trust me is't. Give the Divell his due.
Peg. He pleas'd me well Sir, like a proper man.
Dough. There was a sweet coupling.
Peg. Only his flesh felt cold.[49]

It may sometimes be uncertain, however, whether, as Mephistophilis presents Faustus a "hot whore" and later, Helen, the familiar does not bring in other and inferior devils to serve this beastly turn. *Malleus Maleficarum,* at any rate, ranks the incubus in the lowest order of fallen angels, saying that devils work according to nature and that the abomination of sinful coition suits best the nature of the very lowest order.[50]

In Rowley's wavering play, *The Birth of Merlin,* the devil who begets Merlin is called by his half human son "But an inferior lustful Incubus," with the implication that he is a demon of low order and slight power who cannot resist Merlin's charms. Nor, indeed, can he; for he is shut in a rock by power of an incantation that touches him through an appeal to the power of "tenibrarum princeps," his demonic superior. If this lowliness is inconsistent with Lucina's earlier address to him as "great servant of th' infernal King," it is no more inconsistent than many things in this play that shifts characterization so rapidly and bafflingly from clownishness to high seriousness.

Chapter VI

The Powers and Purposes of Daemons

I

As it was only by their works that spirits could be known to men in the actual world, so it is their works which give them a place in drama. They perform in the play world the same feats ascribed to them in the actual world—feats of possession and revelation and transformation for the most part—and to the same ends of damning or saving men.

The natural powers of daemons—swiftness, knowledge, control over local motion of bodies—were theirs by virtue of their peculiar being as impalpable substance.[1] But whether daemons in the plays are to be conceived as purely spiritual substance, or as quintessence, or as abstractly elementary is a point on which the plays contain slight testimony and one that figures as little in the estimate of daemonic works in the plays as it did in the arguments of the polemists over parallel performance in the actual world.

To witchmongers and magicians alike the important thing about daemons was that they possessed certain real powers. These, contended the orthodox, devils so used as to make them seem greater than they were, oppressing man's senses and swaying his conviction with performance which though it did not equal the promise, yet seemed greater than it was and actually did exceed anything possible to man. There was, even the orthodox insisted, a certain verity in daemonic works; feats of apparition, prestidigitation, and prophecy had enough of substance to excel by far anything in animal nature. Though the bargain of the soul for earthly service of demons was one-sided, the human party to such compact was not without a certain return. But he was likely to receive, even of earthly service, less than he had hoped, for the power of demons was not so great as their profession, and their will to serve was moved by no pledge of theirs, but only by what might be necessary to trap their victims.

Of all Elizabethan play spirits, Faustus' Mephistophilis in his efforts to satisfy the sometimes reluctant Faustus, undoubtedly gives the most extensive exhibition of daemonic powers. Most of his overt works are of display and illusion presented in Faustus' behalf to the senses of others: the figures of Alexander and his paramour and of Helen, the castle shown to the Duke of Vanholt and the grapes brought to his duchess, the horns affixed to the knight's head, and the leg pulled from Faustus by the unfortunate teamster. These marvels Mephistophilis manages by his powers of swiftness and of dexterity, achieving almost instantaneous transfer of objects in space, bodies shaped and moved to his will, the manipulation of men's senses from within. Similarly managed for the most part are the wonders in other plays. Harpax in Dekker's *Virgin Martyr* brings his master, Theophilus, early tidings of the approach of the Roman Emperor by virtue of the same fleetness—a spatially unimpeded shift of spiritual application from area to area—that permitted Mephistophilis to flit in a moment to the tropics and whisk grapes northward for the Duchess. In *Bacon and Bungay* the devil Belcephon at Bacon's command brings the hostess in an instant from Henley to Oxford to humiliate Burden, and later for royalty's banquet delivers delicacies from the far parts of the earth. Similarly in *The Late Lancashire Witches* spirits steal a wedding feast to supply the revels of a Sabbat. Like the figures which Faustus tells the emperor are but "shadows" formed by spirits to "lively resemble Alexander and his paramour," are the spirits of the Saxon magician, Proximus, in *The Birth of Merlin,* and the angels who rout the Saxons in battle. They are but "apparitions Of well-armed troops within themselves are air." They have shape by the condensation of atmosphere, and physical effectiveness by the spiritual power which they represent, though it is not truly through them that it acts.[2]

Similarly to be conceived is the siren spirit which in *The Witch of Edmonton* lures Cuddy Banks to a ducking:

> Enter a spirit vizarded. He throws off his mask, &c., and appears in the shape of Katherine.
>
> *Spirit.* Thus throw I off mine own essential horror,
> And take the shape of a sweet lovely maid
> Whom this fool dotes on. (III, i) [3]

Of an identical stamp, of course, are the spirit-managed forms in *The Late Lancashire Witches* which in humiliating semblances Whetstone, the clown, shows as their fathers to the gentlemen who have offended him.

By similar shadowy bodies, of course, familiars became visible to their masters and sometimes audible as well. Cuddy Banks, present at Mother Sawyer's conference with her 'Tom,' "heard I know not the devil what mumble in a scurvey base tone, like a drum that had taken cold in the head last muster." Although this may refer to the witch's muttered charm, it seems more probable that what Cuddy heard was a demon's assumed voice, which, says Boguet, is usually unhuman, "like that of a man speaking in a tub." [4] He adds that only rarely can a spirit make his utterance by an assumed body sound natural to men's ears. It is, perhaps, for this reason that Faustus will not allow the emperor to speak to the shade of Alexander and exact a reply.[5]

Agrippa, however, says that the speech of spirits requires no organs, either assumed or natural, but that—although they do at times speak audibly from assumed bodies—in ordinary communication with man "they slide into the hearer without any noise, as an image in the eye, or glass" and impress "the conception of the speech in those to whom they speak, after a better manner than if they should express it by an audible voyce." [6] So the Good and Evil Angels speak to Faustus.

Some authorities contended that just as the devil could not surely reproduce the human voice, so he could not disguise himself in a human shape so guilefully that the watchful and godly man might not by the fiery visage, cloven hoof, or some other mark detect the imposture.[7] Thus in *The Birth of Merlin* the clown says:

> Well, I do most horribly begin to suspect my kindred; this brother in law of mine is the Devil, sure, and though he hide his horns with his Hat and Feather, I spi'd his cloven foot for all his cunning.
>
> (III, iv, 144)

Similarly in *The Late Lancashire Witches* the Boy who has fought with the devil relates that he recognized his foe by his "clubb'd cloven feet, like an ox."

In Ben Jonson's *The Devil is an Ass,* the gull Fitzdottrel, meeting Pug immediately after wishing for the devil, says:

> . . . 'Fore hell, my heart was at my mouth,
> 'Till I had view'd his shoes well: for, those roses
> Were big enough to hide a cloven foot. (I, iii, 7) [8]

But Pug has no cloven foot to hide. "That's a popular error deceives many," he tells Fitzdottrel. He had taken not an airy body, but the other sort devils' power permitted them, the corpse of a man dead in sin. In sending Pug to earth Satan says to him:

> But you must take a body ready made, Pug:
> I can create you none: nor shall you form
> Yourself an airy one, . . . (I, i, 135) [9]

By prestidigitation—the bafflingly rapid and invisibly effected disposition of objects—Angelo in Dekker's *Virgin Martyr* deprives Spungius and Hircius of the money in their pockets, and Mephistophilis puts horns upon the brow of the knight Benvolio, and enables Faustus to seem to eat half a load of hay. These feats and others like them, devils managed by deluding the eye, causing it to miss what was there for the seeing and to see what was not substantially present nor actually performed. Not only can Mephistophilis persuade knight and horse courser that Faustus has been dismembered, losing his head to the blow of the former and his leg to a tug by the latter, but he can, even to great prelates' eyes, make Faustus invisible.

Such feats he performed by "glamour," working upon both the exterior and interior channels of vision by his control of the investing medium, the atmosphere, and of the processes of sense transmission within the body.[10]

Daemonic control of the senses from within was an all-inclusive power that permitted daemons to perform in seeming almost any marvel, and to do it without resort to objective machinery. Though hallucination lacked the substantial residue sometimes necessary to works such as transvection, it is of course usually impossible to distinguish in the action of the plays from that objective illusion which daemons also employed often. It is simplest, perhaps, to postulate the objective action wherever possible.

2

In the plays the daemonic feat most difficult to explain, even in general terms, is that of the cryptic Behemoth of *Bussy D'Ambois.* He has been called to resolve Bussy about the doings of his enemies, Monsieur, Guise, and Montsurry. Conjured by the Friar to "Shew us all their persons, And represent the place with all their actions," Behemoth reveals the three conspirators to Bussy and his company though there are, the Friar says to Bussy, "too much distance and too many locks 'Twixt you and them (how near soe'er they seem), for any man to interrupt their secrets." Bussy, though he can see them, may neither hear what they say nor come at them.

In Barnes' *Devil's Charter,* Greene's *Friar Bacon and Friar Bungay,* and Webster's *White Devil* there are scenes that somewhat parallel this. In *The Devil's Charter* Alexander conjures spirits to reveal the murderer of his son and they bring in to him "the ghost of Candie gastly haunted by Caesar persuing and stabbing it. . . ." The action here, however, is neither actually that of the murder nor a reproduction of it, but a pantomime enacted by devils to represent the murder. In *Bussy,* however, the figures Behemoth shows ought, perhaps, to be conceived not as those of impersonating daemons, but as truly the characters they appear; for though their speech is inaudible to the Friar and his proteges, to whom the conspirators are present magically and only to sight, it is audible to the extra-play world audience.[11] The fact that this audience can hear their conversation seems to show that Monsieur and his henchmen inhabit the scene really and not as delusions merely, either objective or subjective, imposed upon the invocateurs. Behemoth's feat, then, is a true overcoming of the spatial obstacles to vision interposing between the Friar's company and its enemies. This is in the face of pneumatology, which indicates that though a daemon could make to seem present what was not present, or make invisible what was present, he could not make truly present to a human sense a thing spatially beyond its range and divided from it by impervious matter. That Behemoth's performance seems beyond the powers assigned by pneumatology to daemons does not, of course, invalidate it for the play, but simply makes it require a special rationale peculiar to its world.

There are, however, alternative explanations that assume special points of view for the audience. If it is thought that the author, in his dramaturgical omnipotence, has allowed the audience to listen to a special recording for its sole ear of a disembodied conversation synchronized with the motions of shadow figures, then we may take it that Behemoth's feat falls within the range of powers allotted to daemons by theoretical pneumatology—though we still have no index to what power. It may be that Behemoth stirs the fancy of the Friar and his fellows, or that he presents them exterior shadows accurately miming the almost simultaneous action of the real conspirators. Obviously, however, if the scene be taken in this way the dialogue of the conspirators falls wholly outside this fiction, the metaphysical play world, since no character in the play world is ever truly present to the audience to utter it. The words amount to a notice to the audience that such and such has occurred verbally simultaneous with the daemonic show presented.

It is as such *tours de force*—though more explicit ones as to means than the *Bussy* scene—that the "prospective glass" scenes in *Friar Bacon and Friar Bungay* may be accepted. Here, as in *Bussy,* there are figures on the stage, completely present to the audience, present only to the sight of fellow inhabitants of the play-world. Looking into the glass, Prince Edward and Bacon behold without hearing a distant passage between Fair Margaret, her Lacy, and Friar Bungay that is presented simultaneously on the stage, complete with dialogue, to the audience. The context seems to show that Bungay, Lacy, and Margaret as they appear on the stage are but shadows in the glass.[12]

Of course this cannot be determined certainly. There is the option that the locale be conceived at once Friar Bacon's cell at Oxford and the Keeper's cottage at Fressingfield with both groups of characters truly present to the audience.[13] And so too it may be in *Bussy* that the Friar and Bussy and Tamyra see their enemies in fantasy whereas the audience by an unusual doubling of its field of view beholds both groups in proper essence.

But there is no certain indication of the rationale of any of these scenes. Obviously so long as the general metaphysical scheme of the scene in *Bussy* remains thus uncertain no pneumatological rationale can be surely detected. Nor can pneumatology here, as sometimes, aid in determining the more general rationale. The comment of theoretical pneumatology upon this scene must be chiefly negative. Its action, like its principal daemonic figure, Behemoth, is fanciful rather than verisimilar. Though circumstantial, it cannot be fitted circumstantially to theory of the actual world. Daemonology here seems ornamental and for the sake of ornament; its reference is too vague to stand more than the most general correlation with contemporary doctrine.

The scene is, nevertheless, elaborate enough in itself to sustain the fiction, the play world, and it is in this, in the richness of a generally consistent detail which induces the willing suspension of disbelief, that it varies from the parallel scene in Webster's *White Devil*. In Webster the scene is discouragingly spare, an undisguised labor-saving device for conveying information to the audience and getting forward the action. Brachiano enters with a Conjuror, who, after declaring his reluctance to use necromantic means, puts an enchanted cap on the duke, to whom and to the audience immediately appear silent shows of the murder of two persons. The magician, who has information exceeding that which the Duke derives from the mere sight of the events, explains the action of the shows.

As to the method of the conjuror's feat, no hint is given. There is no daemon in the scene nor any invocation; in fact almost nothing but the charmed cap which the duke wears supports the fiction. The conjuror's preliminary speech on necromancy seems addressed to the audience rather than to the Duke and is simply a general condemnation of necromancy and those who affect it, says nothing of the present method. Whether the Duke's vision is extended so that he beholds the actual events, or he sees them only in his stirred fancy, or in reflection of some sort, or as reproduced by daemonic actors there is nothing to show. The portrayal is so bare as to amount merely to a notice that by resort to a wizard the Duke has discovered such and such things to have happened. The details of the wizardry are neglected—apparently for the purpose of getting on with the action. The whole situation is aimed directly at the audience and breaks the delusion of the play as a world in itself. It is an obvious extrusion of the awkward requirements of structure through the fabric of the fiction.

3

Since spirit scenes are in plays for dramatic, not expository, ends there is no reason why the scenes should adhere to pneumatology except the reason that always links fiction to a more or less verisimilar subject matter: the need for an understood background. Naturally enough the plays often present spirit action that squares with tradition rather than with theoretical pneumatology. An instance of such use appears in Rowley's *Birth of Merlin,* which contradicts contemporary theory squarely in its principal pneumatological fact: the veritable generation of Merlin by an incubus. Legend, of course, ascribed to Merlin such a father; Agrippa says that "All now believe that Merline, a British Prophet, was the son of a Spirit, and born of a virgin: . . ." [14] Naudé, who defends both Agrippa and Merlin from the charge of using evil magic, seems to follow Agrippa in saying that "all authorities" hitherto have thought Merlin begotten by an incubus. But Naudé then promptly disagrees and mentions several authors—Remy, Wier, Cardan, Molitor—who, because the devil has no seed of his own nor can use human seed, deny that the devil can beget.[15] Most orthodox authorities preferred to say that the devil could use stolen human seed to generate, but they did not grant the child so begotten any extraordinary powers.[16]

In the play, the devil acknowledges his paternity and refers to the child as "this mixture of infernal seed," so that Merlin is undoubtedly to be thought truly the devil's offspring—as he says, half spirit. As those of such a hybrid his feats have no certain place in theoretical pneumatology.[17] Often he seems to act simply as a magician. Thus he uses a charm to enclose his father devil in a rock. He knows his uncle's thoughts before they are uttered, a thing which he might do with the help of the same "little antick spirit" that picks the Clown's pockets so dextrously. He prophesies the death of his rival, Proximus, and a stone falling from nowhere accomplishes it. The pneumatological explanation is that he pre-arranged the event with a servile spirit who dropped the stone, a sport to which daemons were addicted.[18]

But to none of these theoretical explanations is there an overt index in the play—and the ambiguous status of Merlin requires that any very sure rationale base on such index. Merlin must be accounted for by the daemonology of legend rather than by the daemonology that professed to be a science. This means that he is fundamentally unaccountable, even in sixteenth century terms.[19]

II

Though it cannot be said of Behemoth's, most daemonic works in the plays have, as the orthodox held proper, a purpose beyond the earthly, one that was the daemon's and not the man's he served; the purpose is invariably to enlarge the kingdom of heaven or of hell.[20] Angelo of *The Virgin Martyr* and Faustus' Good Angel remind their charges of virtue, and support their good resolution. But devils distract Faustus and Alexander and the witch of Edmonton, play on their evil appetites for power and luxury and vengeance with tricks that are but seductions to enmesh them in sinful association which will augment every day the devil's power over them. Faustus cries: "Hell strives with grace for conquest in my breast," and he means no metaphorical struggle. Agrippa says that every human soul is a battle ground between agents of good and evil and that it lies with the man himself to award victory.[21] So it was with Faustus.

The power of devils to effect their paramount purpose was an indeterminate one and even their weapons uncertain as depending upon the permission of God and the state of grace of the victim. In the plays there are many questions about the limits of daemons' power over the human characters. How does Mephistophilis frustrate Faustus' every inclination to penitence, master the impulses fathered by the Good Angel? Have devils really power to tear to pieces their votaries before the concerted day? Are the convictions that induce despair and acquiescence in Faustus and Mother Sawyer but the subtile sleights of devils who boast more than they can do?

In spite of all the devil's mastery over local motion, his power to do bodily injury to human beings was thought to be severely limited. Gifford says that "all the Diuels in Hell are so chained up and brideled by this high prouidence [of God] that they cannot plucke the wing from one poore little Wrenne without special leaue giuen them from the ruler of the whole earth." [22] Such permission, he goes on, is sometimes accorded, but less often than is thought; and the devil gets more credit with men by shrewdly pretending to be author of such natural ills as his penetration has foreseen than by the works of his own hand.

A more general opinion than Gifford's, however, seems to have been that God's permission usually was ordinary rather than special—though sometimes special too—but that the devil's power over a man was conditioned by the state of grace in which the victim was found. Wier says that the devil's power of affliction is only to enter into a man whose evil disposition has invited him. This power God has given him as He gives it to birds to fly.[23]

At any rate, the devil was thought able to do most against those with whom he had affinity, least against saints; and so it is in the plays.[24]

In *The Birth of Merlin,* Merlin's mother, Joan, is visited by the incubus while she is in a state of sinful vanity. In *The Witch of Edmonton* Mother Sawyer is taken by the devil when she is cursing in an agony of hate; and her neighbor, Banks, the devil cannot touch in his life unless he can catch him cursing.[25] Mephistophilis goes most dubiously against the Old Man whose "faith is great," and Theophilus, in Dekker's *Virgin Martyr,* when Harpax threatens to rend him, finds his penitence and the cross a defense. The Subprior in *If this be not a good play, the devil is in it* is immune to the assaults of Shackle-soule, but the merchant, Bartervaile, is seized when he swears falsely.

Orthodox authorities believed officials of the law to be specially exempt from afflictions caused by the familiars of witches brought before a court.[26] In Heywood's *Late Lancashire Witches* one character says to another who has suffered from *maleficia:*

> Sir I have heard, that Witches apprehended under hands of lawfull authority doe loose their power; and all their spells are instantly dissolv'd. (V, 255)

In court it proves true. The arraigned witches call their familiars in vain and the magistrate says to them:

> Now a shame take you for a fardell of fooles, have you knowne so many of the Divils tricks and can be ignorant of that common feate of the old Iugler; that is, to leave you all to the law, when you are once seized on by the tallons of Authority? Ile undertake this little Demigorgon Constable with these Common-wealth Characters upon his staffe here, is able in spite of all your bugs-words, to stave off the grand Divell for doing any of you good till you come to his Kingdome to him, and there take what you can finde. (V, 257)

The action in *Faustus* seems to show that the Evil Angel's threat that devils will tear Faustus to pieces if he calls on God is a profession exceeding their power, for the Good Angel promises that if Faustus repents, his skin shall not be razed. Pneumatology held that whatever the ordinary powers of a devil over a man, a good angel if permitted by God to interpose, could effectually nullify them.[27] But as the witch, by repeated evil acts and pledges, receded from God and His angels, the devil gained power to harm. Faustus loses being until at the end Mephistophilis can rend his heart for naming of his God, and on the hour slay him.

A devil's most ordinary power against a man was, as Wier

says, that of possession, which amounted in part to the power to tempt, that is, press the interests of the evil kingdom in the soul, and, more manifestly, to a violent bodily and mental disturbance. In drama the only important instance of violent possession is in *The Witch of Edmonton.* The witch's enemy, Anne Ratcliffe, is so afflicted by the devil that with maniacal strength she breaks from her husband's grasp and beats out her brains against a wall. In the play the afflictive action of the devil is denoted by the rubbing of the dog, conceived as invisible, against her. This follows the testimony of many witch tracts.[28]

In *The Witch of Edmonton* there is also an instance of the milder and unmanifest but even more harmful sort of possession. When Frank is debating with himself the murder of the innocent Susan, the demon dog says:

> Now for an early mischief and a sudden!
> The mind's about it now; one touch from me
> Soon sets the body forward. (III, iii)

He rubs against Frank and the evil decision is made. Though oblivious of the dog, Frank is conscious of the sudden access of evil impulse. "The devil did not prompt me till this minute." It is not to be thought, however, that the devil could sway his will. *Malleus Maleficarum* says that no exterior power save God can sway the human will. The setting of the body forward is simply by suggestion to Frank's imagination of the means of escape after the deed which the mind, the will, is already bent to. The devil merely manipulates the fancy. Only indirectly could he move a man's conviction and stimulate him to responsible action.[29] In *Bussy* Tamyra urges Behemoth:

> O honour'd spirit, fly into the fancy
> Of my offended lord, and do not let him
> Believe what there the wicked man hath
> written.

But Behemoth replies:

> Persuasion hath already enter'd him
> Beyond reflection; . . . (IV, ii, 104)

The fancy, however, daemons ordinarily could manage, often to the point of "persuasion," and that without the victim's being aware of it. In *Friar Bacon and Friar Bungay* the hostess of Henley says that just before she was whisked off by Belcephon to Oxford "a motion moved me to look forth of door." When Faustus says that it was not only the words of Valdes and Cornelius that led him into magic "but mine own fantasy That will receive no object; for my head But ruminates on necromantic skill," it may be thought that the devil is silently at work within him. At the end Mephistophilis boasts that it was he who when Faustus read the scriptures turned the leaves and led his eye. By so depriving Faustus of a true reading of God's message the devil swayed him from religion and tricked him to his soul's woe.[30]

Mephistophilis' taunts make it seem probable that throughout the action his hold over Faustus rested almost entirely on trickery, on a skillful playing upon appetites which Mephistophilis could not truly satisfy and upon fears which his real powers could not justify. Whenever Faustus began to think upon the emptiness of his pleasures and the hazard of their purchase, Mephistophilis resorted first to threat of physical violence, and then to insistence upon the hopelessness of Faustus' apostasy. Throughout the play after the conjuration Faustus doubts the possibility of his own redemption—"Now, Faustus, must thou needs be damn'd, and canst thou not be sav'd"—and Mephistophilis does everything to turn this doubt into despair. The Good Angel urges repentance; but the Evil Angel retorts to Faustus:

> Thou art a spirit; God cannot pity thee.

Faustus, startled by this alien thought projected bodilessly into his mind, looks fearfully round, crying:

> Who buzzeth in mine ears, I am a spirit?
> Be I a devil, yet God may pity me;
> Yea, God will pity me, if I repent.
> (II, ii, 14)

But he has no confidence in repentance—or rather, none in his own ability to repent. His words seem to announce his belief in the truth of the Evil Angel's assertion that he is a "spirit"; and Faustus knows well that a spirit cannot repent. Faustus' compact says that he shall be a spirit in form and substance,[31] and though it evidently is not fulfilled so far as transubstantiation of his body is concerned [32] Faustus is subtilely led to feel that he has undergone at least a moral change of state and that the moral rigidity of an unbodied spirit now possesses his soul. This conviction is the work of his persecutors.

On the moral status of a witch as compared with that of a demon, *Malleus Maleficarum* says, following St. John Damascene, that though the sin of the witch is worse than that of Satan, it is theoretically pardonable, whereas:

> . . . since Satan is incapable of repentance, therefore he is incapable of pardon; and this is due to his very nature, which, being spiritual could only be changed once, when he changed for ever; but this is not so with men, in whom the flesh is always warring against the spirit.[33]

What the fall was to the evil angels, and their adherence to righteousness was to the good so far as eternal grace is concerned, death is to man, in that after it he cannot repent and be saved if he has died unregenerate, nor transgress and fall if he has departed in grace.[34] That, created a man, Faustus became supernaturally without death, a spirit in fixity of will alone seems improbable, though undoubtedly his immersion in sin produced an artificial fixity, a fixity of habit against which the Old Man warned. The Old Man urges:

> Though thou hast offended like a man,
> Do not persever in it like a devil;
> Yet, yet, thou hast an amiable soul,
> If sin by custom grow not into nature. (V, i, 41)

And Faustus, in fear and an agony of longing for repentance, cries out:

> Break heart, drop blood, and mingle it with tears,
> Tears falling from repentant heaviness
> Of thy most vile and loathsome filthiness,
> The stench whereof corrupts the inward soul

With such flagitious crimes of heinous sins
As no commiseration may expel,
But Mercy, Faustus, of thy Saviour sweet,
Whose blood alone must wash away thy guilt—

Then, hopelessness renewed in him:

Where art thou, Faustus? wretch, what hast thou done?
Damn'd art thou, Faustus, damn'd; despair and die!
(V, i, 55)

Mephistophilis makes instant offer of a dagger for suicide in this moment of realization and despair, that Faustus may die guiltily without further opportunity for repentance, so confirming the loss of his soul.[35] Had Faustus in any literal sense been already a spirit, been already damned other than potentially, this as well as the rest of Mephistophilis' watchful craft would have been superfluous.

There are some incidental references in the play which show, nevertheless, that in a sense Faustus may be called a devil, or at least for some of his fellow characters was indistinguishable from a devil. Once Faustus is called "devil" by another human character; once the devil, Mephistophilis, is addressed as though he were Faustus, and once Faustus as though he had done a deed that was Mephistophilis'. When the vengeful knight, Benvolio, had as he thought beheaded Faustus only to see his body rise intact, he cried out, "Zounds, the devil's alive again." When Mephistophilis appeared to the conjuring clowns, one cried as though to Faustus that he would never rob his library again. Later the same clowns attributed to Faustus their transformation into dog and ape—a delusory work directly Mephistophilis'.[36]

Of course it is easy to attribute the first use here to an extension of a sort quite normal in language, of the term *devil* to a man who seems devilish,[37] and the second and third to the befuddlement of the clowns—if not to that of the author. Nevertheless, if these references be taken in conjunction with the sentiment of the time, which sometimes seems to identify a man with the spirit that serves and impels him, there may be here (saving the uncertainty of the text) some indication of the sense in which Faustus became a spirit.

Agrippa says on the identification of men with spirits:

> . . . As therefore there is given to every man a good spirit, so also there is given to every man an evil Diabolical spirit, whereof each seeks an union with our spirit, and endeavours to attract it to itself, and to be mixed with it, as wine with water; the good indeed, through all good works conformable to it selfe, change us into Angels, by uniting [with] us. . . . An evil spirit also by evil works, studies to make us conformable to it self, and to unite, as Christ saith of Judas, Have I not chosen twelve, & one of you is a devil? . . .
>
> . . . It is also (as saith Porphyry) the opinion of Magicians, that evill souls are turned into the nature of Divels, and become as pernicious as they; which Christ confirmed, when he spake concerning Judas Iscariot: Have I not chosen twelve, and one of you is a divel? which divels therefore they call adventitious, because of men's souls they are become Divels. Whence the names of wicked men and divels are the same, whether by these we call their souls, an evil Genii, which have taken upon them the names of wicked men, as if it were their persons.[38]

Faustus may, perhaps, be considered to have established an identity of this kind with his Evil Angel and through him with Mephistophilis who, as indicated by his insensible guidance of Faustus' hand and eye, is but an objectification of the Evil Angel. It is unnecessary, of course, to say that the Evil Angel and Mephistophilis are but phases or functions of a single personality. But their spheres of action mingle and their distinctness in play name and figure does not necessarily, in view of the indeterminateness of daemonic appellation and body, divide them as to essential identity.

On the other hand, Faustus' name and form do divide him as to essential identity from all angels, and he cannot, without death, realize his fond wish to be a spirit in form and substance. His unity with his Evil Angel is probably to be thought of as psychological, a oneness of sinful appetites. "The god thou servest is thine own appetite, Wherein is fix'd the love of Belzebub." It is a love that becomes stronger in Faustus' being than the tendency toward goodness and the supporting Good Angel. Agrippa, on the unity of a soul with a spirit, says:

> . . . when a spirit hath influence upon the soul of a man, he scatters the seed of his own notion, whence such a soul being sowen with seeds and full of fury, brings forth thence wonderfull things, and whatsoever are the offices of spirits: for when a good spirit hath influence upon a holy soul, it doth exalt it to the light of wisdom; but an evil spirit being transfused into a wicked soul, doth stir it up to theft, and to manslaughter, to lust and whatsoever are the offices of evil spirits. . . .[39]

The Old Man pleads that Faustus has "an amiable soul, If sin by custom grow not into nature." But with Faustus sin is already so grown; he has union of alliance with hell, tending toward a deeper union that is consummated in his last hour when his essential being is so decayed with sin that his good angel leaves him and only the death of his body remains to plunge him into damnation and oneness of state with fallen angels.[40]

2

It is probably not to be thought, however, that because Faustus' soul was the battle ground and the prize of opposed angels, those angels are in the play but metaphors for the conflicting impulses of his soul. Professor Stoll has said that the Good and Evil Angels in *Faustus* are "as substantive—as substantial one might almost say—as the hero himself," and that to interpret them as "allegorical" is to exhibit prepossession.[41] Such prepossession, though legitimate, is unnecessary; and so far as the play world is concerned Professor Stoll might well have done as he was tempted and referred to the Good and Evil Angels as substantial. As such they correspond to the uses of positive pneumatology, and *Faustus* so abounds in pneumatology undeniably positive that it seems permissible to assume for the Good and Evil Angels the same essentiality that is granted to Mephistophilis.

Perhaps it should be emphasized, however, that although the sixteenth century acknowledged angels as substantial beings, it did not altogether abstain from a metaphorical use of the term *angel* and cognate terms. Bodin, for instance, says equivocally that a man is seized by an evil spirit when he turns to wickedness, by a good when he turns to God; in another place, that by angel he means not essential spirits only, but also all the powers which God gives to men.[42] Like some Elizabethan play ghosts,[43] the Good and Evil Angels in *Faustus* may, without violence to sixteenth century ideology, be taken as symbols of a disturbance purely subjective. Professor Logeman, for instance, so takes them, saying that they are "but the incarnations or representations of Faustus' waverings in his inward soul between good and bad." [44] But although pneumatology permits such interpretation, Professor Stoll indicates with justice that dramatic tradition does not encourage it.

If the assumption of substantiality is made for the Good and Evil Angels, there yet remains a question of their place in the play world. The angels appear on the stage, but never as visible to the human characters.[45] If they are not to be taken as "but the incarnations or representations of Faustus' wavering in his inward soul," that is, are not truly subjective, what is their status? The bodies visible to the audience are not, in the play world, representative of the Angels as Mephistophilis' assumed body is of him, for the Angels are not concreted in the play world, are not in any way present to the outer senses of the human characters. The stage bodies designate the Good and Evil Angels only to the audience. How, then, are these moral prompters active in the play world?

The answer is, of course, that the sphere of their activity is confined to Faustus' mind and that to this extent they are 'subjective'—though 'objective' in that they are personal beings existing apart from Faustus and independently. The stage figures are symbolic not simply of the wavering of Faustus' self-contained judgment, but of the application of exterior angelic powers to the springs of his judgment, directly and without motion to the outer senses.

Most of the time the Good and Evil Angels are closer to Faustus than even hallucination. In this they differ from the play ghosts of the Jacobean drama, who usually take representative form of some sort though it be only in the imagination. The dialogue seems to show that Faustus himself is insensible of the separate presence of the angels and holds their monition to be the seething of his own spirit. Though he says "Who buzzeth in mine ear?" and "Something soundeth in mine ear," he probably is not to be thought to hear the angels with his physical organ.[46]

Twice, it is true, the angels do present things to his senses. First, his guardian makes him see upon his arm *Homo Fuge* as a warning against signing the compact. At the end, the Evil Angel shows him hell. The first, Faustus attributes to no outer object, but to the unrest of his senses, and it is certainly to be thought hallucination, whether natural or daemonically inspired. Even the display of hell, surely the work of the Evil Angel, is probably easiest taken as painted directly upon Faustus' imagination; not, in other words, as an actual view impinging upon the outer senses. The figures, then, that represent the Good and Evil Angels on the stage denote to the audience, if interpreted according to a probable metaphysics of the play world, the insensible activity of these creatures within Faustus' mind.

III

Probably whenever in Elizabethan drama daemonic figures appear in the body of a play, that is, are of the play world, it is proper to conceive them as essential according to the dictates of pneumatology, rather than as metaphorical. Daemons, nevertheless, were uncertain entities, to be known only from their works, which were themselves very difficult of interpretation. In the real world the difficulty of interpretation led rationalists to deny the participation of daemons in temporal affairs. This particular scepticism is seldom reproduced in the plays with any substantiation from the action; but one author in one play does make a telling, if minor, use of it.

Among the works of daemons most difficult to distinguish from natural affliction similar in symptom was possession. The victim of non-violent possession might, like Faustus and like Frank in *The Witch of Edmonton,* be unaware that he was touched at all; and an observer, even of a violent seizure, might be unable to tell it from a natural lunatic condition. Mother Sawyer, accused as author of the frantic state of the possessed Ann Ratcliffe, says sourly in defense:

My work? should she and all you here run mad,
Is the work mine? (IV, i)

In *The Witch of Edmonton* the spectator is not in doubt as to Ann's ailment, for he has seen the dog rub against her. The rationale of the play world on this point of pneumatology is as clear as dramatic action can make it. But in Webster's *Duchess of Malfi* it is otherwise. Of this play's pneumatological rationale there are no certain indices. Here the spectator is not favored over the character. What is revealed is merely what registers on normal senses in the play world. What lies behind it is left to the imagination and the intellect to construct—and there is no special direction for the spectator.

The action in the play which may be connected with daemons is sparse, confined to three incidents in the last act: the lycanthropia of Duke Ferdinand, the ominous echo that answers Antonio, and the Cardinal's delusion that he saw in his fish-pond a thing that seemed to strike at him with a rake. Of all these the readiest rationale is naturalistic; yet the supernatural is not excluded, survives in a doubt just beneath the surface of belief.

The Cardinal muses:

I am puzzell'd in a question about hell:
He saies, in hell, there's one materiall fire,
And yet it shall not burne all men alike.
Lay him by: How tedious is a guilty conscience!
When I looke into the Fish-ponds, in my Garden,
Me thinkes I see a thing, arm'd with a Rake
That seemes to strike at me. (V, v, 1) [47]

That it is his disordered mind, no possessing devil, that so torments him seems an obvious and a plausible interpretation, and even to the most credulous pneumatologist it would have been possibly an acceptable one. But there is no index to give it finality. Bosola says once that the Cardinal has grown melancholy, and again explains as "but my melancholy" the presence like the Duchess that haunts him. Melancholy was a thing that made one see spirits—but whether of the mind's own creation or extraneous, who could say? [48]

Before the Cardinal, Bosola too had thought on a guilty conscience and compared it to

> . . . a perspective [glass]
> That shows us hell!

Here, expressed briefly and in metaphor, is Faustus' experience. His Evil Angel showed him hell and we may take his view as a somewhat more literal one than Bosola's by conscience. But the experiences were alike mental, and truly of a spiritual hell. Saving the point of view, which in Webster dispenses with an essential devil, they may be conceived as identical. Whether the Cardinal, who also has hell in mind, is without the attentions of a real devil becomes uncertain. Other men with soiled consciences, said legend, had seen devils menace them from fish-ponds; [49] and it is the devil, he thinks, who for all his pangs of guilt deprives him of repentance.

> O, my Conscience!
> I would pray now: but the Divell takes away my heart
> For having any confidence in Praier. (V, iv, 30)

Unquestionably the Cardinal, like Faustus and like Alexander in *The Devil's Charter,* is a sinner already suspended over the hell that is to receive his soul, and the powers of evil surround that soul. But he is not like them a conjuror, and on the stage no devil appears. The spectator is left to decide for himself whether the thing in the pond was the work of a devil entering into the temporal world, or of the fevered natural imagination of the Cardinal. The overt indices point toward Scot's sort of rationalism; but a titillating doubt remains.

Similarly handled are the other incidents that hint the supernatural. The horror of the Duchess' murder has unbalanced Ferdinand's mind—or has opened it to devils—and he suffers a violent affliction called from its symptoms lycanthropia, and variously attributable to pathological melancholy and to daemonic possession. The Duke's physician ascribes it, without mention of an alternative, to the former.

> In those that are possess'd with't there ore-flowes
> Such mellencholy humour, they imagine
> Themselves to be transformed into Woolves,

> Steale forth to Church-yards in the dead of night,
> And dig dead bodies up: as two nights since
> One met the Duke, 'bout midnight in a lane
> Behind St. Markes Church, with the leg of a man
> Upon his shoulder; and he howl'd fearefully:
> Said he was a Woolffe: onely the difference
> Was, a Woolffes skinne was hairy on the out-side,
> His on the In-side: bad them take their swords,
> Rip up his flesh, and trie: straight I was sent for,
> And having ministered to him, found his Grace
> Very well recovered. (V, ii, 9) [50]

But though the illusion of thinking himself a wolf does not again assail Ferdinand, the doctor is too sanguine in believing him recovered. His dementia persists in forms that reflect some soul shuddering horror at his inner mind. On the fatal last night a "foul storm" [51] shakes his chamber "like an osier," and Malatesti says:

> 'Twas nothing but pure kindnesse in the divel,
> To rocke his owne child. (V, iv, 26)

This seems but a passing jest, a careless reference to the common superstition that saw the devil's claw in every disturbance of nature; to daemonism in the play world there is no real indication. But the same uncertainty that renders the actual world tolerant of superstition is alive in the play.

Many have supposed, says Antonio's companion Delio, that the echoes from the ruins of the ancient abbey are the answers of a spirit; and it answers indeed very bodefully, though never save as echo of the last words of the friends' speech. Its final repetition is "Never see her more," and Antonio, stricken, cries:

> I mark'd not one repetition of the *Eccho*
> But that: and on the sudden, a cleare light
> Presented me a face folded in sorrow.
> (V, iii, 55)

Delio replies: "Your fancy merely."

So, no doubt, it is to be taken. There are tales of echoes

thought devils—and also of echoes that were the voices of devils.[52] Dramatically, of course, it matters little by what agency the doleful response comes to Antonio—if, indeed, there is from the point of view which the play assumes, a real difference between personal daemonic force and impersonal portentous chance. But here alone in Elizabethan tragedy is pneumatological rationalism given a true balance against credulity.[53] That balance and the means of its achievement are, perhaps, of some importance dramatically.

2

There are other plays in which pneumatological rationalism is prominent. In *The Witch of Edmonton* a modified Wierian doctrine seems to qualify, though not precisely to counterbalance, the prevailing orthodox rationale. In Heywood and Brome's *Late Lancashire Witches* some of the characters express rationalistic views as a foil for the action of *maleficia*.[54] But both plays present essential devils and their works. It may be supposed that in this they do not reproduce the situation in the actual world, thus overset for the play world the position of thorough-going rationalists like Scot. In *The Duchess of Malfi,* on the other hand, there is no certainty of spirits, nor yet any certainty against them.

Probably the most one-sidedly rationalistic treatment of a pneumatological theme occurs, in spite of its presentation of devils, in Jonson's *The Devil is an Ass.* Of course since the devil in this play is, like his allegorical fellow, the Vice, a purely satirical figure, a serious rationale of the play's pneumatology as a whole would be ridiculous. It is without inconsistency, then, that Jonson's personal scepticism about demons, witches, and *maleficium* crops out in the scene of Fitzdottrel's feigned possession. Manly, accused of having bewitched Fitzdottrel, says to the credulous Justice:

> Are you phrenetic, sir?
> Or what grave dotage moves you to take part
> With so much villainy? we are not afraid
> Either of law or trial; let us be
> Examined what our ends were, what the means

To work by, and possibility of those means:
Do not conclude against us ere you hear us.
(V, viii, 91)

One may think that Jonson obviously had scant faith in the means witches had to work by. A passage in *The White Devil* indicates that Webster had a kindred scorn for the pretensions of magicians. A conjurer says just before he begins his practice:

some there are,
Which by Sophisticke tricks, aspire that name
Which I would gladly loose, of Nigromancer;
As some that use to juggle upon cardes,
Seeming to conjure, when indeed they cheate,
Others that raise up their confederate spirits,
'Bout wind-mils, and indanger their owne neckes,
For making of a squib, and some their are
Will keepe a curtall to shew juggling trickes
And give out 'tis a spirit: besides these
Such a whole reame of Almanacke-makers, figure-flingers,
Fellowes indeed that onely live by stealth,
Since they do meerely lie about stolne goods—
Thei'd make men thinke the divell were fast and loose,
With speaking fustian Lattine. (II, ii, 6)

But this peeping of the personal opinions of the authors through the fabric of their plays, if indeed these are instances, is beside the point for the rationales of the play worlds themselves. Judged on the evidence of the action, which includes magic and ghosts, *The White Devil* cannot be taken as presenting rationalism in anything like a balance with the more credulous schemes. As has already been said, *The Devil is an Ass* calls for no pneumatological rationale. The scene of faked possession has the authenticity of that argument upon which rationalism surely based: that fake was usually possible, often demonstrable, on a particular occasion certain.

Chapter VII

Ceremonial Magic

I

In Elizabethan drama many of the activities of spirits on behalf of human characters or against them seem to result from deliberate resort by men to various means of appeal for daemonic assistance in worldly matters.[1] The rationale of appeal and response rests largely on current doctrine as to the efficacy and the responsibility of man's self-initiated relations with daemons, that is, on the doctrines that explain spirit magic.

The plays fall into two natural but not altogether distinct groups: plays dealing with ceremonial magic, and plays dealing with witchcraft, of which the former divides again into plays in which the magicians are pledged expressly to devils, hence are at bottom witches, and those in which the magicians seem genuine thaumaturges. Exalted witches like Alexander of *The Devil's Charter* and Faustus are to be accepted as magicians in one contemporary sense of the word,[2] but they did not rule daemons in the sense occultism claimed for magic. It is very difficult, however, if not impossible, to determine surely from a play's action the efficacy in its world of any magical ceremony presented. The issue is so doubtful that although a fairly consistent rationale of such action can be made by way of suggestive interpretation, it is hardly safe to rest textual criticism on it as some editors have occasionally inclined to do.

In the plays which have scenes of magic or witchcraft, three things are interesting: the method by which the man achieves and sustains a relation with daemons, the worldly fruits of the relation, and the man's responsibility to heaven for it. Some of the plays emphasize one, some another; but since the three are closely interlocked, it is hardly possible that any play wholly neglects any one of them.

Central is the question of the responsibility of the practitioner to a stern heaven; the answer, of course, lies largely in his method and his fruits. There were many guilty methods, but also some not only blameless but meritorious. There were works which the pious could approve, and there were works that were selfish or criminal. In general, as a man drew toward any evil spirit—even though his dependence was but that of a master upon a servant—he correspondingly drew away from God, and his guilt increased. Further, so far as a man associated himself in evil works, though they were not his in doing but only in consent, his guilt increased. Pact was the guiltiest of methods, *maleficium* the guiltiest of fruits.

Most voluntary relations with daemons originated in a conceit of power, in a man's belief that of himself he could bring spirits by attraction or penalty to obey his will.[3] In Elizabethan tragedies, Faustus, Alexander, Mother Sawyer in *The Witch of Edmonton,* and the Friar of *Bussy D'Ambois,* diverse in many things, have in common the belief that they command, if conditionally, daemonic service. For it, all the four but Mother Sawyer exercise themselves in ceremonies, and for it all but the Friar pledge their souls outright. In method and in end they are all of the pattern of the sixteenth century dealer with spirits.

Of their company in works and, fundamentally, in means is the pagan Saxon magician, Proximus, in *The Birth of Merlin* and perhaps the anomalous Merlin himself, and the learned Bacon of Greene's play. Like them in works, though not a sharer in their wilfulness, is the holy Hermit Anselme in *The Birth of Merlin* who routs the Saxon armies with a host of angels, and masters the hell-given spirits of Proximus by his bare presence.

Among these spirit workers there is a seeming variety of method and some difference in means.[4] Most exalted of them all, of course, is the Hermit, whose means is God and whose method prayer, the direct appeal that brings God's special gift upon him as a holy man.[5] These things divide him from the magicians, whose means are creature spirits and whose methods are wilful—either coercive or commercial.[6] Though the Friar of *Bussy* too is, nominally at least, a holy man, his is a sanctity bestowed by formal consecration; his command of spirits is the conventionalized and ceremonially mediated conversion of his priestly virtue, whereas the Hermit's is a direct and special conversion of saintliness.

A greater prelate than the Friar but, in the orthodoxy of his play world, a lesser sorcerer, Alexander addresses himself to devils by devils, as does Faustus—vainly at his first attempt. In the end Faustus and Mother Sawyer and Alexander have their whole power by means, the readiest and deadliest, of rank barter of their immortal souls for the service of devils. More truly successful, less culpable than these witches, yet exposed to damnation by the bare fact of his voluntary commerce with fiends is the mighty Bacon.

All the dealings of these persons with spirits, whether miracle, white or black magic, or bare witchcraft, whether weighed by orthodox or occult standards, have two things in common: (1) a preliminary affinity between the human operator and a superior spirit who either acts in the operator's behalf or delegates subordinates to act, (2) an operation that takes its power from the affinity.

Affinity with spirits rested always upon a sort of worship, a devotion either prostrate or reserved, spontaneous or commercial. Affinity might be, like that of the Hermit, and presumably of the Friar, with the true and infinite God and His angels; or like that of the pagan, Proximus, with false and vain gods; or like that of Faustus and Alexander and Mother Sawyer with the acknowledged Adversary. The Hermit and the Friar have their affinity, the basis of their power over spirits, through piety in the true public worship; the rest link with their fiends by a perverse private worship.[7]

The operation by which the affinity was signified might be the prayer of the miracle worker, a magical rite, or the prayer-aping signal of the witch, such as was Mother Sawyer's *Sanctibicetur in nomen tuum.*

In miracles, of course, the operation is abridged almost to vanishing, for the human instrument of a miracle is selfless and scarcely performs the operator's part, the voluntary initiation of the feat.[8] The witch's prayer to the devil also slights operation; but it is by bargain, whereas the saint's to God is without condition. The Hermit Anselme may be thought to have almost joined his being to God; that union is his whole power, and the operation that applies the power is one with the feat of power and with its source. Agrippa, acknowledging miracles, says:

> . . . so the prophets, Apostles, and the rest were famous by the wonderfull power of God; therefore we must know, that as by the influx of the first agent, is produced oftentimes something without the cooperation of the middle causes, so also by the work of Religion alone, may something be done without the application of natural and Celestial vertues; but no man can work by pure Religion alone, unless he be made totally intellectual. . . .[9]

To Proximus, who has accused him of ruling devils through their prince, the Hermit retorts:

> Know mis-believing Pagan, even that Power
> That overthrew your Forces, still lets you see,
> He only can controul both hell and thee. (II, iii, 108)

The Hermit's feat satisfies the four requirements of the church for a miracle: it is done by God; it is beyond the usual order of nature; it is manifest; it is for the corroboration of the faith.[10]

As the miracle-worker and the witch diminished operation, so the magician magnified it. Friar Bacon, most potent of the play magicians, seems to rely almost entirely upon a coercive ritual. Of affinity between him and the fiends who serve him there is but one hint—the Latin charm by which he conjures Belcephon: "Per omnes deos infernales, Belcephon!"—to show that he rules subordinate devils by agency of the greater. The ultimate question, though, is, of course, of how he won the consent of the greater devils. Although Bacon's first affinity, like that of Bussy's Friar, may perhaps be supposed with the Deity, the emphasis in Greene's play is markedly on the esoteric learning of the spirit practitioner, rather than on the piety of the priest. Though Bacon is a churchman, there is no mention of the spiritual privileges and powers usually attributed to his estate.

In their most reduced and characteristic forms, affinity and operation are those two standard paths to spirit control: pact and ceremony. They are at once allied and contrasting, and each has its field of dominance according to the point of view of the beholder. Among daemonologists the efficacy of pact was universally acknowledged save by rationalists like Scot; but ceremony orthodox authorities held to be nothing more than the witch's signal—or at best a tacit compact—whereas magicians erected the formalities of men toward spirits into a scheme of bonds, attractive to good spirits, painful to evil, the initial efficacy of which rested upon the truths of religion. The ceremonial proclamation of these bonds, occultists said, mediated the magician's affinity with good spirits, and buffered him against the ire of the evil.

Even the occultist confessed, however, that in the baser sorts of magic, those which appealed solely to devils, the ceremonies, though still full of the names of God and the signs of divinity, sometimes included concessions, such as gifts and sacrifices, to superior demons. In these ceremonies the affinity of magician for spirit approaches the witch's pact even on the face of it. Agrippa in his semi-orthodox *Vanity of the Arts and Sciences* says of magicians:

> All these proceed in a twofold manner. For some of them make it their business to adjure and compel Evil spirits to appearance, by the Efficacy and Power of sacred Names; because seeing that every Creature doth fear and reverence the name of its Creator, no wonder if Conjurors and other Infidels, Pagans, Jews, Saracens or prophane persons, do think to force the Devils Obedience by the Terrour of his Creators Name. Others, more to be detested than they, and worthy the utmost punishment of Fire, submitting themselves to the Devils, sacrifice to them, and Worship them, become guilty of the vilest subjection and Idolatry. . . .[11]

The second class here is not that of the "witch," whom Agrippa like Wier considered merely a deluded victim, but that of the black magician, a worker of evil by evil means who yet possessed ritual and some learning to stand between him and the express, unreserved pact of witchcraft. The black magician might be a professing Christian, though he rejected Christianity's ends and wrenched its means to his own evil purposes.[12]

II

The express pact or the operation that established a man as, respectively, witch or magician was but a culmination of his progress toward a subliminal affinity with some spirit. To any formal rule of spirits there were certain prerequisites. Speaking of the magus, but with some application, too, to the black magician, Agrippa says that before a man can operate in magic he must undergo dignification in two ways: (1) by renunciation of the carnal things that encumber the understanding, (2) by participation in the learning and practices that elevate the understanding.[13] By learning in nature, mathematics, and divinity he moves toward "Knowledge of the truth"; and by the practices of religion he solicits virtue of the intellectual world. Thus he who is a magus has freed himself of passion by discipline, become receptive by study, finally won affinity by religious observances.

> . . . what dignity is acquired by the art of Religion is perfected by certain Religious Ceremonies, expiations, consecrations, and holy rites proceeding from him whose spirit the publike Religion hath consecrated . . . who hath power . . . of initiating with Sacramental power, by which the Character of the divine vertue and power is stampt on us which they call the divine consent, by which a man supported with the divine nature, and made as it were a companion of the Angels beareth the ingrafted power of God. . . .[14]

So, perhaps, Bussy's Friar is or believes himself a companion to the angels, fulfilling in his priesthood the prerequisites of abnegation and practice, and in his study that of knowledge.

There was yet another prerequisite which, it may be supposed, he had also fulfilled: initiation. Agrippa says that to consecrate—an indispensable work in ceremonial magic—a man had to have holiness of life, which "nature and desert perform," and "the power to consecrate," which is acquired by "initiation and dignification." [15] No man, save in miracle, rules spirits from the direct power of God. Whoever by discipline, knowledge, and observances has won the stamp of power, that is, established affinity, converts it into act—unless he be a saint—only by further observances that are the esoteric operations of a particular ceremony of invocation. These require that the magician know not only the One God and the rites of the public religion, but all the inferior spirits who convey His rule to the world and whose finite excellence accords with the magician's necessarily incomplete merit. These "gods" must be moved with "holy rites conformable to the condition of every one"; for whoever "invocates the gods and doth not confer on them their due honor, rightly distribute to them what belongs to them, shall neither enjoy their presence, nor any successful effect from them." [16]

There were other magicians than those who won the divine signet by the difficult novitiate which Agrippa describes. There were those who, aiming, though by the same general means, at an easier affinity than the theurgist's, prayed and sacrificed to devils. This, though an evil and dangerous derogation from the glory of God, was not necessarily an outright abnegation of true religion, as was witchcraft. Rather it was, like the theurgist's operation, the paying to inferior spirits of the honor they required. The difference was that the spirits were admittedly evil.

Such observances fell far short—in the operator's view, at least—of the witch's deliberate and express renunciation and pact. They were merely a kind of superstition, a confusion or extension of the rites of true religion. Agrippa says that superstition is potent for magic. As whoever worships truly may receive virtue sanctioned by God, attractive to angels, so whoever worships improperly may yet by his credulity bring his mind to "be assimilated to those spirits who are the chief leaders of that Religion, may work those things which nature and reason discern not." [17]

Every superstition, according to Agrippa, has a rudiment of truth, partakes a little of the virtue of religion, has its power—though ever so wrongly and remotely—from God. The magician who sought to work by the devil and propitiated him with worship, yet in operation used as instruments of compulsion holy names and the sanctified materials of Christian rite, was not, to his own way of thinking, reversing his worship as the witch did, but merely adulterating it as, unaware, the pagan did. The magic Faustus practices after Valdes and Cornelius is not yet the magic of pact, for all that he fears it will damn him. It is the magic of the theurgist, but without the prerequisite discipline and practice which, according to occult theory, would in themselves have so modified Faustus' ends as to make his magic wholly good, would have given him affinity with good angels. Faustus, unwilling in his pride and his haste to submit his soul to God, relied on learning and initiation alone.

Faustus, great scholar, had indeed knowledge of nature, mathematics, and divinity; and he was schooled also in the secret operations of magic. But this learning, exoteric and esoteric, was not enough, he discovered, to establish even the hasty affinity he sought—one with the great devils, Lucifer and Belzebub. In his orthodox world there was no virtue in operation. In Faustus' world his learning led not to coercive spirit magic, for there was no such thing, but to pact. Witchcraft as well as magic had its prerequisites, and they were, says Remy, for the learned ambition, and for the ignorant envy, malice and despair.[18] Ambition broke down the moral defenses of Faustus and Alexander and let the devil in upon them; and malice and despair began Mother Sawyer's affinity with her demon.

2

According as the rationale of a particular feat of spirit command is orthodox or occult, the act, no matter how signalized, is at bottom one of pact or of efficient operation. Now Faustus has, by an occult scheme in which he rests hope, prayed and sacrificed to devils and acknowledged Belzebub as chief.[19] Upon the affinity he believes this to have established with infernal rulers he has relied for the efficacy of his adjuration to Mephistophilis. "Did not he charge thee to appear to me?" he asks Mephistophilis of Lucifer. But though Faustus' preliminaries have indeed made a sort of bond with hell, it gives virtue to his operation only *per accidens.* To rule devils, Faustus must be of their kingdom by express compact. For nothing less sure would Lucifer give his servants. Thus the play's orthodox rationale of magic resolves the masterful operation of the magician into the affinity of the witch, the ceremony into the pact.

In *The Devil's Charter* this absorption is not quite so evident, for Alexander perseveres in ceremony after express compact, which does not relieve him, as it does Faustus, of the labor of incantation.[20] "Now must I sweat like a collyers horse," says the Pope, preparing his ritual. But there are many indications that there is no virtue in his labor *per se.* The dumb show of the signing of Alexander's covenant signifies that his lust for power led him into occult arts and that he paid his soul to render them effective. The devils with whom he bargains give him the papacy and a "magical book."[21] That the operations directed in the book are to be conceived as more than a sign to which the demons responded by the terms of their bargain seems unlikely. At the end, when confronted by the "Diuill" come to announce damnation, "Alexander taketh his booke of Magike" to exorcise the spirit; but he can find no names of exorcism; his "date is expired," his "power determined." The devil need no longer simulate obedience, and the Pope's charms have no more power than Mother Sawyer's mumbled and jumbled *Sanctibicetur.*

Between the magic of Faustus and Alexander on one hand and the witchcraft of Mother Sawyer on the other, there is, in the predominantly orthodox rationale common to their play worlds, no essential distinction. It is true that the devil "goes a nearer way to work" with her ignorance and malice than with their learning and ambition; but like her they in the end deny God and pledge their souls for a service that is only at the will of the servitors.

The only true power the witch possessed was that to give or to withhold an express lien on the soul. By giving it he obtained a certain mandate in wickedness, a choice of evil deeds. "What will not I do to obtain his soul," exclaims Mephistophilis. When Faustus had pledged himself, he did indeed have a kind of rule of Mephistophilis in all things not against hell's kingdom, in all things that would damn Faustus.[22]

Ostensibly, at least, this rule was by virtue of the disposition of Mephistophilis' superior—he swears to Faustus "by hell and Lucifer"—that is, by virtue of the order which devils observed in their war with mankind. This was an order that brought certain devils, though only *per accidens,* to answer conjurations when they heard one rack the name of God, to attend whatever magician used "such means whereby he is in danger to be damn'd."

It is for this, perhaps, that Mephistophilis answers the words of Faustus' incantation even as garbled in the mouth of the illiterate Robin from a purloined book. But a glance shows him that here is no hope to get a glorious soul, for Robin is too simple and too canny to do this thing truly in despite of God. Like his fellow, Dick, who says that for Nan Spit he will feed Robin's devil with horse bread of free cost as long as he lives, and like Cuddy Banks, who entertains Mother Sawyer's devil only for a dog, the "damn'd slave" Robin must be brought to hell by a more routine means than the covenant of witchcraft. Mephistophilis' exclamation:

> You princely legions of infernal rule,
> How am I vexed by these villains' charms!
> From Constantinople have they brought me now
> Only for pleasure of these damned slaves,
>
> (BIII, iii, 33)

signifies not compulsion beyond that ordinary to his duties as a subordinate demon, but vexation at the comic creatures who have distracted him from the great business of devouring Faustus' "amiable soul." Robin and his fellow have no pleasure of their conjuration. That Mephistophilis is bound by it *per se* no more than by Faustus' earlier conjuration is, perhaps, shown by the cavalier treatment he accords the clowns. Such inept conjuring as theirs was not thought, even by occultists, to bind devils, but rather to release them to do physical harm to the conjuror.[23]

This reading of the scenes is, of course, by no means exclusive of others. But Mr. Boas is perhaps mistaken when he says that the inconsistency between this scene and Mephistophilis' earlier declaration that he responds to conjuration but *per accidens* cannot be resolved. There are at least two other fairly plausible ways of resolving it. First, it may be assumed that in denying the efficacy of magic *per se* Mephistophilis lied to Faustus. Devils, even coerced devils, did constantly deceive their conjurors in every possible way. If this solution is accepted, an occult rationale underlying the action regains much validity. Second, it may be assumed that the book Robin conjured from was not that of Albanus, or whatever ritual Faustus used originally, but that which Mephistophilis had given to Faustus, containing the secret of many magical powers. In the manuals on magic there is much information on such books.[24] Usually they bore the seals and pledges of devils with whom the conjuror had established relations. A citation from such a volume was supposed to be compelling to the spirit who had sealed it. Mephistophilis at any rate would have been especially alert to answer, that Faustus might not complain of him. If it be supposed that Robin conjured from such a book, the 1604 text with its new conjuration is more acceptable than the 1616 text, which Mr. Boas prefers because its incantation seems a jumbling repetition of Faustus' original spell.

But however the scenes be interpreted not much weight can be given to the contradiction between them.[25] Unshaken, too, remains the general orthodoxy of the rationale, which makes out Faustus, whatever the extent and genuineness of the power he acquires, to be surely a witch at bottom in his dealings with Mephistophilis.

3

Very different from this witch bond seems the relation between Friar Bacon and the demons he rules. Channels of magic which Faustus explored in vain—the use of divine names and of figures and symbols—led Bacon to genuine power, and that, apparently, without Faustus' dark concession of preliminary prayer and sacrifice to fiends.[26] Bacon's ultimate repentance is not for such offenses, nor for a witch's express compact, but for his irreverent use of holy names and signs to "countervail his God" with demons. Of the efficacy of Bacon's means the play leaves no doubt.

The great arch-ruler, potentate of hell,
Trembles when Bacon bids him, or his fiends,
Bow to the force of his pentageron. (ii.)

Bacon, says the devil which Vandermast has conjured up, "bridles headstrong Belcephon, And rules Asmenoth, guider of the north," so that though Vandermast conjures

By all the thrones and dominations,
Virtues, powers, and mighty hierarchies,

the spirit dare not obey him against Bacon's command. Never before, says Vandermast, had he known

That men held devils in such obedient awe.
Bacon doth more than art can, or else I fail.
(ix.)

Then at Bacon's bidding the German is whirled away to Hapsburg "to learn by travail, 'gainst the spring, More secret dooms and aphorisms of art."

But though Bacon thus does as much as any occultism claimed in the coercion of fiends, his art cannot be conceived that art of the theurgist which Iamblichus and Agrippa affirm and justify, the magic that elevates the operator toward the First Cause and is truly a religion of the elect. For Bacon deals not with angels but with fiends and in the end confesses that his art, though effective, is damnable and damning. Bacon is no Prospero.[27]

It is to be thought, then, that Bacon's world is but little less orthodox than Faustus'. The difference is that Bacon's blasphemy is effective *per se,* whereas Faustus' is not. Bacon's art is that of the "practical" Cabala, of the Solomonic rituals. It is all that they claim to be except truly reverent.

The "cabalism" which Bacon undertakes to demonstrate to the doubting Burden is his initiate's art, which rests upon manipulation of sacred symbols weighty with the truth of Christianity, terrible to devils confronted with them. To this art he adds the infusive, developed personality of the prepared practitioner—though his dedication, despite his friar's gown, has been to learning rather than to piety. Vandermast says:

Lordly thou look'st, as if that thou wert learn'd;
Thy countenance as if science held her seat
Between the circled arches of thy brows. (ix.)

Less the budding scientist, and more the ecclesiastic, hence more the theurgist, seems the Friar of *Bussy D'Ambois.* He may, perhaps, be supposed to have undergone the arduous "dignification" necessary to the magus and to have won what he calls his "power of learned holiness Vouchsaf'd from above." Like Bacon, he acts with no hint of express pact. The Friar's processes, however, are but vaguely delineated in the play. The indices are both equivocal and scanty, and can establish no thaumaturgical rationale.

Agrippa warns that one must not enter rashly upon the exercise of magical ceremony.

> . . . whosoever beyond the authority of his office, without the merit of Sanctity and Learning, beyond the dignity of nature and education, shall presume to work anything in Magick, shall work in vain, and deceive both himself and those that believe on him, and with danger incur the Displeasure of the Divine powers.[28]

The Friar who will justify upon his soul his pander's work for Bussy, may easily delude himself as to the "authority of his office," "the merit of Sanctity and Learning" "vouchsaf'd from above." But in these matters there is little to clear the rationale.

III

The magical ceremonies in *Bussy, The Devil's Charter,* and *Faustus* make a less detailed appeal to the literature of magic than their sometimes explicit presentation and their obvious general modelling after contemporary magical practice might lead one to expect. In *Bussy* though the whole action of the exorcism is directly staged, there is of the ceremony but a fanciful rudiment comprised almost wholly in a finely poetical Latin incantation. In *Faustus* and *The Devil's Charter* the ceremonies are extremely condensed—although, in the latter play especially, highly circumstantial—and are almost entirely divested of the verbal piety that marks even goetic rituals. The reasons for such deviation are, of course, fairly obvious. The vagueness of the ceremony in *Bussy* is consistent with the whole pneumatological action of that play. The length and tiresomeness of magical ceremonies precluded, even for *Faustus* and *The Devil's Charter,* any very full reproduction on the stage; the pious expressions of the rituals were out of keeping with the wickedness dramatically requisite to the operations of Faustus and Alexander; the censor, in the interests of religion, probably forbade much direct transcription from manuals whose devotion was looked upon as a subtile profanation as bad as their basic apostasy. Finally, both author and audience may have been not without fears of a genuine demonic response to too genuine an invocation.[29]

The Devil's Charter, nevertheless, does levy very considerably on one well-known ritual, the *Heptameron* attributed to Peter of Abano, and Mr. McKerrow conjectures a connection with another, the pseudo-Agrippa's *Fourth Book of Occult Philosophy.*[30] From the *Heptameron, The Devil's Charter* takes many terms and incidents of ceremony. It does not, however, by any means adhere to the rationale the manual implies for its ceremonies, and it distorts the ceremonies themselves to conform to an orthodox rationale.

Faustus shows no certain debt to any known ritual, though its ceremony displays general characteristics common to many. Valdes' instructions to Faustus to take with him to his conjuring "wise Bacon's and Albanus' works" may be held to indicate that Faustus, a novice at magic, was using the *Heptameron,* professedly a manual for beginners. The reference does not mean, of course, that Marlowe knew or used the *Heptameron.* The names Bacon and Albanus were constantly coupled as of authors on sorcery; Agrippa in his *Vanity of Arts* twice thus couples them, and no doubt they were generally so known to many who never saw the books reputed theirs.[31]

Like *Faustus, Friar Bacon and Friar Bungay* shows no sure levy on any particular magical book. Its references link it closest, perhaps, to the two Solomonic rituals: *The Key of Solomon* and *The Lemegeton. Bussy's* connection in its conjuring scene with the literature of magic is even vaguer.

2

The parts of magical ceremony were roughly two: (1) the preliminaries, which out of general virtue previously acquired, fashioned power for a particular operation by affirming and focussing whatever spiritual affinity the magician intended to rely on; (2) the invocation itself, which with its symbolic gestures and figures gave specific direction and application to the power which the preliminaries had concentrated. Needless to say, these two parts of ceremony are largely coalesced in performance.

The most detailed conjuring scene in Elizabethan tragedy is that in *The Devil's Charter,* Act IV, scene i, and it contains a considerable display of preliminary operation. *Faustus,* however, has only incidental allusion to the preliminaries, and *Bussy* but the barest hint of them. *Friar Bacon and Friar Bungay,* which has no full-blown scene of ceremony, but many references to ceremony, contains allusions which show that Bacon may be supposed to have practised the usual preliminaries.

As the powers which the ceremonial magician brought to bear were of three kinds: natural, celestial, and intellectual—so his preliminary preparations were of things elementary, mathematical, and religious. By fumigation with natural odors attractive to the spirits whom he intended to invoke he made the place of his operations agreeable, even fascinating, to the spirits, and by the form of fumigation did ceremonial honor to the overseeing spirit of the operation.[32] Thus Alexander adjures his assistant, Bernardo, to cense well, since "Festatiui ["the name of the earth in Summer"] must haue her honour." Later, alone by the circle just before he begins his invocation by the four kings, Alexander takes his incense, "Red Sandall," and probably is to be thought to burn it over the "fire in an earthen vessell" which he has ordered Bernardo to bring him.[33]

In *Faustus* the dialogue gives no hint of fumigation nor of any other natural means employed in the ceremony except Cornelius' remark that among other requirements for magical operation a man need be "well seen in minerals." The use in magical ceremony of such knowledge was chiefly in the preparation of certain instruments according to affinities in the celestial and intellectual worlds.[34]

More important in ceremony than any acquaintance with minerals was mathematical knowledge, of which a part was that good grounding in astrology that Cornelius commended to Faustus. Astrology is probably here to be taken as an inclusive term signifying all the knowledge pertinent to understanding formations of the heavenly bodies, their signs and seals and occult affinities in intellectual and elemental realms.

In *Friar Bacon and Friar Bungay,* Mason, sagely swallowing Bacon's vaunting of his Brazen Head, admits:

> No doubt magic may do much in this;
> For he that reads but mathematic rules
> Shall find conclusions that avail to work
> Wonders that pass the common sense of men. (ii.) [35]

Professor Ward says that " 'mathematic' merely signifies astrology" in this and similar passages; and there can be no doubt that for the magician astrology was indeed the sum and center of mathematics. Agrippa's book on mathematical magic makes it clear, however, that for magic there were important studies subsidiary to astrology: geometry and numerology. Faustus' good grounding in astrology and Bacon's reading in "mathematic rules" involved the figures and theorems of geometry for the framing of the many designs ceremonial magic required and, more urgently, the Neo-Pythagorean theories of numbers and of celestial harmonics [36] for determining time of operation and for bringing every move into accordance with prevailing influences.

In *The Devil's Charter* Alexander rejoices that the season is auspicious for "nocturnal ceremonies" since "Bright Armatas," the moon, "increaseth" and "is not combust," that is, waxes, is no longer in the same degree of the zodiac with the sun; and he reckons the hour of the night with its angels. Then according to his reckoning he makes his fumigation and orders his conjuration.

Of the time of Faustus' ceremony nothing is said save that it is night,[37] but he has amply employed his mathematical knowledge in framing his circle and within it "Figures of every adjunct to the heavens," that is, of the fixed stars "conceived of as being joined to the solid firmament of the sky"; [38] and "characters of [zodiacal] signs and erring stars." Alexander, too, fashions a circle and, in addition, a pentacle, and Bacon has his "Strong pentageron." These things, Agrippa says in his book on mathematical magic, are of the utmost moment in conjuration, for geometrical figures arise from numbers and are of no less power.

> . . . Of these first of all a Circle doth answer to Unity, and the number ten; for Unity is the Center, and circumference of all things; and the number ten being heaped together returns into a unity from whence it had its beginning, being the end of all numbers . . . hence a circle being the largest and perfectest of all [geometrical figures] is judged to be most fit for bindings and conjurations; Whence they who adjure evil spirits, are wont to environ themselves about with a circle. A Pentangle also, as with the virtue of the number five hath a very great command over evil spirits. . . .[39]

It is obvious that these figures are mystical symbols, and impose not only a harmonic bond, working upon the spirits, as Agrippa says all symbols taken from the celestial world do, "by admonition and example," [40] but, as symbols of deity, impose also a religious bond by "command and power." They connect with the third and foremost means of magic—religion.

The persuasive virtue of any compelling magical operation with spirits came eventually, according to occultists, not from natural bodies or mathematical signs, but from the sympathetic soul of the magician, the microcosm's correspondence to the intelligible world.[41] This was a correspondence fostered only by worship. Religion, therefore, whether the true or a false one, was a crowning means to spirit magic, the vivifying element in ceremony. In the preliminaries it was the forms of religion that gave confirmation to all the natural and mathematical operations.[42] These operations lent themselves to the practices of worship and were fortified by consecration and by alliance with the actions of devotion and with the verbal symbols of deity such as the names of God and his saints and angels, or of what other spirits, being propitiated, gave power.

The Friar in *Bussy* "puts on his robes," and Alexander says to his assistant, "Bernardo bring hither thy white robes of sanctity" and later calls for his own robes, and for his pentacle and "fashioneth out his circle and then taketh his rod." *The Heptameron* says that the vestment should be a priestly or at least a pure white garment of linen. Its purity, and the mathematical excellence of the circle and pentacle, and the "virginity" of the wood of the rod [43] resemble and attract spiritual virtues in themselves; to them the magician adds yet other symbols—divine names and the sigils of spirits—brings all together at a propitious time, fecundates them with consecration and prayer.

The consecrations and prayers of magicians drew their first efficacy from their form, which, it was usually contended, was according to divine prescription; and from the grace possessed by the operator.[44] But if the operator was not sanctified, he might rely upon the forms alone,[45] first to provoke daemonic response, then to protect him; [46] and upon some kind of compromise with avaricious demons to gain their service. No matter what ultimate response the Christian magician aimed at, his operation began with God as the origin of all. The superstition which fertilized magic was, as Agrippa says, never entirely devoid of at least the signs of religion.

But *The Devil's Charter,* which derives many details of its conjuring scenes from *The Heptameron,* by no means duplicates the manual's rationale of those details that touch upon worship. The orthodox rationale of *The Devil's Charter* puts upon the operations described in *The Heptameron* the interpretation which the church put upon them, altering and suppressing parts that might, to an audience, have sounded all too pious from so black a character as Alexander was intended to be.

As a priest Alexander possessed the forms of consecration of the Christian religion, and if, though a dealer with devils, he had closely followed the ritual of *The Heptameron* he would have had ample opportunity in the preliminaries to use his priestly power, for *The Heptameron* refers to God for its first efficacy and presupposes for the operator at least a formal affinity with God.[47] In *The Devil's Charter,* however, there is but a hint of this. Alexander orders Bernardo to bring "white robes of sanctity" and to "cense about this sanctified place." But in what devotion the robes and the place are sanctified there is no clue. Of the prayer which in *The Heptameron* refers the virtue of the robe to the merit of Holy Angels by the consent of God, there is nothing. Into the exorcism itself creeps none of the devout expressions of *The Heptameron*.

In Alexander's invocation the only vestiges of *The Heptameron's* piety are certain Hebrew names of God so strange to an English ear that they pass as barbarous jargon of the sort which some occultists declared efficacious in magic.[48] Some of these names the play mingles—as, indeed, *The Heptameron* also does—with exclamations that appear to be gibberish, and it omits all comprehensible mention of God, His angels or saints, Solomon, or any other who might connect with piety. Consequently the dominant impression from the play's conjuration is of that utter nonsense which orthodox authorities so scornfully insisted magicians relied upon. The corollary, of course, is that the magician's ceremony is but a signal to devils.

It may be thought, then, either that Alexander's conscious practice was rather more diabolical than the actual rituals of the time required, or that the scene in the play is addressed to the audience as a stripping of magic to its insensate fundamentals, Alexander being conceived as left in the magician's self-fostered delusion that his operations were between him and the fiends not only a link but a bar in some way that might in the end permit him to preserve his soul from their clutches. In either event, it is clear that Alexander is very remote from God, fructifies his operation by affinity with fiends.

Not quite so abandoned in his ceremonies is Faustus, between whom and Alexander exists the difference that, in his initial operation at least, Faustus is not expressly contracted to hell, whereas Alexander at the time of his ceremony is already so contracted. It is true that among the preliminaries to Faustus' invocation was observance to evil spirits; he says that he tries if devils will obey his hest, seeing that he has prayed and sacrificed to them. But this, as the further enormity of his bond proves, is by no means the ultimate in abandonment, embodies a reserve which, because conceivably it might admit salvation to Faustus' soul, is rejected by Mephistophilis.

3

Prayer and sacrifice to spirits, even to evil spirits, was by no means so horrific a thing from the point of view of the rituals as, on the face of it, it may seem. In the preliminaries it was, as Agrippa says, a matter of paying to each inferior spirit the observance that was its due, and so long as this worship did not exceed the degree of *dulia* and was directed to angels or saints it was within the bounds of orthodox Catholicism.[49] The magician, it is true, might distort this license considerably, both as to the degree and the direction of the worship. But even so, neither the prayer nor the sacrifice was intended to be in despite of God any more than Odysseus' sacrifice of blood to the shades of Cimmeria was in despite of Zeus. Nor was the sacrifice an enshrinement of cruelty and horror designed so to attract those beings who were the opposites of God's mercy and tenderness.[50] Rather, if it was to evil spirits, it was simply a catering to the vanity and the avarice of such spirits, and a binding of them as by gifts. "May this sacrifice which we find it proper to offer unto ye, noble and lofty Beings [so might even devils be addressed], be agreeable and pleasing unto your desires; be ye ready to obey us, and ye shall receive greater ones." [51] The sacrifice itself need by no means be of blood; the *Clavicle* mentions burnt offerings of various kinds of wood, and gifts of food and drink. The only distinction it makes as to the nature of the spirits served is that "sometimes white animals are sacrificed to the good Spirits and black to the evil." [52]

In his ceremonies, although Faustus conjures by the great devils he still openly recognizes the fact that power is ultimately God's and he seeks by using the forms and symbols of Christianity to tap this universal power and apply it to his ends. Though in the interest of his pleasure he has "abjured the Scriptures and his Saviour Christ" for magic and Belzebub, a path and a deity readier to his purpose, his instrument and application yet contain tacit acknowledgment of God's supremacy. In his circle "by which the spirits are enforc'd to rise" are, together with astrological figures, "Jehovah's name forward and backward anagrammatiz'd" and "The abbreviated names of holy saints." His incantation, too, contains the name of Jehovah and he scatters holy water and makes the sign of the cross.

It is true that such use of these things may be rationalized as profanation attractive to the adversaries of God. Mephistophilis, indeed, so took them, and the orthodox so took them, and the language of Faustus indicates that as an accomplished divine he himself had few illusions as to the legitimacy of his observances, either in the use of holy things or in the worship of creature spirits. But whatever he may truly have believed, his ceremonies were not, *within the scheme of magic he professed to follow,* a deliberate flouting of Christianity, and were not, *within the scheme of magic,* a mortal offense against God's deity. Voluntary outrage to religion was, the occultist contended, a thing reserved to witchcraft. Faustus had thought "desperate thoughts against Jove's deity," but not yet arrayed himself formally with the foes of God. His sacrifices to creature spirits to win their favor were a dangerous derogation from God's glory, but not deliberately inimical to God. The use of God's names in the circle was not, in the theory of magic, an anagrammatizing, a racking—though Faustus with an orthodox bluntness uses these derogatory terms—but a reverent employment of reverently varied and euphemistic names of power.[53]

In other words, Faustus' practices are an attempt, in which he does not himself very strongly believe, to work magic by means of superstition. Whatever as a divine he may privately have thought to be the nature of his observances—and obviously he thought them guilty—they were not, even to him, even to Mephistophilis or the orthodox, as yet that deliberately contrary worship, that express alliance with evil, which was witchcraft and which *Malleus Maleficarum* declares a sin more unforgivable than Satan's.[54]

But as in *The Devil's Charter,* so in *Faustus* the rationale is so topplingly orthodox that only by a *tour de force* can the vestiges of verisimilar magical procedure be rescued and put in their places in the submerged occult rationale that is represented in the misguided promises of Valdes and Cornelius and in Faustus' abortive ceremony. It does indeed seem that as Taylor insists, the *Valeat numen triplex Jehovae* of the incantation must mean "I bid defiance to the three-fold deity of Jehovah"; for, as he points out, Mephistophilis himself says that "the shortest cut for conjuring Is stoutly to abjure the Trinity." [55] How then could the Latin passage mean, as on the face of it it may, "The three-fold deity of Jehovah aid me"? Mr. Taylor says that the words cannot in this sense be an actual part of the incantation. Faustus' subsequent use of Jehovah's name shows, nevertheless, that reference to God's power was not excluded from his conjuration, and the dozens of conjurations by the Trinity that may be cited from sixteenth century rituals show that appeal to the Trinity was by no means foreign even to magic as black as Faustus'. Wier in his *Pseudomonarchia Daemonum* where he recites the charms of the *Magiciens infames* gives the invocation by the Trinity as the form most general, and many of the charms in Scot are by the Trinity.[56] Faustus urges the rise of Mephistophilis *per Jehovam, Gehennam, et consecratam aquam nunc spargo, signumque crucis quod nunc facio.*

Superstitious the operation surely was by any canons, even those of magic—and doubly so to a Protestant audience in its use of holy water and the sign of the cross.[57] But it need not be conceived so diabolical that it necessarily opens with a defiance of the Trinity rather than, as the most obvious sense of the words is, with a citation of the Trinity as a source of power.

Faustus' words are by no means a prayer to the Trinity—in the rituals many of the citations are in essence prayers—but rather, like the names of God in the circle, a simple presentation to the demons of that which, it was presumed, they feared and which enforced them to rise. It was the ritualized, the arcanely energized, utilization of a thing somehow keyed to the spiritual vibrations of the world. This appears the more plainly if the *numen triplex Jehovae,* which Mr. Boas says "presents some difficulty" but which he with Taylor believes to mean the Trinity, is taken to mean rather "the triple power of God," that is, the power of God in the three worlds: the intellectual, the celestial, and the elementary.[58]

But whether *numen triplex Jehovae* be taken as "the triple power of God," or as periphrasis for the Trinity, still reasonably evident is the fact that Faustus need not be thought in his conjuration to denounce and reject the power of God as an aid. He is far from praying to God, as a miracle worker would do, for an extraordinary exercise of power in his behalf; his prayer for such special answer is directed to other spirits. But he seems surely trying, in part at least, to avail himself of that ordinary power of God which flows into the world through channels that are fixed and that do not run dry, magicians held, even when illicitly tapped.[59]

Faustus' magical operation may be thought paradoxical in details, perhaps hopelessly so; but the general rationale is moderately clear. Though Faustus, learned in divinity, can hardly be thought to credit intellectually the superstitious processes into which Valdes and Cornelius induct him, his appetites, secretly stirred by Mephistophilis, imbue him with an unreasoning hope. As a theologian he knows in his soul that the forms he observes are indeed blasphemy which estranges his guardian angel and attracts, though but *per accidens,* the enemies of God.

> Faustus, begin thine incantations,
> And try if devils will obey thy hest,
> Seeing thou hast pray'd and sacrific'd to them.
> (I, iii, 5)

He is essaying a thing whose efficacy without damnation he doubts, yet in which he has hope. His operation, if not his faith, is in harmony with occult rationale of spirits and their relations to men. At his first success he is exultant, like one who has seen a long chance realized.

> I see there's virtue in my heavenly words:
> Who would not be proficient in this art?
> How pliant is this Mephistophilis,
> Full of obedience and humility!
> Such is the force of magic and my spells:
> Now, Faustus, thou art conjuror laureat. . . .
> (I, iii, 29)

Yet when Mephistophilis denies the force of his spells, Faustus is not greatly surprised nor dismayed, but vaunts his sacrilege as a better title than spells to the service of demons.

So Faustus hath
Already done; and holds this principle,
There is no chief but only Belzebub;
To whom Faustus doth dedicate himself.
(I, iii, 57)

From this point, the rationale of his relations with spirits is uncontestedly orthodox; Faustus does not again have either power or the hope of it but by the witch pact.[60]

4

Much more successful than Faustus at tapping by magical operation the power which God infuses into His creation is Friar Bacon. His methods are much like those which Faustus tried without avail. He has prayed, he says, to the "five-fold powers of Heaven," "wresting" the holy names of God, and with "stole and alb" conjured devils. Although these things "are instances that Bacon must be damned" for his blasphemy and his presumption in "using devils to countervail his God," they have nevertheless served him as instruments of veritable power over devils. Further, Bacon seems rather less guilty in his operation than was Faustus, for of prayer and sacrifice to fiends nothing is said in Greene's play. Many references make it clear that the spirits are to be thought truly coerced by a power outside their hierarchy, a power resident in forms observed by the magician. Whereas Faustus' highest hopes rested largely on a worship-won acquiescence of superior fiends, and only in part upon use of divine symbols, Bacon possessed ceremony that roughly constrained even "proud Asmenoth, ruler of the north."

Bacon's magic, so far as the mode of it is apparent from the passing allusions of the play, apparently comes closer to the thing which the rituals claimed than that of any other play magician. The "five-fold powers of heaven" to which he has prayed may perhaps be taken to be the "Five Intelligible substances" given in Agrippa's scale of the number five. The first three of these substances are the three supernal hierarchies. The fourth comprises the "Souls of Celestial bodies," and the fifth "Heroes or blessed souls,"—notably, of course, saints whose names Faustus abbreviated in his circle.[61] Bacon has evidently in the pious manner which the rituals prescribed appealed to angels to command fiends in his behalf. These appeals he has supplemented with the uttered names of God, "As Sother, Eloim, and Adonai, Alpha, Manoth, and Tetragrammaton"[62] and with "tossing" of "papers full of necromantic charms," *i.e.*, of consecrated leaflets inscribed with symbols of deity. These were "necessary," says *The Fourth Book of Agrippa,* "as well for the defence of the invocant and his fellows as to serve for bonds which shall bind and constrain the Spirits."[63]

For all their success, however, Bacon's means are confessed in the end to be only desecration. Like Faustus, Bacon knows in his soul that the "art" he practices is a guilty one; and like Faustus he persists, deluding himself as best he can. Unlike Faustus, however, he does not lose his soul, for the success of his magic *per se* has relieved him of the necessity for that last, irretrievable iniquity, the express compact. Ceremony was, even to the orthodox, but tacit compact, a seeking of devils, whereas express compact was a consenting to devils. The general scheme of Bacon's play world is clear. It is occult in that it admits the real power of magic, orthodox in that it insists upon the guilt of magic, though in a degree less than mortal.

5

Much more obscure is the rationale of the ceremony in *Bussy D'Ambois.* However contradictory the indices to the rationale of Faustus' ceremony may be, they are plentiful; and when allowance is made for the facts that (1) the occult rationale is set up only that it may be destroyed, hence could not be allowed to carry much conviction; (2) censorship, both formal and informal, limited impieties on the stage, we have reasons, at least, for the contradictions. It is possible to make a fairly consistent rationale of Faustus' operations, both as he intended them within the scheme of magic, and as they turned out. For the ceremonies of the Friar of *Bussy D'Ambois,* however, this is never quite possible. As a churchman engaged in magic he is the counterpart of many a legendary and historical figure of the Middle Ages and Renaissance. Further, he is, or deludes himself that he is, a sanctified practitioner. But his part in the play as a magician is, unlike that of Faustus, not central to the action, but incidental, and the indices to its rationale are both few and non-committal.

The ceremony itself consists chiefly of an ornate invocation. Of preliminaries we are told only that "He puts on his robes." Though nothing is said of it, there is probably a circle, for the Friar orders his companions to "Stand sure together then, whate'er you see, And stir not, as ye tender all our lives," a precaution usually directed to keeping everyone within the safety of the circle.

The invocation itself bears only the most general resemblance to the invocations found in the rituals. It is classical, contains no names of God. The spirit is adjured by "the inscrutable secrets of the Styx, by the irretraceable windings of Hell," "by the secret depths of Night and Darkness, by the wandering stars, by the stealthy march of the hours and Hecate's deep silence." [64] This is reminiscent of a passage in Agrippa:

> Now good spirits, if they may be divers wayes called up, yet can by no bonds, or very hardly be allayed by us, but we must by some sacred things beseech them, as we read in Apuleius, by the Celestial Stars, by the infernal deities, by the natural elements, by the silence of the night. . . .[65]

But these correspondences, probably fortuitous, give little clue to the thaumaturgical rationale of the incantation. The Friar calls on the power neither of God nor of an inferior spirit to make Behemoth respond, but on impersonal things.

Analogies in various works permit the supposition that the Friar had previously raised Behemoth and bound him by oaths given upon the "secrets of Styx" and the "windings of Hell," and the other things by which classical gods swore, and that now the citation of these things compelled the apparition. But this is gratuitous and in the face of the charm's obvious graceful meaninglessness. Equally uncalled for is any attempt to read diabolism into the Friar's feat. It is true that an orthodox rationale can be imposed; but there is nothing to give it preference over the occult. The Friar's magic, like Behemoth and the Friar himself, remains an enigma.

Chapter VIII

Witchcraft

I

IN ANY PLAY that deals with a witch pact, a large part of the dramatic interest must rest in the question of whether or not the dreadful covenant will hold; that is, on how the devil will fulfill his engagement and whether he can exact his toll at the end. Upon this question turns the tragic conflict of *Faustus*. In its answer is such pity and terror as *The Devil's Charter* can boast, and from the same implacable answer stems much of Mother Sawyer's pathos, and the dulled but occasionally effective horror of Mrs. Generous' plight in *The Late Lancashire Witches*. Beings pledged to God and confirmed with His baptism have deliberately renounced that sacrament, the promise of the kingdom of God, for promise of immediate kingdom in this world. Each has his wilful guerdon, and each, struggling, pays the awful penalty. Yet it is not without yearnings, without crafty evasions, without remorse tottering sometimes on the verge of repentance that they live out their chartered time. Might they, despite their so express pacts, have saved themselves? The worth of the dramatic struggle requires that though they did not, they might have; and theology says that though witches did not, yet they might have turned to God and received mercy.

It was the popular opinion in the sixteenth century that if the devil received the soul of a witch at death it was primarily because his bargain gave him a right to it; that if he failed of the soul, it was because the witch or some heavenly advocate had found a flaw in the covenant.[1] The compact was accepted as formally binding aside from the further merits or demerits of the human party to it. This was not, however, the theological view. A witch went to hell not because the devil had an express lien upon her soul, but because she had been wicked enough to grant the lien—to renounce the redemption for which Christ died, to turn deliberately and wholly from God for alliance with the Adversary. Such was the sin against the Holy Ghost, and covenant or no covenant it was damning and to be forgiven neither in this life nor after.[2] This doom did not, in theory, contradict the doctrine of Divine mercy, for even such a sinner God would receive again if he came penitently. But one who had put himself so into the hands of Satan could never win to repentance.

King James says that both magician and witch commit the sin against the Holy Ghost. The magician is culpable so soon as he acts in full knowledge that his ceremonies are strengthless except by pact, and that it is the devil he deals with. If he persists after he has sure knowledge of his means and his confederate, doom encloses him.[3] Faustus, there can be no doubt for all his occult show, knew Mephistophilis for a devil and had also a sure presentiment of the falseness of his means. It was for this, then, that he felt himself already damned, and willingly conceded a pact. Yet before covenant his soul was not irretrievable; it was not until the magician had persisted, or until he had capped his offense with express compact that he had mortally offended God and was past repentance.[4]

One of the chief differences between Marlowe's Faustus and the Faustus of the source book is the greater sophistication which the former shows in his prompt acceptance of Mephistophilis' terms. The Faustus of the *Faust Book* would, he said, have his request and yet he would not be damn'd. He was astonished at the failure of magic and troubled at the prospect of witchcraft, so that to Mephistophilis' proposal he answered "faintly for his soul's sake." [5] But Marlowe's Faustus, long since determined to brave it through to the satisfaction of his appetites, whether by magic or witchcraft, boldly continues from his sophistical learning to justify his wild and wilder courses. Though magic, the "art" in which he professed faith, has failed him, witchcraft shall not; and as for the penalty:

> This word 'damnation' terrifies not me,
> For I confound hell in Elysium:
> My ghost be with the old philosophers!
> (I, iii, 61)

So Faustus' ambition and Mephistophilis' invisible guidance with its constant monition that damnation lies already upon him bring Faustus to the pact.

The pact as a pact does not damn him. But as a sin it makes his damnation certain; it becomes another psychological weapon to club down his impulses to repentance. Boguet says:

> As a brave soldier disarms his enemy so that he may become his prisoner, having nothing with which to defend himself; so, when Satan wishes to become our master, he makes us to renounce God, Baptism, and Chrism, because these are the weapons with which we can guard and defend ourselves against him, and the Evil One well knows this.[6]

Thus Faustus is forbidden to name God or Christ. His agonized cry:

> O, Christ, my Saviour, my Saviour,
> Help to save distressed Faustus' soul!
> (II, ii, 85)

brings upon him the great devils Lucifer and Belzebub and their stern rebuke:

> We are come to tell thee thou dost injure us.
> Thou call'st on Christ, contrary to thy promise.
> (II, ii, 93)

So the compact is an instrument by which the devils fatally weaken Faustus' resistance, twist his own conscience to put a face of injustice upon his desire to repent. Later, after the Old Man's exhortation has brought Faustus to call again upon Christ only to be overwhelmed by the conviction of damnation, he seizes the dagger Mephistophilis proffers, and cries:

Hell claims his right and with a roaring voice
Says, 'Faustus, come; thine hour is almost come,'
And Faustus now will come to do thee right.
(V, i, 5)

Yet Lucifer's claim is false when he says:

Christ cannot save thy soul, for he is just:
There's none but I have interest in the same.[7]
(II, ii, 87)

Not the bargain as such damns Faustus, but the evil of which the bargain is but a symbol. Not any justice of God that must allow the pact, nor wrath of God that refuses grace to true repentance damns Faustus, but his own sin and the toils of the serpent, which enwind him as hopelessly as Laocöon. "Never too late, if Faustus will repent," says the Good Angel. But Faustus does not repent; for the devil whom his evil deeds and desires have given dominion over him hardens his heart.

Scarce can I name salvation, faith or heaven,
But fearful echoes thunders in my ears,
'Faustus, thou art damned.'
(II, ii, 19)

Remy says that though witches may, like Judas, know bitter remorse, they are cut off from repentance, which is a true turning to God, because devils are unremitting in their vigilance over a witch and frustrate every impulse toward good.[8] Faustus says: "I do repent; and yet I do despair." In his efforts to free himself of Mephistophilis' rule he is blocked at every turn. Threats cow him, pleasures distract him, and above all a constant and deadly insinuation stifles all confidence in Divine mercy. When Faustus calls upon Christ, the great devils first look fiercely upon him, then urge that God has abandoned him, finally show him some pastime that effectually draws his mind from the question Mephistophilis would not answer: "Who made the world?"

Theologians were insistent that the evil which hardened the heart of the witch against repentance was not traceable to

God, and that the repentance, even of a witch, deserved mercy of God and would receive it. Calvin says in a discussion of the sin which it was generally agreed witches were guilty of, the sin against the Holy Ghost:

> To some it seems harsh and at variance with divine mercy, utterly to deny forgiveness to any who betake themselves to it. This is easily disposed of. It is not said that pardon will be refused if they turn to the Lord, but it is altogether denied that they can turn to repentance, inasmuch as for their ingratitude they are struck by the just judgment of God with eternal blindness. . . . The promise to those who call upon him will never fail; but the names of conversion and prayer are improperly given to that blind torment by which the reprobate are distracted when they see that they must seek God if they would find a remedy for their calamities, and yet shun to approach him.[9]

The judgment of God that blinded sinners was not, however, a vindictive domination by God of the sinner's will, but that universal judgment that permitted the sinner his evil and justly left him in the toils of it.[10] Faustus had wilfully entered a serpent's folds from which God would indeed receive him again, but from which he could not extricate himself.

The struggle, nevertheless, is no paltry one. Faustus is of "amiable soul," one into whom the grace of God has been strongly breathed, and in those moments free from the domination of the demon and of the doubts and appetites that give the demon community with him, he knows his peril with that sober certainty more vital to repentance than any clamor of prayer.

> What art thou, Faustus, but a man condemn'd to die?
> Thy fatal time draws to a final end,
> Despair doth drive distrust into my thoughts.
> (A, IV, v, 29; B, IV, v, 22)

But, as was the witch's way, Faustus cherished a weak and superstitious hope of a divine mercy to be his without desert, bestowed in a miracle of conversion at the final moment.[11] He shakes off his fearful mood:

Confound these passions with a quiet sleep.
Tush! Christ did call the thief upon the Cross;
Then rest thee, Faustus, quiet in conceit.
(B, IV, v, 26; A, IV, v, 32)

Indeed the powers of good have not abandoned Faustus. The Old Man sees hovering over his head an angel with a vial of grace, "Offers to pour the same into thy soul"; and Faustus feels hell strive with grace for conquest in his breast. The outcome is dependent not upon the pact and its formal capitulation to hell, nor upon the withdrawal of mercy by an angered God, but upon Faustus' will and the alliance that theoretically it yet may choose. Uppermost in Faustus' fancy Mephistophilis presents all the immediate worldly advantages of the pact, and Faustus is caught. He keeps by him for comfort his miserable hope of ultimate evasion; on the very day of his damnation Mephistophilis says that "his laboring brain Begets a world of idel fantasies, To over-reach the Devil." But by then the devil has so nearly prevailed that he can boast his triumph to Faustus' face.

'Twas I, that when thou were i' the way to heaven,
Damn'd up thy passage; when thou took'st the book,
To view the Scriptures, then I turned the leaves,
And led thine eye . . .
What, weep'st thou? 'tis too late, despair, farewell!
(V, ii, 97)

Faustus' being is so decayed, distrust of salvation and predilection to evil so far developed in him, that he can indeed but despair. He labors in "desperate lunacy" to repent, to achieve the miracle of grace, the drop of Christ's blood. But his own "heart-blood dries with grief, His conscience kills it." Call upon the offended God "whom Faustus hath abjur'd! on God whom Faustus hath blasphem'd" he cannot. The devil that has entered into him and almost become him, draws in his tears and holds down his hands. At the preconcerted hour that part of Faustus that can indeed become one with evil departs the body.

2

The persuasion with which the witch comforted himself that he could revoke his deed to Satan by resort to God's mercy, was delusory in that it was a practical (though not an absolute) impossibility for the sinner against the Holy Ghost to approach the refuge which, could he come to it, would indeed shelter him as well as all others.

> It is not strange [says Calvin] that God should be implacable to those whom John, in his Epistle, declares not to have been of the elect from whom they went out (John ii, 19). For he is directing his discourse against those who imagined that they could return to the Christian religion though they had once revolted from it. To divest them of this fake and pernicious opinion, he says, as is most true, that those who had once knowingly and willingly cast off fellowship with Christ, had no means of returning to it.[12]

The fond hope of a ninth hour recourse to mercy was supposed especially prevalent among Catholics, since the doctrines of intercession and absolution marked for them a path not open to Protestants.[13] The Protestant scorn of such subterfuge is reflected in *The Devil's Charter*. Alexander, sick to death of the poison he had intended for his cardinals, lies in his study with the cardinals attending. They have urged penance and penitence, "compunction with contrition and remission" for all his sins; and his laboring mind grasps at the promise though he can scarce bring himself to receive it at their hands and refuses their prayers.

> You talke of pennance and of penitence,
> Compunction with contrition and remission
> For all my sinnes; I pray you thinke of yours
> You vex your selues too much I cannot thanke you,
> Haue patience sirs; oh tis a goodly exorcisme
> Quem penitet pecasse poene est innocens.
>
> (V, vi.)

He then asks time to meditate; the cardinals shall return at his summons, "eyther mere fooles or good phisitians all" for his soul. He thinks desperately upon repentance, but can muster no confidence in it, and turns for comfort to his pact by which he looks for seven years yet of life. But drawing the curtain of his study to invoke again the "Angells of eternall darkenesse," he is confronted by the "Diuell sitting in his pontificals," who, jeering at Alexander's startled sign of the cross, says:

> What dost thou start foule child of reprobation
> Vaine are thy crosses, vaine all exorcismies,
> Those be no fruites of faith but mere hypocrisie:
> . . . .
> Thy date expired is, thy powre determined.
> (V, vi.)

The devil then exposes the pact's fraudulent wording, which cheats Alexander of seven years, and demonstrates to him in a long dispute that his soul, though God's, has by sin been withdrawn from God and now, corrupt, falls to the devil's clutches. Alexander's last effort is to arouse himself to repentance, to convert his desperate remorse to that true sorrow which will win him mercy; but his "stubborne, stonie, stiff, indurate heart" cannot "arise." The devil says:

> . . . by free-will to sin thou slaue,
> Hast sold thy soul from happiness to hell.
> (V, vi.)

That deadly bargain Alexander cannot now find the goodness of will to revoke.

Similarly, in *The Late Lancashire Witches* Mrs. Generous is inexorably doomed. ". . . th'art a lost woman," says her horrified husband when he knows her for a witch. But against his better judgment he is beguiled by a feigned repentance. "Why," he asks, "hast thou any hope?"

> *Mrs. Gen.* Yes Sir, I have.
> *Gen.* Make it appear to me.
> *Mrs. Gen.* I hope I never bargain'd for that fire,
> Further than penitent teares have power to quench,
> . . . .

[tears] Tinctur'd in blood, blood issuing from the
heart,
Sir I am sorry; when I looke towards Heaven
I beg a gracious Pardon; . . .[14]

But this contrition Mrs. Generous speedily disavows to her confederates.

Some passionate words mixt with forct tears
Did so inchant his eyes and eares
I made my peace, with promise never
To doe the like; but once and ever
A Witch thou know'st. (IV, p. 236.)

As Mr. Generous feared, she has indeed "extermined" herself "Out of the blessed society Of Saints and Angels."

II

It has often been remarked that as *Faustus* and *The Devil's Charter* are plays of the darksome and pretentious witchcraft of the continent, so *The Witch of Edmonton* is a play of homely English witchcraft. It is indeed a play of a witch of low station who has but a vulgar familiar and slight service by an offhand kind of compact. More clearly than either Faustus or Alexander, Mother Sawyer is cheated and cozened; unlike them she wins no worldly honor or goods, and is taken at last by the law. Whereas they are great in place and knowledge and may assume before the world that resounding, if dubious, title 'Magician,' she is indeed but the old woman the like of whom, Scot says, are "poore and needie and go from doore to doore for releefe, have they never so manie todes or cats at home. . . ."[15]

King James asserts that though to the greatest magicians Satan will oblige himself to teach many arts and sciences, to carry news from any part of the world, reveal secrets, aid them to creep into favor with princes, and otherwise to serve, he appears to the baser sort but as a dog, ape, or other vermin and gives short answers and swift abuse.[16] Faustus' soul is a prize hard to win for which Mephistophilis says he will do anything;

but Mother Sawyer in her misery and ignorance can drive no bargain for more than the bitterness of a petty revenge.

This, it is true, was not more vain in the sight of theologians than the riches and honor Faustus won, nor was Mother Sawyer held less culpable for the meanness of her worldly winnings. Faustus was cheated no less than she, since bargain of the next world for this was utterly unprofitable; she guilty no less than he, since it was utterly sinful.

James says that the devil never tempts a witch until he finds means of entrance by her ignorance or contempt of God, nor ever offers anything but riches or false learning or revenge—the empty or the wicked. He comes to her when he finds her solitary, in bed or in the fields.[17]

So, indeed, Mother Sawyer's devil takes her—alone in the fields cursing her enemies—and proceeds with her as was the devil's way, cajoling, threatening, tempting. Tormented by her enemy, Banks, who has beaten her as a defense against her charms,[18] shunned by others, she has cried:

> Would some power, good or bad,
> Instruct me which way I might be revenged
> Upon this churl, I'd go out of myself,
> And give this fury leave to dwell within
> This ruined cottage ready to fall with age.
> (II, i.)

Her sincerity has indeed given the devil the entrance she proffers; "I have found thy love unfeigned," he says. So, taken in malice and ignorance, Mother Sawyer is mastered by the devil, who tempts her with the revenge she longed for, wheedles that "The devil is no liar to such as he loves," and threatens to tear her to pieces if she denies express pact.

There can be little doubt that the devil who appears to Mother Sawyer is to be conceived an essential devil, no neurasthenia; but the rationale of their relations is not so clearly an orthodox one as that of Faustus' with Mephistophilis and Alexander's with Astaroth. Perhaps Mother Sawyer's situation is that laid down by Wier and Gifford rather than that which King James and Perkins and their continental allies insisted upon. *The Witch of Edmonton* is tinged with humanitarianism, with pity for the witch.

Wier and Gifford say that the *sorcière,* the woman witch against whom the fury of the witchmongers chiefly raged, was indeed usually but a feeble and ignorant outcast, suffering under the condemnation of the community and the delusions of the devil. So Mother Sawyer describes herself—"poor, deformed, and ignorant," spurred by the "scandalous malice" of her neighbors to wish the thing they accuse her of, though she scarce knows what it is save as they have taught her.

> Some call me witch,
> And being ignorant of myself, they go
> About to teach me how to be one; urging
> That my bad tongue—by their bad usage made so—
> Forspeaks their cattle, doth bewitch their corn,
> Themselves, their servants, and their babes at nurse.
> This they enforce upon me, and in part
> Make me to credit it. (II, i.)

Then when Banks has beaten her, she breaks out:

> What is the name, where and by what art learned,
> What spells, what charms, or invocations,
> May the thing called Familiar be purchased?
> (II, i.)

It is this confusion and distress mingled with hate that makes her a ready victim to the devil's wiles and threats.

Among pneumatologists a point of contention on the pact was whether or not the witch could effectively renounce the redemption which divine grace proffered universally to the baptized. Wier insists that the witch could not renounce the benefits of baptism and that in this as in all else the pact was an empty formality designed by devils to mislead the ignorant. This, of course, was simply the orthodox contention with altered point of view and emphasis, and to it the tacit reply of the witchmongers was that baptism did not revoke the individual's freedom to sin and that the most heinous sin was to strike a bargain, whether or not inherently binding, with the Adversary, wilfully to turn the back upon salvation.

Now, this orthodox opinion unquestionably meets with Faustus' sin. He writes a deed of gift: "Faustus gives to thee his soul," and the blood congeals. But in his obstinacy he persists: "Why shouldst thou not? is not thy soul thine own?" And unquestionably it fits Alexander's sin. Disputing desperately for his soul with the Devil, he says:

> I will not do that violence to God,
> Taking that which is his from him
> To be bestow'd on his great enemy.
> (V, vi.)

But Satan is the better disputant and proves the soul lost to salvation by the pollution of sin Alexander has heaped upon it. Similarly in Heywood's *Late Lancashire Witches* Mrs. Generous says she has engaged to the devil but so much of her soul as was hers. But her husband replies orthodoxly that having any of her soul he has all. Like these compacts seems Mother Sawyer's in that she gives all her soul, testifies her free will to sin completely.[19]

> Then I am thine; at least so much of me
> As I can call mine own—
> *Dog.* Equivocations?
> Art mine or no? speak, or I'll tear—
> *M. Saw.* All thine. (II, i.)

But Mother Sawyer seems obviously here the helpless and nigh blameless victim in whose behalf Wier argued. Whereas Faustus and Alexander and Mrs. Generous are portrayed as wretches who meet their deserts, Mother Sawyer wins the compassion of the spectator. Wier and Gifford did not deny the possibility of compact, nor even the guilt of a person who consented to it. They did ask pity for the ignorant and aged women so unevenly matched against both devils and a hostile humanity. Obviously *The Witch of Edmonton* asks the same thing, though somewhat hesitantly in spots. Of Mother Sawyer's compact, the audience is surely to understand that as it is forced and empty, it is fraudulent.[20]

The Wierian rationale for the play is strengthened by the fact that Mother Sawyer is not, at the end, taken by the devil, but by the law into whose hands he betrays her, charged with the deeds that are his. According to Wier and Gifford, the aim of the devil was by spreading belief in witchcraft, to spread the attendant injustice and cruelty of its persecution and the infidelity of resort to superstitious defenses against it. Consequently, Gifford says, "Satan doth gaine more by their confession, than by their deniall, and therefore rather bewrayeth them himself [to the law], and forceth them to confession, oftener than unto deniall." [21] Orthodox authorities usually insisted that the devil protected the witch as well as he could against justice, making her insensible to torture and encouraging her to hope for rescue.[22] But Mother Sawyer's Tom abandons her to the hangman.

> Out, witch! thy trial is at hand:
> Our prey being had, the devil does laughing stand.
> (V, i.)

It is to be remembered, though, that the efforts of Wier and Gifford in behalf of the woman accused of witchcraft were chiefly for her better treatment in this world. They denied her power truly to perform the deeds for which she was arraigned, hence the justice of the legal arraignment. Wier's attacks upon the genuineness of the covenant were intended principally to demonstrate it fraudulent, that the devil needed alliance with no mortal to do his evil deeds, and deceived, as though they were insane or children, those who thought themselves compacted. Even Wier and Gifford, however, had to confess the responsibility to heaven of those who made a truly wilful covenant.

It is probable that Mother Sawyer is to be conceived abused and pitiable and powerless as Wier and Gifford would have her, but at the same time damned by her consent to wickedness. ". . . thou art so ripe to fall into hell" says the dog, "that no more of my kennel will so much as bark at him that hangs thee." And earlier the spirit who is deluding Cuddy Banks to a ducking says that though hell can do nothing serious against that light-hearted and canny youth:

> We'll sport with him; but when we reckoning call,
> We know where to receive; the witch pays for all.
> (III, i.)

It is fitting, nevertheless, that such payment as she makes within the play is but to earthly vengeance. *The Witch of Edmonton* is, as contrasted with *Faustus* and *The Devil's Charter,* not only the play of a homely and English witchcraft, of a crone rather than a magician, but also the play of the worldly rather than the theological aspects of witchcraft, of *maleficium* rather than of pact.

III

The characteristic phenomena of *maleficium* were storms, sexual impotence, blighted crops and diseased cattle, lycanthropy, possession and similar evils. *The Witch of Edmonton* displays some of them on the stage, has references to others. A distinction is requisite, however. *The Witch of Edmonton* is not a play of *maleficium* in the same crude sense that Heywood's *The Late Lancashire Witches* and Middleton's *The Witch* are plays of *maleficium.*[23] In these latter plays the point of view is that of the uninstructed layman, intrigued and frightened by the malicious marvels of witchcraft, to which he gives an unquestioning and irrational credence. To him the essence of *maleficium* is hostility asserted beyond fair human means. *Maleficium* is any phenomenon referable at once to human malice and superhuman power. Its importance and its interest are in direct proportion to its harmfulness and its marvellousness.

The point of view in *The Witch of Edmonton* is the more philosophic one from which most daemonologists approached the matter. The orthodox theological view was that *maleficia* were the deeds of pure evil in which the devil associated witches with himself the more securely to damn them.[24] The emphasis remained where any complete orthodox rationalization of witchcraft required it to be: on Satan's preying upon human souls. This emphasis is clear in all the deeds Mother Sawyer sets her dog to. When their compact is first confirmed he says:

> See! now I dare call thee mine!
> For proof, command me; instantly, I'll run
> To any mischief; goodness can I none.
> *M. Saw.* And I desire as little. (II, i.)

And at last when he abandons her to justice he taunts:

> . . . thy time is come to curse, and rave, and die; the glass of thy sins is full, and it must run out at gallows. (V, i.)

In *The Witch of Edmonton* every deed of evil is bent to the development of the witch's deadly relation with her familiar. In Heywood's and in Middleton's plays, on the other hand, the *maleficia* are for the sake of physical horror and wonder. Perhaps the simplest way to make the distinction is to say that *The Witch of Edmonton* permits insight into the final cause of *maleficium,* the other plays present merely the phenomena, for the sake of sensation.

As already pointed out in the matter of the rationale of the pact, *The Witch of Edmonton* is orthodox with a strong tinge of the moderate rationalism of Wier and Gifford. This tinge is quite apparent in the treatment of *maleficium.* Wier and Gifford were in agreement with orthodox authorities that *maleficium* was always the devil's work, that the witch, despite her mummeries, was no participant in fact; but they did not agree that her confederacy in the deeds was nevertheless a genuine one merely because voluntary. Their denial linked, of course, with their denial of true pact; and their precise position as to the witch's moral responsibility when she was a consenting party to *maleficium* is as uncertain as their ultimate position on the pact. What is certain is that they (1) minimized and excused the witch's connection with *maleficium,* and (2) extended the devil's purpose in it to include not only the damnation of the witch through her more or less imaginary participation, but that of her persecutors by the sin of a superstitious hounding of witches or defense against them. Wier and Gifford inclined, too, so far as they dared, to Reginald Scot's bold denial that the phenomena of *maleficium* were supernatural in cause. If tempest or death or failure of crops seemed witches' work, said Scot, it was but coincidence; and lycanthropy and possession were natural diseases.

As previously mentioned, it seems evident that in *The Witch of Edmonton* the final cause of *maleficium* is the orthodox one: the devil's purpose to damn Mother Sawyer by allying her with himself in will to commit offenses against her neighbors' goods and bodies.[25] It is with her approval that he touches Old Banks' fields and cattle, nips the sucking child, strikes lame a horse, prevents coming of cheese,[26] and—worst of all, the deed that brings her to gallows—possesses and drives to suicide Ann Ratcliffe.

But though Mother Sawyer chuckles her spiteful delight, she can hardly be thought the true instigator of even the least of these. The tone of the play leaves no doubt that the devil dog—who performs evils such as his assault on Frank Thorney without her knowledge—has taken advantage of the hate her heart was filled with to lead her to most of her evil commands. This was the thing Wier pled in extenuation for the witch.

It is to be noted, too, that though many sins of *maleficium* could be truly laid, in the orthodox sense, to Mother Sawyer's door, her credulous rustic enemies foolishly accuse her of many things surely not her doing. As she is led to execution a countryman says:

> I'll be sworn, Master Carter, she bewitched Gammer Washbowl's sow to cast her pigs a day before she would have farrowed: yet they were sent up to London and sold for as good Westminster dog-pigs at Bartholomew fair as ever great-bellied ale wife longed for. (V, ii.)

In another place when Banks has told how his horse is stricken, a country-man says:

> I took my wife and a serving-man in our town of Edmonton thrashing in my barn together such corn as country wenches carry to market; and examining my polecat why she did so, she swore in her conscience she was bewitched: and what witch have we about us but Mother Sawyer? (IV, i.)

These ridiculous accusations—inserted though they also are, no doubt, for a laugh from the pit—serve to spice the play with that rationalism which derided the superstition that saw the devil's claw in everything the least out of the normal order.

Of their kind, in part, is the strange mania of which Old Banks tells the Justice. Banks says that ever since he "fell out with" "this grumbling devil," Mother Sawyer, she has owed him no good-will, that he consequently imputes to her malice the seizure that has forced him repeatedly to kiss his cow behind.

> So, sir, ever since, having a dun cow tied up in my back-side [out-building], let me go thither, or but cast mine eye at her, and if I should be hanged I cannot choose, though it be ten times in an hour, but run to the cow, and taking up her tail, kiss—saving your worship's reverence—my cow behind, that the whole town of Edmonton has been ready to bepiss themselves with laughing me to scorn.
>
> *Justice.* And this is long of her?
>
> *O. Banks.* Who the devil else? for is any man such an ass to be such a baby, if he were not bewitched?
>
> *Sir Arthur.* Nay, if she be a witch, and the harms she does end in such sports, she may scape burning. (IV, i.)

This has a close resemblance to a passage in Gifford. Samuel, the rustic interlocutor, tells the tale as he heard it when serving on a jury:

> . . . A third man came in, and he sayd she was once angry with him, he had a dun cow which was tyed up in a house, for it was in winter, he feared that some euill would follow, and for his life he could not come in where she was, but he must needes take up her tayle and kisse under it. . . .[27]

To this the wise interrogator, Daniel, replies that the victim's suspicion of the woman was no proof of her power to do him that harm, and that:

> . . . he was farre in loue with his cow. Let such men learne to know God, & to expell fantasies out of their mindes that the deuill may not haue such power ouer them, for he worketh in the fantasies of a mans mind, and the more strongly where they fear him, as it appeareth this man did. Satan did worke in this mans minde many foolish imaginations, and to make him beleeue he was bewitched he maketh him fall out with one that may be suspected.[28]

Gifford does not deny the supernatural agent behind so extraordinary an obsession; nor does he expressly assert that no old woman was a strengthless ill-wisher to the victim and ally to the spirit. Simply he pleads that the true enemy of men, the true worker of *maleficium,* is the devil; that the so-called witch is merely an equal sufferer with any other victim of demonic wiles. Obviously this merciful rationale is strong if not dominant, in *The Witch of Edmonton.*

On the other hand, the chief argument of Gifford, that the devil used fear of *maleficium* to lead people into unjust prosecution of supposed witches, is not very strongly apparent in the play. It is true that Mother Sawyer answers the magistrate's accusations with bitter recrimination, asserting the injustice of his prosecution of her when other and worse 'witches,' *i.e.,* harlots and lechers, go unpunished. But it is not apparent in the action of the play that her prosecution is sinfully conducted either in superstition or injustice.

An enigmatic incident with a bearing on the grounds of witch persecution is the burning of Mother Sawyer's thatch by the countrymen. One of the superstitious tests for witchcraft, against the like of which Gifford protests, is that which was based on the belief that a witch would be drawn to the spot at which thatch from her roof was fired. Even the orthodox authority, Perkins, confesses that such tests are so insufficient as to be themselves a sort of witchcraft.[29] But in the play when Banks and his fellows fire a handful of Mother Sawyer's thatch, she does indeed "come running in." The Justice, who represents educated opinion—or at least legal opinion—on such things, calls the proof ridiculous; but the issue seems rather to discredit his superior view.[30] The action leaves it decidedly uncertain whether Mother Sawyer's pursuit of the thatch was truly for the occult pain its burning induced in her, or for rage at the destruction of her roof. The supposition seems in favor of the former.

If, in the light of Mother Sawyer's conscious and malignant traffic with an essential devil, and her sin-ridden end, Wier's humanitarian rationale cannot be completely established for *The Witch of Edmonton,* the action has, nevertheless, many rationalistic balances, and especially that sympathetic consideration of the witch's plight that was characteristic of Wier and his followers. The play seems to abate nothing, however, of the orthodox stand that for her pact and the *maleficia* that confirm it the witch is damned; this fact is central, though not so emphatic as to overbalance the play into the apathetic.

Mother Sawyer goes to execution obviously unrepentant for all her striving; the settled gloom of hell seems already about her. But the emphasis is still on the pathos of her worldly plight as her neighbors continue their persecution even in her last desperate moments, until she longs for her familiar to tear them all to pieces.

> *Mother Sawyer.* These dogs will mad me: I was well resolved
> To die in my repentance. Though 'tis true
> I would live longer if I might, yet since
> I cannot, pray torment me not; my conscience
> Is settled as it shall be: all take heed
> How they believe the devil; at last he'll cheat you.
> *Carter.* Thou'dst best confess all truly.
> *M. Saw.* Yet again?
> Have I scarce breath enough to say my prayers,
> And would you force me to spend that in bawling?
> Bear witness, I repent all former evil;
> There is no damned conjuror like the devil.
> *All.* Away with her, away! (V, ii.)

So she is led out to execution. Whether devils come for her soul the play does not say. There remains just the possibility that after all Wier was right, that Mother Sawyer's pact and *maleficia* laid no mortal sin upon her.

2

More positive and by so much the less discriminating than *The Witch of Edmonton* in its portrayal of *maleficium* is Heywood and Brome's *Late Lancashire Witches.* Plainly and ungrudgingly orthodox, it yet displays *maleficium* rather for the sake of marvels to make the pit gape than for the sake of deeper dramatic values or of godliness.[31]

As a foil for its marvels the play presents superficially in some of its characters a Scotian rationalism. But it is a rationalism that speaks feebly and is utterly routed in the event.

The play opens with a party of gentlemen returning from a hunt in which they have unaccountably lost the hare. One fumes, saying the hare was a witch or devil, its escape from before the very noses of their dogs a prodigy. The others reply that the escape was merely chance and by some natural means simply not at the moment visible to them. But Master Arthur, like most in his time who testified for spirit wonders, is not to be put off by the mere possibility of a natural explanation. He says:

> Well well Gentlemen,
> Be of your own faith, but what I see
> And is to me apparent, being in sence,
> My wits about me, no way tost nor troubled,
> To that will I give credit. (I, p. 172)

But this proclamation—which contains the soul of orthodox testimony to spirit marvels, the principle that when the senses are nonplussed the means is more likely to be supernatural than natural—did not move Arthur's companions, for presently Shakestone is declaring:

> It seemes then you are of opinion that there are Witches, for mine own part, I can hardly be induc'd to think there is any such kinde of people. (I, p. 174)

His friend, the good Mr. Generous, when told that some believe a certain odd state of affairs brought about by witchcraft, says:

> They that thinke so dreame,
> For my beliefe is, no such thing can be,
> A madnesse you may call it; . . . (I, p. 179)

But all the sceptics are riding for a fall, Mr. Generous heaviest. He ridicules a servant who claims to have travelled to London and back in a night upon a demon steed; but the same servant shows him his own wife transformed into a horse by witchcraft, of which she confesses to have been the author.[32] Later he finds his forgiveness vain and her repentance simulated. In the likeness of a great cat she has, at her witch's sport, attacked a miller and lost a paw to a stroke of his blade. In the morning the paw has become a hand with a ring upon it which Generous well knows. As he holds it, he feels his former incredulity punished:

> . . . dost this last age
> Afford what former never durst beleeve?
> O how have I offended those high powers?
> That my great incredulity should merit
> A punishment so grievous, and to happen
> Under mine owne roofe, mine own bed, my bosome.
> (V, p. 249)

The transformations of Mrs. Generous and the other witches and Robin variously into horses, dogs, and cats are certainly to be conceived according to orthodox explanations of such sleights. Most authorities held that devils could not truly transform a natural body, but could so obscure it with an airy shape as to delude the senses of all save especially sanctified beholders,[33] and to convince even the subject.[34] Her victims the witch ordinarily made beasts of burden, horses or asses; herself assumed predatory shape, usually wolf or cat. Any injury received by the beast form persisted in the corresponding part of the witch's anatomy when she resumed her human appearance. So Mrs. Generous is betrayed by her wound.

Some orthodox authorities held that the witch did not physically participate in the deeds of her *alter ego,* but lay at home in trance while the devil ran abroad in the beast shape; afterward the devil fastened in her imagination as hers whatever experiences he had encountered, and confirmed them with the hurts his airy body had taken.[35] It seems certain, however, that Mrs. Generous is to be thought to have suffered in the more spectacular manner, since she is personally on the scene—though in her own form—a moment before the miller enters saying to himself with satisfaction:

> One of them I have pay'd
> In leaping out oth' hole a foot or eare
> Or something I have light on. (V, p. 245)

The deeds which witches or their victims did in the likeness of animals often exceeded human strength; but it was supposed that the devil invisibly assisted.[36] So, no doubt, Robin carries his mistress to the witches' feast [37] and she him back again.

A characteristic and constantly discussed phenomenon of *maleficia* was impotence. *Malleus Maleficarum* says that the witch, through her devil, could balk copulation in a number of ways. A feat of prestidigitation might seem to deprive the male of the essential member, or manipulation of the humors might obstruct its proper responses. One party might be made to seem loathesome to the other, or an invisible obstacle might be interposed between them.[38] The most spectacular and consequently most talked of sleight was that which seemed to deprive the man entirely of his organ. So in Heywood's play, Bantam and Shakstone discuss the woes of a newly married couple:

> *Shak.* The quarrel began they say upon the wedding night and in the bride bed.
>
> *Bant.* For want of bedstaves?
>
> *Shak.* No but a better implement it seemes the bridegroome was unprovided of, a homely tale to tell. (IV, p. 231)

But Lawrence, the impugned groom, pleads:

> . . . But keepe her off and search me, let me be searcht as never witch was searcht, and finde ony thing mor or lasse upo me than a sufficient mon shold have, and let me be honckt by't. (IV, p. 233)

The supposition, therefore, must be that the devil took some other means with him than Shakstone had believed. In the end the unfortunate Lawrence found the signal of his affliction to be a codpiece point given him by Mall, a jealous witch. It being destroyed, his woe vanished. We are not to suppose, probably—though the play gives no certain clue—that the point itself had any power over either Lawrence or the devil, merely that it was the symbol of the witch's collaboration.

But the play does not invite its audience to be more curious in the matter than the ignorant Lawrence himself. Its full dramatic purpose seems achieved with the simple portrayal of witchcraft in its instrumental cause. With the deeper relations of the witch to her victim and to her means there is no concern. The hostility and the wonder of the practice are sufficient in themselves.

3

Of greater dignity than the treatment of *maleficium* in *The Late Lancashire Witches,* but equally superficial, is that in Middleton's *Witch.* A continental locale and the hint of a classical rationale give it dignity; it is superficial because, despite the title, the witch scenes are but incidental.

Middleton's Hecate is witch on rather a grander plan than anything in *The Late Lancashire Witches* and she possesses to obstruct the venereal act a more fearsome apparatus than Mall's codpiece point. She has skins of serpents and of snakes, knit with charms and "retentive knots"; in what house they are conveyed "Neither the man begets nor the woman breeds, No, nor performs the least desires of wedlock." She has, further, magical stones and herbs of impressively long names, which she could "sort to villainous barren ends"; a needle that has been used to sew up a shroud is as effective if thrust into a pillow of the wedded pair; "a privy gristle of a man that hangs After sunset" will serve the purpose. Many other dread secrets of the baser part of nature[39] are hers; and she knows Latin.

These acquirements seem to take her from the class of the mumbling rural crone such as was Mother Sawyer, and make of her a goetist like the foul witch Sycorax of *The Tempest.*[40] She is certainly no feeble victim of the devil, but a grand Satanist, a worshipper of the evil spirits of old times—perhaps (since she worships the moon) a member of that fabled cult of Diana, existence of which Christian authorities denied.[41]

It is important to remember, perhaps, that doctrines of witchcraft and daemonology were ancient and cumulative; that every authority of the sixteenth century cited dozens of classical tenets and instances, and that no authority of the sixteenth century was troubled by historical perspective. A witch, therefore, might well be conceived according to a classical rationale in many particulars if it suited the occasion.

Indeed, writers with a leaning toward occult views on spirits were ordinarily inclined to deny almost *in toto* the existence of the sort of witch against whom King James wrote. The witch whom they acknowledged was the goetist, a learned and powerful though utterly evil practitioner like Lucan's Erichtho and the Thracian witches of Apuleius.[42] Of such witches Agrippa, who regarded the *Malleus Maleficarum* as a stupid and malicious work, says that they are users of:

. . . a sort of Natural Magick, which they call witchcraft; the effects whereof are wrought by Potions, Philters, and other compositions of Medicaments.[43]

These natural means—chiefly poisons—were but a step in the goetist's equivocal command of evil spirits for evil ends. Such witches occultists inclined to credit with real power of themselves, analogous to the power through good of the theurgist.

Whether Hecate is so to be credited, and her *maleficia* ascribed to her true powers in natural filth, is left uncertain in the play. Her *maleficia* are those of Mother Sawyer and the witches of Lancashire, though done with a finer air. But the *maleficia* of Apuleius' witches were the same; the phenomena of sorcery are constant throughout its history.[44] Hecate's *maleficia* seem veritable in the issue; but so were those of the humbler English witches. Her spirits do not appear in the action; but she refers to them often and was certainly under compact, for she says of one of her deeds:

'Tis for love of mischief I do this,
And that we're sworn to the first oath we take.
(I, ii.)

Further, she tells her lout of a son that her death "will be Even just at twelve a'clock at night come three year." The reference is undoubtedly to the settlement of her bargain with hell.

Since she has a compact it must be thought that, in part at least, her spirits act for her. Speaking again of witchcraft, which to him meant goety, Agrippa says:

No man is ignorant that evill spirits, by evill and prophane Arts may be raised up as Psellus saith Sorcerers are wont to do, whom most detestable, and abominable filthiness did follow, and accompany, such as were in times past in the sacrifices of Priapus, and in the worship of the Idoll which was called Panor, to whom they did sacrifice with their privy members uncovered. Neither to these is that unlike (if it be true, and not a fable) which is read concerning the detestable heresy of old Church-men, and like to these are manifest in Witches and mischievous women, which wickednesses the foolish dotage of woman is subject to fall into. By these, and such as these evill spirits are raised, as a wicked spirit spake once to Iohn, of one Cynops a Sorcerer; all the power, saith he, of Satan dwells there, and he is entred into a confederacy with all the principalities together, and likewise we, with him, and Cynops obeys us, and we again obey him. . . .[45]

So, perhaps, Hecate has her power by the devil—scarcely as his victim, but as an ally by right of a malignance as great and almost as ingrain as his own.

Like Hecate in many ways, and more fortunately suited with a classical environment, is Erichtho of Marston's *Sophonisba*. They have in common the repulsiveness of squalid evil and the impressiveness of mysterious power. They are alike, too, in the detail of their lust for young men who have engaged them to win love by charms. Hecate's love charm, however, works perfectly; whereas Erichtho confesses to her cosened patron her powerlessness against love.[46]

Neither Hecate nor Erichtho quite fits the characteristic pattern of the sixteenth century witch, though each corresponds to it in many details. To the scenes in which they appear there is an antique flavor quite different from anything in *The Witch of Edmonton* and *The Late Lancashire Witches*. Yet it is, perhaps, not entirely proper to think that Marston and Middleton are simply using what has been called "the mythology of witchcraft"[47] in contradistinction to a more prosaic contemporary doctrine which the age accepted as descriptive and explanatory of actualities, and which consequently appears in the later and realistic plays of Ford and Heywood. To sixteenth century pneumatology the spirit data of antiquity were not mythology, but the stuff of man's experience on which science might base as surely as on more modern observation. For all their differences from such realistic spirit traffickers as Mother Sawyer and Mall, Hecate and Erichtho are not less literally witches of a kind, and were as credible in their special kind to a sixteenth century audience as the humbler English crones. They were further from home, hence the fitter for romance; but to their audiences they were, perhaps, upon the plane neither of allegory nor of myth.

Chapter IX

Ghosts

I

The ghost-figures in Elizabethan drama have been much commented upon by scholars and carefully analyzed from every point of view, though the emphasis has been rather on their dramatic function and modelling than on their essential conception and their place in the play world. So far as the latter have been discussed, however, three general matters seem to have drawn most attention: (1) the question of the "objectivity" of the play ghost; (2) the question, first broached by T. A. Spalding, of the further nature of an apparition taken to be objective, that is, as to whether it was returned soul or impersonating devil; (3) the question as to the motive or reason of whatever apparition should be confirmed as the continuing personality of a man. These questions suggest pretty fully the field of pneumatological comment on play ghost-figures.

The non-human figures of Elizabethan drama are hardly subject to the first question. On any level of understanding that takes the play as fiction, the daemonic figures are for the most part of a self-evident objectivity. Their roles are usually extensive, their works unaccountable as coincidental or imaginary.[1] With the majority of ghost-figures, however, it is otherwise. Many appear very briefly. Most appear to those agitated by remorse or by hatred. Some do not speak, many are beheld by only one person, and an overwhelming majority are sceptically received by the persons they visit. Further, they are usually in the forms either of victims or of lamented relatives or friends, forms which a man's aroused feelings might reasonably be expected to project into his imagination.

On the other hand, there was an authoritative pneumatology which, taking all this into consideration of instances in the actual world, yet affirmed the true apparition of souls. It would certainly be a mistake to believe that the Elizabethan play-goer received a ghost-figure as subjective simply because circumstances permitted the interpretation.

When a play ghost-figure has been assumed objective, the question of whether it represents a soul or a daemon sometimes presents itself and occasionally assumes considerable importance to an exact comprehension of the play. As Miss Lily Bess Campbell and Professor J. Dover Wilson have demonstrated, an understanding of *Hamlet* is largely dependent on the doubt in which Hamlet stands as to the nature of the ghost.[2] Not quite so pivotal, but illuminating in its answer by Professor W. C. Curry is the question of the Banquo specter in *Macbeth*.[3] It is true that no other Elizabethan plays have ghost scenes in which pneumatology is so critically and competently keyed to dramatic uses as it is in these works of Shakespeare; nevertheless the conception of some other ghost scenes may perhaps be serviceably sharpened by the comment of pneumatology.

Almost indispensable in the estimating of a ghost-figure as soul or daemon is the motive or reason that seems to move it. Catholic pneumatology uses this criterion as by far the most satisfactory of any. But in the plays, literary tradition and dramatic usage obscure it. The traditional motive of the play ghost was revenge, and with the mark of that motive a ghost may be comprehended under a rationale that is literary and classical, does not seriously touch contemporary theological doctrine. The upshot is that the Senecan ghost is virtually withdrawn from the consideration of pneumatology, and that his traits confuse the issue in appraisal of his dramatic descendents. On the other hand, this progeny appears in some plays largely enfranchised in essential conception from the Senecan convention. As has often been pointed out, Jacobean play ghost-figures are drawn from a model less stagey than the

Senecan, represent a considerably modified concept of the nemesis which it was the ghost's customary function to bear.[4]

II

In 1907 Professor Stoll expressed the opinion that virtually all of Shakespeare's ghost-figures are to be accepted on the footing which the inclination of the times accorded them. This footing was, he insisted, that which we call the "objective"; they are "the ghosts of popular superstition."[5] Nineteenth century critics had preferred to interpret Shakespeare's ghosts as "subjective," had both expressly and tacitly denied their existence in the play world except as abstract symbols or as figments of the aroused consciences and imaginations of the bodily human characters. Professor Stoll established the fact that there was no more reason, either in folklore or in the action of the plays, to take such ghosts as Banquo's and Caesar's as "subjective" than to take the elder Hamlet's as such. Since Professor Stoll's monograph little has appeared to confute his opinion on Elizabethan play ghosts in general,[6] and a good deal has been written that confirms it. Except on that level of criticism where a play is interpreted as a continued metaphor, there is rarely any certainty that an Elizabethan play ghost is "subjective." Perhaps it may be said, nevertheless, that of many Elizabethan play ghosts it can be no more certain, pneumatologically, that they are "objective" than that they are "subjective."

Mr. Stoll argues not only from "folklore" but from the characteristics of Elizabethan drama and the predilections of the dramatists. The ghosts are "objective" because the Elizabethan dramatic conception of nemesis was as a personal revenge; the personal ghosts of the injured dead are a literal part of it, and Shakespeare habitually delineates it so.

These are weighty and probable arguments. They return, however, inevitably to construction from the action of the individual plays, that is, to interpretation of the play worlds from the theories of their model, the contemporary actual world. Unquestionably any such interpretation may be checked against that element in the actual world which is called "dramatic convention," and even against that nebulous, uncertain thing, the historical conception of an author's characteristics and tendencies. The objectivity of Shakespeare's ghosts may be a moral certainty in view of the dramatic tendencies of Shakespeare and his time as estimated by competent authorities. It may have some importance, however, even for their estimate, that a bald correlation of play world with contemporary theory of the actual world cannot by any means make certain the "objectivity" of many of the ghost figures which Mr. Stoll in incidental reference remarks as "objective." Most often it may be surmised that the intention of the dramatist was that the ghosts be taken as "objective." But the bare sense of the action sometimes permits as freely an alternative explanation, and the beliefs of the time do not forbid it.

As the problem of apparitions in the actual world was a thing that did not admit of sure solution except by faith and dogma, so in the play worlds it is as uncertain sometimes. In the presence of the dominant Elizabethan conviction of the reality of phantoms we ought not, perhaps, to overlook the mild yet potent insistence of Elizabethan rationalism and the even more telling emphasis of orthodox pneumatologists upon the frequency of self-delusion among witnesses to apparition.[7] It was not this, perhaps, that led nineteenth century editors and critics to make such statements as that of John Churton Collins that the ghost of Montferrers in *The Atheist's Tragedy* is an "imaginary delusion."[8] The fact, nevertheless, gives some ground to their views, or at least, to kindred views.

In the course of his article, Professor Stoll says that "the mind of the Elizabethans . . . was far from clear on the head of the subjective and the objective." It is certainly true that as the Elizabethans lacked our word *psychology* they also lacked our conception of the science that word stands for; similarly, perhaps, they lacked our conception of the cleavage between the objective and the subjective. But it was not that they were without a theory of mental process, or neglected to distinguish the forms impinged upon the intellect by the outside world from combinations of these forms which the soul itself originated. It was rather that they were not so sure as we of the inviolability of the personality, not sure that alien personalities could not come into the mind in a manner much more immediate than anything our theories of suggestion and hypnotism admit of. The subjective as "what is considered as belonging to the perceiving or thinking self" was an uncertain category in a day when authorities held that a percept might indeed be peculiar to a man as shared with no other and having no existence outside his mind, yet originate with and represent a foreign substance. A spirit might manifest itself to a man so as to offer nothing to his outer eye; it did not for that lose its independent metaphysical being. We can and do say of a hallucination that it is a subjective thing. But we cannot, except in a limited sense, say this certainly of a hallucination as the Elizabethans conceived it. The Jesuit, Delrio, in detailing how ghosts manifest themselves to men, says:

> The ancients distinguished a vision [*visio*] from a phantasm [*visum*]. A vision is thinking that we see immediately that which afterwards happens just as it had appeared to us. Phantasms are certain forms and figures which present themselves to the eyes of him who is either awake or asleep. We shall dispute of Visions in the following books. Let us talk now of the Phantasm, which Christians prefer to call Apparition [*apparitio*], of which there are three sorts according to St. Isidore, to wit, Intellectual [*intellectualis*], Imaginary [*imaginaria*], and Corporeal [*corporata*]. The Intellectual apparition occurs when separated substances come to insinuate themselves into the understanding, not in form foreign to them, but in their proper form. This, which happens rarely, is like a certain image of the eternal vision of blessedness, and is very remote from this treatise. The Imaginary, also called Spiritual [*spiritualis*], occurs when there are no bodily spirits which serve the senses, as Cardan also thinks, but when the spirits themselves, separated from their bodies, present certain forms foreign to them before our internal senses by means of which we are conducted and driven to a knowledge of them. Finally, the Corporeal occurs when such images are represented to exterior senses. And it is of these two last that we dispute, and we find that neither one nor the other is contrary to the laws of nature.[9]

There is, of course, despite this, no confusion whatever in Mr. Stoll's application of the terms "objective" and "subjective." Within his meaning the play ghost is objective if whatever image conveys it to the intellect of the character be conceived to originate, no matter how, not with the man's mind but with something separate from it. The ghost is subjective if it originates wholly within the mind itself, that is, if it be either simple hallucination on the character's part, or the dramatist's symbol for some imponderable element in the character.

But in spite of the clarity of these terms so employed, they do not perfectly serve for a correlating of pneumatology with the play ghost-figures. In the first place, the terms have connotations not agreeable to strict employment thus; and in the second, they do not allow adequately for reference to the various phases of manifestation and apprehension by which Elizabethans held man to have cognizance of spirits.[10]

A *bona fide* ghost—the soul of a dead man returned to earth, Scot says[11]—comprised (1) the spirit, an intelligible essence transcending human sense, (2) an image that represented it in the fancy of a man. There might, in addition, be (3) an exterior shape that gave rise to the image. If the ghost consisted of all three, that is, was what Delrio calls a *corporeal phantasm,* the exterior shape, at least, was certainly *objective;* but if it consisted only of the image and the managing soul, was thus *imaginary phantasm,* it was *subjective* in the ordinary modern sense of the word, *i.e.,* wholly distinct from any exterior sensible object.

On the other hand, the subjective ghost in Mr. Stoll's usage—the empty image, unbacked by the separated spirit of a dead man—was to Elizabethan psychologists quite as definite an object for the understanding as though induced by a spirit. For Elizabethans, perhaps, there was no certain demarcation between the understanding and the matter of it. There was the world of sense and the world of intellect; but the world of sense was of the inner senses—imagination, memory, common sense—as well as of the outer, and the personality receded with the division of function in the soul.[12]

To say, then, that a ghost is "subjective" may mean (1) that it is a groundless image in the fantasy, or (2) that it is what Delrio calls an *imaginary phantasm.* These are, of course, opposites in Professor Stoll's usage. To say that a ghost is "objective" may mean either that it is an *imaginary phantasm* or that it is a *corporeal phantasm,* is presented to the interior senses only, or first to the exterior senses.

It is not difficult, of course, to keep the meaning clear so long as the modern terms are not crossed with Elizabethan concepts. But the correlation of pneumatology with the play ghost-figures requires the Elizabethan conceptions. Perhaps, therefore, the discussion is on a footing better suited to its purposes if it relates not to the "subjectivity" or "objectivity" of play ghosts—for these are terms of which the modern sense came into use only with Kant—but simply to whether or not the ghost-figures are to be conceived as substantial, that is, possessing being in themselves, or as mere accidents of the mind.

Obviously for this pneumatological consideration, which tries to translate "play ghost-figures" into pneumatological equivalents, certain other terms also need to be fixed. It is as much a contradiction in terms to speak of an "unsubstantial ghost" as of a "subjective ghost," since *ghost* by definition is autonomous substance. Conversely, it is tautological to say "substantial ghost." It may, therefore, be decided, more or less arbitrarily, that the apparition, whether accidental to the mind or representing substantial being, and whether *imaginaria* or *corporata,* is a *phantasm.* A phantasm plus an unbodied spirit, either human or daemonic, that manages it is a *spectre.* A phantasm plus a separated human soul that manages it is a *ghost.* The question on the nature of the ghost-figures in Elizabethan plays resolves itself, then, first to the question of a managed or an unmanaged phantasm, one representative of substance or not so representative. The "objective" ghost-figure may be designated *substantive,* or *supernatural* or a *spectral phantasm;* and the "subjective," a *native, natural* or *idle phantasm.*[13]

2

There are many ghost-figures in Elizabethan drama of whose status it is unnecessary to inquire since they can hardly be assigned a place within the play world. These are the almost purely Senecan prologue ghosts such as grace *The Misfortunes of Arthur, The True Tragedy of Richard, Fuimus Troes, The Battle of Alcazar,* and most prominently, of course, *The Spanish Tragedy.* Distinctions have been made between these prologue ghosts as to artistic function, but any pneumatological distinction applied to them is virtually worthless, since they all appeal for understanding primarily to what had become a strictly literary conception.

All these ghosts, mingled as they are with allegorical figures such as Revenge and Truth and Poetry, are clearly outside the play world. They take no overt part in the action, are but introducers and commentators, are on the stage for the sake of informing the audience directly, rather than of fostering the fiction. *The Spanish Tragedy* offers a partial exception to this since its ghost, as Mr. Whitmore points out, never descends to mere exposition, is circumstantially conceived, oversees the action to the end.[14] But the complete Senecan conventionality of its play world rationale bars that convincing reality achieved by later treatments of ghosts, brought to a peak in *Hamlet.*

Exclusive of Shakespeare's work, the Elizabethan plays whose ghost-figures participate most fully in the body of the action are Marston's *Antonio's Revenge,* Chapman's *Bussy* and *Revenge of Bussy,* Tourneur's *Atheist's Tragedy,* Peele's *Old Wives' Tale* and *Locrine,* the anonymous *Second Maiden's Tragedy,* and *The Tragedie of Caesar's Revenge.*[15] Ghosts appear more fleetingly and less actively in Marston's *Sophonisba,* Webster's *The White Devil,* Greene's *Alphonsus,* Heywood's *Iron Age,* Middleton's *Changeling,* Ford's *The Witch of Edmonton,* Massinger's *Unnatural Combat* and *Roman Actor,* and many other lesser and obscure plays.[16]

When the action of the plays is correlated with pneumatology, it becomes clear that most of the phantasms in these plays may be considered to have their efficient cause in some substantial spirit, and that many are evidently to be supposed manifest to what Elizabethans called the exterior senses. Equally clear is the fact that some of the phantasms may with as much justice to the Elizabethan point of view be accepted as gratuitous creations of the fevered minds of human characters. Often there seems no sure choice. The matter is very much more in doubt than the substantiality of play daemons, because the play ghosts frequently only appear, do not perform the residuum-producing feats that more surely substantiate the daemonic figures. Only occasionally do the ghostly phantasms attach to any dramatic action that might not be ascribed entirely to the diseased imagination of a character plus coincidence.

Of the more active ghost-figures, the only one much in doubt, perhaps, is that of the murdered Montferrers in *The Atheist's Tragedy*. Professor Stoll declares it surely "objective" since it appears first to one person, then to two, then again to one and finally to another. The first appearance is on a stormy night to the murdered man's son, Charlemont, who with another soldier has been standing watch "above five hours together." Charlemont says:

> I know not why I should be thus inclined
> To sleep. I feel my disposition pressed
> With a necessity of heaviness.
> Soldier, if thou hast any better eyes.
> I prithee wake me when the sergeant comes.
> *Soldier.* Sir, 'tis so dark and stormy that I shall
> Scarce either see or hear him, ere he comes
> Upon me. (II, vi) [17]

The phantasm then enters and urges Charlemont's return to France. This apparition is certainly to be conceived *imaginaria,* to Charlemont in his sleep, for he starts up crying: "O my affrighted soul, what fearful dream Was this that waked me?"

The Soldier, questioned, says he's seen nothing, assures Charlemont it was a dream. Charlemont then speculates on the causes of dreams, decides this cannot be a natural one. But on second thought he inclines to a rationalistic interpretation.

> Tush! these idle dreams
> Are fabulous. Our boyling fantasies
> Like troubled waters falsify the shapes
> Of things retained in them, and make 'em seem
> Confounded when they are distinguished. (II, vi)

But instantly a phantasm appears to both Charlemont and the Soldier.

Soldier. Stand! Stand, I say! No? Why then have at thee,
Sir. If you will not stand, I'll make you fall.
(*Fires.*)
Nor stand nor fall? Nay then, the devil's dam
Has broke her husband's head, for sure it is
A spirit.
I shot it through, and yet it will not fall. (*Exit.*)
(*The Ghost approaches Charlemont who fearfully avoids it.*)
Charlemont. O pardon me, my doubtful heart was slow
To credit that which I did fear to know. (*Exeunt.*)
(II, vi.)

On the face of it this second apparition is spectral and *corporata* to boot, since it is to two persons. But it does not speak, nor do anything which a shred of wind-driven mist or smoke might not. The possibility of a delusion shared by Charlemont and the Soldier remains. The apparition is to men weary and overstrained, with imaginations aroused on a night so foul that the Soldier can scarce see or hear his sergeant's approach.[18] The circumstances meet completely the explanation of self-delusion which the scoffer, Reginald Scot, proposed as the sole way to see "spirits."

Unquestionably, however, they meet as well the conditions which the orthodox moved as propitious for a genuine seeing of spirits. The storm blackness that may have deceived the Soldier's outer senses also made the occasion the fitter for spectres. The strain that may have played tricks with Charlemont's imagination, gave spirits readier access to his mind. Professor Stoll takes the appearance to more than one person as indicative of "objectivity," and this agrees with orthodox pneumatology. Taillepied says some authors are inclined to hold that when men see a phantasm, what appears to be its body is but a figment of the imagination, but that this cannot be generally true "inasmuch as it is known that many persons at once have beheld an apparition, and a number of individuals could not all at the same moment be collectively deceived in the same way."[19] But to this sort of reasoning Scot retorted, of course, with insistence on the contagion of credulity.

This second apparition, therefore, considering the circumstances, does not completely settle the question,[20] and the two subsequent ones are the first to Charlemont singly, and the other to his wicked uncle in sleep. In neither is there any circumstance not attributable simply to the mood of the character. That D'Amville is apprehensive and conscience stricken enough to see groundless phantasms is shown in an earlier scene.

> O behold!
> Yonder's the ghost of old Montferrers, in
> A long white sheet climbing yon lofty mountain
> To complain to Heaven of me.—
> Montferrers! pox o' fearfulness! 'Tis nothing
> But a fair white cloud. (IV, iii)

Significant, perhaps, for a rationalized interpretation is Charlemont's speech to Castabella when later she takes him for a ghost.

> Within this habit, which thy misinformed
> Conceit takes only for a shape, live both
> The soul and body of thy Charlemont.
> *Castabella.* I feel a substance warm, and soft and moist,
> Subject to the capacity of sense.
> *Charlemont.* Which spirits are not; for their essence is
> Above the nature and the order of
> Those elements whereof our senses are
> Created. (III, i)

This last speech contains Scot's argument to the letter. But it is not surely to be taken as Scot's sentiment, for it was also a preliminary admission of the orthodox, who always proceeded then to qualify it heavily as regarded assumed or imaginary bodies of spirits.[21]

Perhaps the most convincing point for substantivity is that the phantasm conveys true information to Charlemont. He returns home expecting to find his father dead as the ghost had reported. In the church he comes first upon his own tomb where he had looked to find his father's.

> What's here?—"In memory of Charlemont"?
> Some false relation has abused belief.
> I am deluded. (III, i)

But he presently discovers his father's tomb also, and the phantasm's information is borne out. On the whole, although there seems room for a rationalistic interpretation of the ghost scenes, there is certainly no necessity for it and greater inducement in the circumstantial evidence, to say nothing of the general cast of the play, to consider the phantasm the work of an autonomous spirit.

Churton Collins says that Charlemont's attempt "to give a scientific explanation of an imaginary delusion may be compared with Clermont's" [22] in *The Revenge of Bussy D'Ambois* where just before the apparition of Bussy's shade, Clermont says to Guise of a phantom voice:

> 'Twas but your fancy then, a waking dream:
> For as in sleep, which binds both th' outward
> senses,
> And the sense common too, th' imaginary power
> (Stirr'd up by forms hid in the memory's store,
> Or by the vapours of o'erflowing humours
> In bodies full and foul, and mix'd with spirits)
> Feigns many strange, miraculous images,
> In which act it so painfully applies
> Itself to those forms that the common sense
> It actuates with his motion, and thereby
> Those fictions true seem, and have real act:
> So, in the strength of our conceits awake,
> The cause alike doth [oft] like fictions make.
> (V, i, 41)

But a moment later the "Umbra Bussy" is manifest to Clermont, who stands, as Guise says, and applies his "ears and eyes to nothing." It is Guise's turn then to urge groundless hallucination.

Clermont. Saw you nothing here?
Guise. Thou dream'st awake now; what was here to see?
Cler. My brother's spirit, urging his revenge.
Guise. Thy brother's spirit! Pray thee mock me not.
(V, i, 99)

The facts that earlier the phantasm has been independently on the scene and later is manifest to other eyes than Clermont's seem plainly to mean that it is to be taken as representative of some substance. Of what substance will be considered later. But no more than the *Umbra* of the Friar in *Bussy,* which also appears busily to many persons, can it be conceived as an "imaginary delusion."

Even more certainly substantive is the phantasm of Andrugio in *Antonio's Revenge.* For it there is no hint anywhere of a rationalistic interpretation, and as clearly as the ghost in *Hamlet* it is the guiding power to vengeance. Further, it appears independently and to more than one person. Like it in most of these things is the phantasm of Albanact in *Locrine.* It, however, although of the play world, is in essential concept so completely Senecan, with its cry "Vindicta" and its recitation of the tortures of Hades, that there can hardly arise a pneumatological question of its substantivity. As Senecan is its fellow apparition, that of Corineus. And though it takes no overt part in the action, does not manifest itself to the characters,[23] it too is surely supernatural.

Quite as literal, though not Senecan, is the ghost-figure in *The Second Maiden's Tragedy.* It appears first to the lover, Govianus, then to him again together with the Tyrant, and on both occasions speaks. Neither Govianus nor the Tyrant makes any effort to rationalize the apparition, which at last accompanies its body to the grave.

3

But if the substantivity of these active spirit-figures can hardly be called in question, it is otherwise with some of the less active. Of the two phantasms in Webster's *White Devil* one does nothing whatever; the other makes but a symbolic gesture. The "spirit of Susan" in *The Witch of Edmonton* silently stares the murderer, Frank, out of countenance; and the phantasm in *The Changeling* only appears to the guilty, without speech or action. In *The Unnatural Combat* likewise, the apparitions are silent and come to a man sore in conscience. In *The Iron Age,* out of two persons present only an overwrought boy sees the apparition.

Of these phantasms none is certainly groundless; yet none is demonstrably substantive. Most clearly put, perhaps, is that situation which in *The White Devil* produces the ghost of Isabella. Her brother, Francisco, is meditating vengefully on her murder at her husband's hands. He says:

> Let me remember my dead sister's face:
> Call for her picture? no, I'll close mine eyes,
> And in a melancholic thought I'll frame
> (*Enter Isabella's ghost.*)
> Her figure 'fore me. Now I ha't:—how strong
> Imagination works! how she can frame
> Things which are not! Methinks she stands
> before me,
> And by the quick idea of my mind,
> Were my skill pregnant, I could draw her picture.
> (IV, i, 103)

Since he sits with closed eyes, the apparition is evidently to be conceived *imaginaria.* The fact, then, to which Professor Stoll attaches weight, that the figure appears upon the stage, cannot in itself be taken to signify surely that it is substantive.[24]

But the phantasm becomes so clear and compelling that Francisco is impelled to explain it away:

> Thought, as a subtle juggler, makes us deem
> Things supernatural, which yet have cause
> Common as sickness. 'Tis my melancholy.—
> How cam'st thou by thy death?—How idle am I
> To question mine own idleness! Did ever
> Man dream awake till now?—Remove this object;
> Out of my brain with't: what have I to do
> With tombs, or death-beds, funerals, or tears,
> That have to meditate upon revenge.?
> (*Exit Ghost.*)
> So, now 'tis ended, like an old wife's story.

Obviously Francisco's settled view is that the phantasm is groundless; and indeed it fades when he sets his mind against it. But it fades, too, simultaneously with his declaration of devotion of himself to revenge, a thing usually satisfying to a spectre. The question of the substantivity of this apparition is unanswerable.

The phantasm of Brachiano later in *The White Devil* is, as Mr. Stoll points out, "actual enough to throw earth at Flamineo."[25] But that this action also is not part of a natural hallucination becomes unsure when the earth vanishes with the apparition. "He's gone; and see, the skull and earth are vanished." A moment earlier Flamineo had said that he has felt "the maze of conscience" in his breast. He was in mood to delude himself and to accept the self-delusion as supernatural. He did indeed accept the ghost, for he says when it has vanished: "This is beyond melancholy."

But there seems a veiled doubt, almost derision, in his words to the apparition:

> What a mockerie hath death made of thee! thou
> look'st sad.
> In what place art thou, in yon starrie gallerie,
> Or in the cursed dungeon? No? not speake?
> Pray, Sir, resolve me, what religion's best
> For a man to die in? or is it in your knowledge
> To answere mee how long I have to live?
> That's the most necessarie question.
> Not answere? Are you still like some great men
> That only walke like shadowes up and downe,
> And to no purpose? say:—
> What's that? O fatall! hee throwes earth upon
> mee.
> A dead man's scull beneath the rootes of flowers.
> I pray speake Sir, our Italian Church-men
> Make us believe, dead men hold conference
> With their familiars, and many times
> Will come to bed to them, and eat with them.
> (V, iv, 119)

But it is perhaps only a desperate half mockery which Flamineo uses to keep a grip upon his courage. Neither in his words nor in the actions of the phantasm is there a sure clue to its nature.

As baffling is the situation in Middleton's *Changeling*. To Beatrice and her instrument, De Flores, tense in the moment before murder, enters a shade in the likeness of a former victim. De Flores first sees it.

> Ha! what art thou that tak'st away the light
> Betwixt that star and me? I dread thee not:
> 'Twas but a mist of conscience; all's clear again.
> (*Exit.*)
> *Beatrice.* Who's that, De Flores? bless me it slides by! (*Exit Ghost.*)
> Some ill thing haunts the house; 't has left behind it
> A shivering sweat upon me; I'm afraid now.
> (V, i) [26]

That it was indeed but a "mist of conscience" seems indicated later when De Flores, confronted by the murdered man's brother, says:

> I cannot strike; I see his brother's wounds
> Fresh bleeding in his eye, as in a crystal.
> (V, ii)

But though this may be the work of conscience, it may as easily be the work of a persecuting spirit. The earlier appearance of the ghost in the dumb-show of Beatrice's marriage festival, which begins Act IV, is non-committal. "De Flores after all, smiling at the accident: Alonzo's ghost appears to him in the midst of his smile, and startles him, showing the hand whose finger he had cut off." This can hardly be taken as action in the play world, but is rather an expository indication of it; the ghost, whether it later be taken as substantive or not, is here perhaps simply indicative of nemesis or of the pangs of conscience.

Equally wrought upon by conscience is Malefort, murderer of wife and son, in Massinger's *Unnatural Combat*. Only for a moment, however, does he credit the phantasms of his victims as anything but hell's answer to a mad challenge to augment his terrors.

> They cannot add an atom to the mountain
> Of fears and terrors that each minute threaten
> To fall on my accursed head,—
> *(Enter the Ghost of young Malefort, naked from the waist, full of wounds, leading in the Shadow of a Lady, her face leprous.)*
> Ha! is't fancy?
> Or hath hell heard me and makes proof if I
> Dare stand the trial? Yes, I do; and now
> I view these apparitions, I feel
> I once did know the substances. For what come you?
> Are your aeriall forms deprived of language,
> And so denied to tell me, that by signs
> *(The Ghosts use various gestures.)*
> You bid me ask here of myself? 'Tis so:
> And there is something here makes answer for you.
> You come to lance my sear'd up conscience.
> (V, ii)

It is difficult to believe that these ghosts are intended to be merely an overwrought state of mind in Malefort and not, as he certainly believes, substantive apparitions of his wife and son come from another world to further disturb that state of mind, "to lance his sear'd up conscience." Nevertheless his state of mind was, according to Elizabethan doctrine, a sufficient explanation of such phantasms.[27] The state of mind preceded the ghosts on the scene. There can be little doubt that Reginald Scot in the audience might have put his rationalistic interpretation upon these ghosts and made as good an argument from it as he made in the actual world.

Less doubtfully substantive are the phantasms in another of Massinger's plays, *The Roman Actor*. "The apparitions of Junius Rusticus and Palphurius Sura rise, with bloody swords in their hands; they wave them over the head of Caesar, who seems troubled in his sleep, and as if praying to the image of Minerva, which they scornfully seize, and then disappear with it." The Emperor rises in great agitation, harassed by conscience, but thinking the apparition a natural dream until he misses the image of his goddess.

> Where is my goddess? vanished! I am lost then.
> No; 'twas no dream, but a most real truth,
> That Junius Rusticus and Palphurius Sura,
> Although their ashes were cast in the sea,
> Were by their innocence made up again,
> And in corporeal forms but now appeared,
> Waving their bloody swords above my head,
> As at their deaths they threatened. (V, i)

The ravishing of the image seems to put the substantivity of the phantasms beyond doubt. They are, too, since they perform what was threatened before death, more consequential than the apparitions in *The Unnatural Combat, The White Devil,* and *The Changeling* which are without warning or direct issue, seem but an ornamental part of a general retributive action.

As well substantiated as these ghosts in Massinger are the ghost of Asdrubal in Marston's *Sophonisba* and that of Calchas in Greene's *Alphonsus*. They are two among the few ghosts in Elizabethan drama that do not rise in the interests of vengeance. Each is the bearer of a fulfilled prophecy.

Doubtful in itself, but perhaps resolved by the general rationale of its play world is the scene in *The Witch of Edmonton* in which the murderer, Frank Thorney, is afflicted by a phantasm like his dead wife, Susan. Frank lies in bed of self-inflicted wounds which, together with his wife's murder, he has fathered upon a jealous rival. Mother Sawyer's devil-dog, who has inspired him to slay Susan, comes invisibly to his bedside, dancing for joy at Frank's approaching exposure. "The Dog runs off.—The spirit of Susan comes to the bed's side; Frank stares at it, and then turns to the other side, but the spirit is there too. Meanwhile enter Winifred as a page, and stands sadly at the bed's foot.—Frank affrighted sits up. The spirit vanishes."

> *Frank.* . . . Kneel by me here.
> On this side now! how dar'st thou come to mock me
> On both sides of my bed?

Winifred. When?
Frank. But just now?
Outface me, stare upon me with strange postures,
Turn my soul wild by a face in which were drawn
A thousand ghosts leapt newly from their graves
To pluck me into a winding-sheet!
Winifred. Believe it,
I came no nearer to you than yon place
At your bed's feet. . . .
Frank. Then 'twas my fancy;
Some windmill in my brain for want of sleep.
(IV, ii)

In his distressed state of mind he then confesses to her the murder and a moment later her indiscretion has revealed it to Susan's father, already suspicious, and Frank's doom is sure.

The scene itself affords as much ground for rationalistic interpretation as does that of Isabella's ghost in *The White Devil.* The apparition does not act except to stay in Frank's vision, as a phantasm, whether substantive or not, might certainly do. When he makes a strong effort and sits up in bed, it disappears. There is ready truth in the explanation which he makes: that there is turmoil in his brain.

But the presence of the demon at the bedside suggests the alternative that the apparition was his creation, intended to do what it did: drive Frank to a confession. Certainly the issue was what the demon wished and fostered. If the phantasm of Susan be conceived his doing, the connexity of the action is sustained. It is to be noted, nevertheless, that once before the demon had been willing to leave a sinner, well launched, to the gnawings of his conscience. It may be thus with Frank also.

Mr. Stoll asserts that "the crucial test of the objectivity of any Elizabethan ghost" lies in whether or not it appears to the audience; ". . . then the audience was never made a prey to an illusion."[28] This seems a sound principle and one backed by general usage in Elizabethan drama. So far as it applies to ghost-figures, nevertheless, its inductive demonstration follows on its assumption as true in particular plays. Pneumatology, at any rate, cannot always make a separate demonstration of the substantivity of phantasms presented on the stage. The very number of ghost scenes that carry their own rationalistic explanations in the mouths of the characters is indicative of the force of rationalism at the time.

Rationalism, however, never comes off with better than a dogfall except perhaps where the ghosts considered are such unstaged ones as those in *The True Tragedy of Richard III* of which Richard says that whatsoever he does they come "gaping for revenge"; or that of the Duchess of Malfi which Bosola says he thinks yet haunts him, then attributes to his melancholy. Orthodox pneumatology would probably put the stamp 'genuine' on every spectre that has been here discussed, and for purposes of further discussion that verdict may be accepted.

III

Among believers in the manifestation of spirits the foremost question about an apparition in the likeness of a dead man was not as to its substantivity but as to its further nature. Was the phantasm representative of a separated human soul or of a daemon? If of a daemon, good or evil? If of a soul, was it from the Christian havens of the dead, or was it an earth-bound vestigial personality after the pagan doctrine?

The spectre in the likeness of a known dead man professed by the resemblance to be the continuing personality in a new manner of that man, to continue his memory and understanding, and perhaps his passions in a state of being that was superearthly. If the profession was a true one it gave to the spectre and all its works a surer identity and a more individual motive than was ever attributable to a daemon. If the profession was false, identity faded, the motive became general. There were two ways in which the profession could be false: the phantasm might be daemonic in origin; or it might, according to an occult view, be a perishable shape, a man's astral body, a thing that temporarily survived the dissolution of his elementary body, wandered without conscious memory or volition, a mere drifting vestige.

To distinguish the human from the daemonic spectre, orthodox Catholic pneumatologists had many tests; but none of them is conclusive in application to play-spectres. Delrio says that if a spectre alleges a wicked reason for its appearance, or if it seem passionate or vindictive, or if it disappear with a great noise or stench, it is demonic.[29] These tests would infallibly convict the Andrugio phantasm in Marston's *Antonio's Revenge;* for at its first apparition it leaves behind an odor of sulphur, its carriage is certainly passionate and vindictive, and its counsel correspondingly wicked. But its vindictiveness is so purely Senecan, its whole essential being is so surely in the tradition which Seneca and his imitators conventionalized from classical doctrine, as to baffle any very strict application of Delrio's tests. Andrugio's ghost must be accepted at face value, and the pneumatology that comments on it is not that of Delrio and Le Loyer, but one, like that of Agrippa, in which classical doctrine is less tempered by Christianity. In a similar, though not identical, way the tests of Delrio and Taillepied and Le Loyer fail with other ghost-figures.

Some play ghost-figures, nevertheless, may be taken as daemons.[30] In fact, any that are not too plainly stamped with the classical label may be so taken, though certain demonstration that any one need so be taken is, perhaps, never possible. The principal ghost-figures that may be construed as daemons are those in *The Atheist's Tragedy, The White Devil, The Witch of Edmonton, The Unnatural Combat,* and *The Changeling.*

It has been mentioned that the "Spirit of Susan" in *The Witch of Edmonton* may best be understood as an apparition managed by Mother Sawyer's devil. This is not because the figure accommodates itself to the tests; for silent, brief, nebulous, it is too indefinite for that. The key to the rationale is in the antecedent probability supplied by the mischievous presence of the demon-dog and in pneumatology's confirmation that conscience-harrowing phantasms were indeed often the work of demons. There is no proof for such a rationale; it can be only an assumption that fits all the facts of the play world and draws them somewhat more nearly into a unit than they would be in the supposition that the "Spirit of Susan" is either ghost or idle phantasm.[31]

Similarly, perhaps, the apparitions in *The White Devil* may be explained, though here the presumption is by no means so clearly offered since the demonic agency explicit in

The Witch of Edmonton is nowhere so in Webster's play. Perhaps indicative, however, is the fact that neither of the spectres in *The White Devil* had, if the souls of the persons they seemed, any reason from their mortal history or passions for appearing as they did. The phantasm of the Duchess spurs vengeance against a husband to whom in life she was abjectly devoted and in whom she forgave the most flagrant offenses. That the departure of her soul to heaven should have changed this is not in reason,[32] nor yet conformable to the general atmosphere of the play. The spectre in her shape does nothing to show itself accordant with the Catholic scheme of ghosts; yet on the other hand it is certainly not Senecan. The easiest explanation of it—if the phantasm be taken as indeed spectral, not baseless—is as the work of that force of spiritual evil which imbues all the action of the play. Similarly explicable is the phantasm like Brachiano that appears to Flamineo. No reason personal to Brachiano required the apparition—neither vengeance nor love, nor any of the offices a Christian ghost might serve. Only the mounting horror in Flamineo's mind required it. Whether spontaneously out of that mind or introduced by the personal forces of evil, it came.

Mr. Stoll in his *John Webster* comments on the nebulous and symbolic nature of these ghost-figures as compared with the robuster ones of Marston and Chapman, and says that they are not *dramatis personae* but "a vague and environing influence, and an atmosphere of fate." [33] It would be entirely too brusque, perhaps, to say that the "environing influence" is demonic. Not that such influence is unworthy of the dramatist's art—*Macbeth* proves the contrary—but that it is here unexpressed. Webster's play is too veiled for an interpretation so direct to be agreeable to it. The comment of pneumatology on the action of *The White Devil,* as on that of *The Duchess of Malfi,* must be at one remove from the explicit since the play offers to it little, though tantalizing, material.

Not so attractive of speculation and far less, though no more uncertainly, responsive is the ghost material in Massinger's *Unnatural Combat.* The sinner Malefort, challenges hell to "open Her wide-spread jaws, and let out all her furies." The immediate answer is the appearance of a spectre like Young Malefort, "naked from the waist, full of wounds," accompanied by another spectre, "the Shadow of a Lady, her face leprous." Malefort's instant conjecture is that hell has heard him and makes proof if he dare stand the trial. But his conviction that the phantasms are infernal quickly fades as he recognizes their shapes:

> . . . and now
> I view these apparitions, I feel
> I once did know the substances. For what come you?
> (V, ii)

Professor Stoll cites this as illustrative of the Elizabethan conception of nemesis as personal revenge. He says that "It is no uncommon thing on the Elizabethan stage for ghosts and the heavenly or the infernal powers to answer words of appeal, defiance, or blasphemy with outcries or with thunder and lightning," and that here "ghosts" have answered the murderer's challenge.[34]

Pneumatology strongly supports the view of nemesis as a retribution fostered by a vital agent of some kind, rather than as the issue of an impersonal course of events. But nemesis was not—in the participation of apparitions, at least—always quite so personal as it sometimes appeared. Not always does apparition like the murdered to the murderer, even of young Malefort's shape to his father, signify simply a "blood-feud carried beyond the confines of the grave"; it is not always, "in the body or out of the body, the murdered one himself."[35] Though Elizabethans conceived punishment to be shed on the head of an offender, they were not, perhaps, so naïve as invariably to look upon it as retaliation between man and man. They possessed, after all, a conception of providence which allowed for a moral law that of itself, though through personal agents, acted against the sinner. Certainly the ghosts in Chapman's work and in *The Atheist's Tragedy* are drawn according to a less primitive conception of nemesis than the Senecan ghost that declares it will carry on its feud in Hades.[36]

Whether the spectres in *The Unnatural Combat* are human or demonic cannot be certainly determined, and is perhaps dramatically unimportant. What seems sure, however, is that they are instruments of God's vengeance rather than, like Senecan ghosts, of their own. They act in concert with a power greater than that accorded to man's vindictiveness, even beyond the grave. They disappear when Malefort asks whether repentance can save him, and a moment later he is blasted by lightning as he blasphemes his "cause of being." Devils were a more customary channel of God's wrath than ghosts, though pneumatology affirms the use of both.

2

The conception of a play ghost-figure as the returned soul of a murdered man fostering a personal revenge is perhaps at its lowest ebb in the Montferrer's spectre of Tourneur's *Atheist's Tragedy*. Mr. Charles Whitmore has declared this figure, which does so little to forward the action, to be an artistic nullity. Its conception, he says, is "not one which has any real dramatic value," [37] and Miss Lily Bess Campbell has since pointed out that it is in essential characteristics the least Senecan, most Christian, ghost in Elizabethan tragedy.[38] It demands no revenge, just benevolently warns Charlemont of a menace to his heritage, charitably restrains him from violence to his offending uncle and cousins, finally in a dream apparition to the wicked uncle dispassionately predicts his fall by his own unwisdom. This certainly has no hint of personal retaliation so far as the spectre is concerned. The ghost but stands by while D'Amville is destroyed by his own evil worked out in God's providence.

The play draws an obvious contrast between this evil, which roots in the atheist's withdrawal from God, and a divine grace that abides in the bosom of Charlemont, bolstered by the ghost—or almost being the ghost. According to pneumatology a spirit which so served a human soul was the guardian of that soul and usually was thought a non-human essence. But Agrippa, at least, seems to hold also that the spirit of a dead man might return after death and permanently attend a living man as his good genius.[39] This is a pagan tenet traceable in Greek literature to Hesiod.

Sometimes, however, Agrippa seems to leave the matter open:

> We read that some men are called Gods and angels and devils. So the names of them which are endowed with any singular excellency

of vertue, or with some desperate wickedness have departed this life, have obtained a place amongst the names of good and bad Demons, and are reckoned amongst them, whether we shall think that the souls of those men or the Genii whether good or bad are signified.[40]

The occultist was content that there should be little practical distinction between daemons and separated souls. In this he followed the precedent of antiquity, which had held the human soul a daemon, though it might understand also by the term spirits that had never vitalized a body.[41]

Orthodox writers were more insistent than Agrippa upon keeping clear a distinction between human and superhuman spirits, but just what the distinction was, in the apparition, between a ghost and an angelic spectre they were hard pressed to say. Delrio after citing some proposed tests for determining whether an apparition is ghost or good angel, discards them all as unserviceable, and says he will—with St. Augustine—confess his ignorance. It is, he asserts, sure that guardian angels can and do present themselves in the shapes of those whom they guarded, but to detect them as angels there is no way.[42] In the play, then, it may be that the spectre is Montferrers' good angel come to renew its guardian's role, this time with Charlemont, or that it is Montferrers himself in that role.

Charlemont takes the ghost at its first appearance as what he calls his "Genius," and indeed its words: "Return to France, for thy old father's dead, And thou by murder disinherited," attach no nearer identity to it. At its last apparition to Charlemont, however, the spectre refers directly to "my murder." But even this cannot be conclusive, since to judge from Delrio a good angel appeared in the similitude of its dead charge in language as well as shape.

The generality of the evidence, however, seems to be in favor of taking the spectre as indeed what it appears—Montferrers returned to earth. It is perhaps noteworthy that the rascally and discredited Puritan chaplain, Languebeau Snuffe, rejects ghosts in accordance with Protestant doctrine. When Charlemont, supposed dead, enters and proclaims himself "The spirit of Charlemont," the chaplain cries:

No. 'Tis profane. Spirits are invisible. 'Tis the fiend i' the likeness of Charlemont. I will have no conversation with Satan. (III, ii)

Later when D'Amville thinks to have seen a ghost, Snuffe says:

> Tush! tush! their walking spirits are mere imaginary fables. There's no such thing *in rerum natura.* (IV, iii)

Since Snuffe is throughout presented as a false, ignorant, and misguiding ministrant in things religious, his doubt of ghosts may be simply another instance of his wrongheadedness, and the action may be interpreted to refute him as solidly as it does the atheist, D'Amville.

3

One thing about the Montferrers spectre seems reasonably sure: that it conforms to a Christian orthodox doctrine. Whether ghost as it seems, or guardian angel as it may perhaps be intended, it offends in no particular against that general Catholic pneumatology from which Protestant pneumatology was but a partial dissent. There is nothing pagan, nothing Senecan, in the ghost of *The Atheist's Tragedy.*

Equally remote from the pagan conception in everything except a scrupulous—or perhaps merely pretentious—designation by the word *umbra,* a word which the orthodox Delrio specifically eschews as pagan,[43] is the ghost of the Friar in *Bussy D'Ambois.* Its sentiments are highly Christian; it urges on Bussy forgiveness of his murderer, and between Tamyra and Montsurry a "Christian reconcilement," finally seems to retire to purgation.

So far as pneumatology is concerned, the *Umbra Friar* partakes largely of the obscurity, not to say confusion, that marks the conjuring and the daemonic figure in its play; [44] but clearly it seems intended to signify the continuing personality of the Friar seeking after death to carry on his confederacy with Tamyra and Bussy.[45] Bussy himself at one time takes the spectre to have been a demonic delusion. When Montsurry comes to him in the Friar's habit, apparently the Friar living and to the discredit of Behemoth's information, Bussy says, "Oh, lying spirit! to say the Friar was dead; I'll now believe nothing of his forged predictions." But the Friar is dead, and in view of its busy personal concern in Bussy's behalf the apparition in his likeness seems truly to represent him.

To judge by its own words the ghost is from purgatory, acting by that special license which Catholic pneumatologists agreed the purgatorial soul had to receive before it could return to earth. Like Behemoth, the Friar is restrained by fate from divulging to Bussy the information that might have saved him. "My power is limited; alas! I cannot," it answers Tamyra when she urges it to convey its warning to Bussy.

After Bussy is slain the *Umbra* commands Montsurry to be reconciled to Tamyra, "or be assur'd Never to rest free from my haunt and horror." Though Montsurry refuses, the *Umbra* threatens no more, but in the play's concluding speech says:

> My terrors are strook inward, and no more
> My pennance will allow they shall enforce
> Earthly afflictions but upon my selfe.
> (V, iv) [46]

Taillepied notes cryptically that "it sometimes pleases the hidden counsel of God that for certain mysterious reasons disembodied souls endure their purgatory, either among mountains or in waters, or in valleys, or in houses, and particularly are they attached to those spots where on earth they sinned and offended God." [47] Thus, perhaps, the Friar endures an "Earthly affliction." But whatever the truth of this, the *Umbra* seems certainly what Delrio preferred to call *anima separata* according to orthodox Christian doctrine.

Of its successor, the *Umbra Bussy,* in *The Revenge of Bussy D'Ambois* not so much can be said, for though it speaks well of Christianity and is surely Christian by time, it is not so by mission nor, apparently, by nature or by place—for all that Clermont devotes his brother's soul to heaven. Yet it is certainly not recognizable as pagan in the way that, for instance, the ghost of Asdrubal in Marston's *Sophonisba* is pagan.

4

The ghost of Asdrubal does not fit orthodox Christian doctrine, for it is by its own testimony a spirit wandering because "ungraved," hence rejected from Hades. It has, however, in the play the warrant of a classical milieu. Though the truth probably is that an Elizabethan audience made little account of historical discrepancies and could easily swallow anachronism, yet in plays such as *Sophonisba, The Iron Age, The Roman Actor, The Tragedy of Caesar's Revenge,* the ghosts fit well enough into the play-world time. But ghosts like that of Andrugio in Marston's *Antonio's Revenge* and that of Bussy in *The Revenge of Bussy* are not so simply suited to their play-world time. They retain too many marks of antiquity to seem from purgatory or heaven, yet show also too much stamp of Christianity to be classical wanderers and so acceptable as frank anachronisms. The question to be asked of them, then, is: what was the sixteenth century conception of that ghost which did not fit orthodox Catholic doctrine? Probably no very clear answer can be made, for appropriation of antique opinion by sixteenth century writers and their adjustment of it to Christianity was very various.

The general pagan doctrine which Le Loyer sketches from Trismegistos, Homer, Tertullian and other authors as widely divergent in aim, time and historicity, was, roughly, that the soul of the good man became after separation a free intellect or even a god, that of the evil man (*i.e.,* the man addicted to the vices of the body) a wanderer tormented with a perpetual unquiet search for its body to recover it.[48] Le Loyer further notices the opinions of the common people that "the souls of those dead before their due age become vagabonds until the time when their bodies would naturally have died," and that those who had suffered death through violence were daemons and bad ones.[49] All this Le Loyer and the rest of the orthodox stoutly reject; but the influence of the general doctrine upon Elizabethan tragedy has, of course, long been recognized.

Agrippa, who is not intent like Le Loyer to expose ancient error, quotes Ovid that a man is of four things, which at his death disperse to the states severally fitting them: the corruptible flesh, earth receives; the ghost (*Umbra*) hovers over the grave; the soul (*manes*) descends to Hades; the spirit (*spiritus*) rises to the stars.[50] Without specifically saying so Agrippa accepts this analysis and applies it to Christian doctrine. If the soul (substituting *anima* for Ovid's *manes*) has done well in its earthly life, it "rejoyceth together with the spirit" [51] and "passeth freely to the quires of Heroes," ascends in full possession of all its faculties into heaven to a perpetual felicity from which as if it were an immortal God it freely bestows gifts upon its inferiors. But if the soul has done ill:

> . . . the spirit judgeth it and leaves it to the pleasure of the divel, and the sad soul wanders about Hell without a spirit, like an image. . . . Wherefore then this soul being voyde of an intelligible essence, and being left to the power of a furious phantasy, is ever subjected by the torment of corporeall qualities, knowing that it is by the just judgment of God, for ever deprived of the divine vision (to which it was created) for its sins: the absence of which divine vision, as the Scripture testifies, is the ground of all evils, and the most grievous punishment of all which the Scripture calls the pouring down of the wrath of God. This image therefore of the soul (*Haec animae imago*) enters into the ghost (*umbra*) as an Aerial body which being covered doth sometimes advise friends, sometimes stir up enemies. . . .[52]

All this has a general sort of echo in both Marston's and Chapman's plays. In *Bussy* the shade of the Friar says when Bussy has died:

> Farewell, brave relics of a complete man;
> Look up and see thy spirit made a star,
> Join flames with Hercules. (V, iv, 147)

"Relics of a complete man" perhaps may be taken to signify the tripartite make-up of the personality which Agrippa cites from Ovid and which was Platonic in philosophic origin. If this be so, it may be perfectly consistent that Bussy's mighty spirit soared to the stars, to "the quires of Heroes," though in *The Revenge of Bussy* his soul (*anima*) rises "from the chaos of Eternal night" to animate his *umbra* and appear to men.[53]

In *The Revenge of Bussy* when a party of ghosts led by Bussy's have danced about the corpse of Montsurry, Clermont undertakes to explain the apparitions. He says:

> That spirits should rise in these times yet are fables;
> Though learned'st men hold that our sensive spirits
> A little time abide about the graves

Of their deceased bodies; and can take
In cold condensed air the same forms they had,
When they were shut up in this body's shade.
(V, v, 133) [54]

Whether Clermont intends to cite the belief of "learned'st men" in contradiction of his first assertion that rising of spirits is fabulous, or to offer it as an explanation of what seemed risen spirits, *i.e.*, ghosts, re-manifested souls of the dead, is not clear. Whatever he intended, the instant news that Guise and his brother, whose ghosts Clermont had taken for "true shadows" "Fore-running thus their bodies," are already dead seems finally to resolve Clermont's persistent doubt that spirits "rise in these times." At any rate, it may certainly be held that the *Umbra Bussy,* which directs the action of Montsurry's slaying so strongly and persuasively, is not a mere will-less shadow, the "sensive spirits" abiding about the grave, but, in Agrippa's words, "this image of the soul" come up as it says "from the chaos of Eternal night," and entered, though without its intellectual part, now in the stars, "into the *umbra* as an Aerial body, with which being covered [it] doth sometimes advise friends, sometimes stir up enemies."

As he prepares to slay himself, Clermont speaks again on the composition of man:

The garment or the cover of the mind,
The human soul is; of the soul, the spirit
The proper robe is; of the spirit, the blood;
And of the blood, the body is the shroud.
(V, v, 170)

Unquestionably, of the five terms here three are physical: "spirit," "blood," and "body." The "mind" evidently is the *mens* or *spiritus* of Agrippa, the portion that is blameless, and plunges back into the universal, whatever the conduct of the individual on earth. The "soul" in Clermont's usage is Agrippa's *anima,* and "Spirit" refers to the bodily liquors or vapors, the "sensive spirits" of Clermont's earlier speech, which sixteenth century physiology held to conduct the soul's powers into bodily action. As such it is equivalent to Agrippa's *umbra,* or "ghost," which Agrippa also calls the "sensitive or animal soul," the physical remnant that at death lingers will-less and without memory or power in itself, about the grave until dissolution overtakes it.[55]

It is true that Bussy at his death has seemed to speak of man as a dichotomy, "two sweet courtly friends compact," body and soul. Certainly the speeches of both Bussy and his brother are rather rhetoric than reliable commentaries on the metaphysics of their play-worlds, and the action gives little key. But it is sure, at least, that the ghost-figure *Umbra Bussy* is somehow strangely wrought of Christian and pagan ideas, related perhaps closely to what we find in Agrippa.

5

Far more Senecan, in its savagery and its vaunting, than Bussy's ghost is Andrugio's in *Antonio's Revenge.* With its Senecan manners, however, and its general Senecan place in the action are compounded the same nondescript kind of Christian characteristics that mark Bussy's ghost. Though its cry is the Senecan cry, *Vindicta,* it leaves behind it the odor of burning sulphur suggestive of hell or purgatory. The ghost rises first from a grave in "Saint Mark's Church"; but "the banks of rest" it says it is to touch may rather be Elysium than heaven. Certainly its final sentiment after the murder of its enemy is no Christian one:

> 'Tis done, and now my soul shall sleep in rest:
> Sons that revenge their father's blood are blest.
> (V, v, 115) [56]

The rest in which it is to sleep can hardly be heaven.

Antonio addresses his dead father as a spirit hovering in remote celestial regions:

> Thou royal spirit of Andrugio,
> Where'er thou hover'st, airy intellect,
> . . . .
> O, in what orb thy mighty spirit soars . . .
> (III, i, 17, 27)

But Andrugio himself professes to come but from the grave:

> Thy pangs of anguish rip my cerecloth up,
> And, lo, the ghost of old Andrugio
> Forsakes his coffin. Antonio, revenge!
> (III, i, 32)

This is, of course, another echo—though fainter than that in *Bussy*—of the doctrine Agrippa cites from the ancients. The "soul" of Andrugio that can "sleep in rest" only after the satisfaction of revenge is not the "airy intellect," but that lower soul hovering with the *umbra* near the coffin.

Obviously this is a surmise which, general as it is, is yet too particularized for the situation and the action it would explain. Yet obviously, too, both the situation and the action here are surely of the cast of Agrippa's hybridized doctrine, lack only a more thorough conception to become one with it.

IV

The central question of the dispute between Catholics and Protestants on ghosts was the place of ghosts in God's providence, and this not so much as to their nature—for both sides held that no return of souls could be conceived save as miracle, special act of God—but as to their reason. Protestants denied that there was any reason for souls of the dead to return; Catholics named many reasons, all of them valid within the scheme of Catholic theology and some not altogether without the pale of the reformed theology.[57]

The missions which Catholics ascribed to ghosts hinged, many of them, on the doctrines of purgatory and intercession. These no Protestant could admit, and they do not appear in English plays with ghosts. There are occasional allusions that seem to show ghosts purgatorial—the shades of the elder Hamlet and of the Friar in *Bussy* are examples—but no English play ghost ever comes to beg candles and prayers.[58] Not dramatic interest, dramatic convention, nor the religion of the land would have been served by such a motive in a play ghost.

The traditional motive of a play ghost was revenge, and revenge is certainly the motive most prominent in Elizabethan drama. Mr. Stoll notes five classes of Elizabethan play ghosts, according to "purpose." [59] The end, above all, for which they came, he says, was "to wreak revenge by appearing either to the victim or to the revenger." The other four purposes were "to protect some loved one," citing the Friar's *Umbra* in *Bussy;* "to prophesy," citing Asdrubal's ghost in *Sophonisba;* "to crave burial," citing the Ghost of the Lady in *The Second Maiden's Tragedy;* and finally, "simply in the capacity of an omen of death, to appear," citing Brachiano's ghost in *The White Devil.* Of these last four classes all save the first are reducible to the revenge class—not, certainly, to a heading of personal revenge, but to a heading of divine retribution. Asdrubal's prophecy is of disaster to the evil Syphax. The ghost of the Lady craves rescue for her body from one who sinfully abuses it; the central function of the ghost is not to achieve its body's reburial but to bring the downfall of the tyrant who has dared run "so fearfully in debt to black eternity." Brachiano's appearance announces death to one ripe for it and well worthy the torture of the portent.

Catholic pneumatology gives as the ultimate reason for ghosts the glory of God, which the apparitions serve, and allows under it two divisions: the mercy of God and the justice of God. The mercy of God permits souls of the dead to guide and warn their survivors, the justice of God strikes at sinners through ghosts.[60] Sixteenth century Catholicism emphasized the former reason almost to the extinction of the latter—partly because it was more generally consonant with Christianity and was a shift from the pagan emphasis, but partly, no doubt, because the ghost as a minister of wrath was difficult to distinguish from the demon, gave a handle to Protestant polemists. A consequence of this, perhaps, was Catholicism's abandonment of the tenet that souls could return from hell as well as from heaven and purgatory.[61] Catholic interest was pinned to the special matters of purgatory and intercession, and these did not hinge on the ghost as an instrument of punishment. As such an instrument the ghost receives but passing reference from Catholic writers who feel the need of pagan testimony to establish the general fact of return.

Pagan doctrine of ghosts had admitted in substance the two prime Catholic reasons, providential care for the good and punishment for the evil. Apuleius says that the souls of the worthy become *lemures* and assist their living progeny, souls of the evil become *larvae,* and terrorize offenders.[62] But paganism, of course, added a wealth of matter which Le Loyer and his fellows very properly reject as non-Christian. The identification of the dead with daemons, the cycle theory of the soul, the confirmation of necromancy, the tripartite make-up of the personality, the Hadean idea of the after-world—all these things were anathema to Catholic doctrine of ghosts, just as any conception of purgatory or mass-begging was foreign to pagan doctrine. Common to them, nevertheless, was the fundamental concept of the ghost as minister of divine reward or punishment.

In Elizabethan plays the emphasis, as has been said, is upon retribution as certainly the more dramatic of the two reasons for ghosts. This is in itself a pagan emphasis, and as it appears in the strictly Senecan dramas with prologue ghosts and in *Locrine*—equally Senecan so far as the essential nature, though not dramatic place, of its ghosts is concerned—it is without any tinge of Christian pneumatology. But with the development of the ghost-figure away from the Senecan in essential concept as well as in dramatic place, the point of view becomes Christian so that although the emphasis remains predominantly on the ghost as minister of justice, it is God's justice and no longer Rhadamanthus' that sends the soul back to earth. The harrying of sinners appears less vindictive and more inscrutable than in earlier plays.

There is a distinction to be made, of course, between the motive personal to the ghost, and the providential reason that permits the apparition and uses it. But the ghost as separated intellect was ordinarily conceived to possess an insight into the ways of providence, or at least a sense of the constraint of its providential function and a surety of its place. In the plays, at any rate, among the more active ghosts it is simply a question of whether the emphasis is Senecan, hence upon the ghost's personal animus, or shifts toward the Christian concept of the ghost as a relatively disinterested tool in God's hands. The revenge ghost shaped to Christian doctrine may be conceived almost as impersonal an instrument of providence as the idle phantasm rising out of a disturbed conscience; yet, like the demon, which though it serves God's wider plan in its every action, serves also its own will, the ghost was a vital agent capable of motive. But that its motive coincided with the will of heaven, Catholics thought sure of every soul which was saved, that is, came from purgatory or heaven.

2

It is probable that *Hamlet* has the only extensively active Elizabethan play ghost which, though conceived according to Catholic pneumatology, is artistically very effective as a supernatural figure. Mr. Whitmore says that the predominant reason for the introduction of the supernatural in tragedy is the desire to inspire terror;[63] this Chapman's ghosts, busy and loquacious, and Tourneur's, mild and restraining, can do in no great measure. Perhaps the vicious Andrugio with his crude Roman terrors of blood and pain is more effective, though he do no more than repel and frighten. But no rounded conception of Andrugio's ghost is possible, for it depends from pagan pneumatology very much at second hand, via Seneca. What effectiveness it has does not come truly from its nature as a ghost. The ghost of Montferrers, on the other hand, is soundly backed by Catholic pneumatology; if it fails of the effectiveness of the *Hamlet* ghost it is not for being less authentically grounded. Chapman's ghosts, almost as rhetorical as their vehicles, are less consistently authentic than Tourneur's and Shakespeare's; but this is not because of the classical conceptions that tinge them, for those conceptions are not strained through Seneca, but come into the pneumatological rationale as validly as the Christian tenets with which they mingle.

The ghost of Montferrers in *The Atheist's Tragedy* has been remarked as the last enfeebled heir of the Senecan tradition of revenge ghost. Its dramatic forebear is unquestionably the ghost in Kyd's *Hamlet*,[64] and enfeebled it may be by comparison of its sentiments with what we may suppose his to have been. But its sentiments fit its role, and its role is pneumatologically justified. How they consort with the dramatic is another question, and a question to be put about the whole play, not merely of the ghost.

Montferrers' is a revenge ghost in that it is the soul of a murdered man returned to the world to figure in the further courses and eventual downfall of the murderer. It is not a revenge ghost in any act of personal retaliation, nor even as a conveyor of the wrath of God. In other words, as a revenge ghost it is refined almost past recognition.

The role of the Montferrers ghost is to assert the glory of God against the challenge of D'Amville's atheism and Snuffe's Puritanical hypocrisy. To play this role the ghost had the warrant of all pneumatology, which held apparition of spirits to be one of the most positive reproofs which the phenomenal world afforded to materialists and kindred doubters of immortality.[65] Of course its very presence might be construed as a reproof, also, to Protestantism; but the uncertainty of whether the phantasm represents a returned soul or its good angel softens that thrust.

The ghost's role is fundamentally identical with Charlemont's. It is the supernatural, as his is the earthly, testimony to the benefits of faith and the goodness of God. As has been mentioned, it is virtually one with him, may be taken, perhaps, as merely the promptings of his virtuous nature, the grace of God working in a chosen servant to thwart by a spiritual bar D'Amville's Machiavellianism. It is better, no doubt, within the Elizabethan scheme of the play, to take the phantasm as substantive than as idle; but its role is the same either way, and is a positive and definitive role, though supplementary to Charlemont's larger one. Even if the phantasm is idle, it is a thing distinct enough from Charlemont's own natural powers almost to be in itself *dramatis persona.*

It has been noted by others that the conflict in *The Atheist's Tragedy* has a general resemblance to that in *Faustus.* In both plays an infatuation of personal power leads the protagonist to misread the nature of things and wilfully affront God past forgiveness. In each the tragic conflict is between the forces of salvation and damnation for the soul of the protagonist. It is needless to point out that in *Faustus* the conflict is developed, in *The Atheist's Tragedy* merely postulated. The struggle for D'Amville's soul takes the form of a parade of his evil deeds and a counter-parade of the godliness that rebukes them. The emphasis is less on the fight within D'Amville than on the justification of religion against atheism, so that the conflict assumes a wider stage than D'Amville's soul without truly enlarging the scale of the action. It becomes general between religion and misbelief, is hardly less impersonal than the conflict in a morality play.

In this dramatically malformed contest, the place of the ghost is that of Faustus' good angel if it should be attached to the Old Man instead of to the protagonist. The ghost is, indeed, the antagonist of D'Amville in that it stands with Charlemont for faith against apostasy, but not as Mephistophilis is the antagonist of Faustus, fighting for his soul, nor certainly as Andrugio's ghost was the foe of the murderer, Piero, bearing wrath to his body. To the protagonist, D'Amville, the ghost of Montferrers bears neither God's wrath nor his mercy, nor yet any personal wrath. It is merely the witness of the religious truths which D'Amville contemns, is God's mercy to D'Amville's enemy, Charlemont.

3

Less passive, and closer in function to Senecan progenitors is the ghost of Bussy. Its mission is to convey to offenders eternal justice. It acts with a dignity and detachment proper to that mission, is, nevertheless, the soul of a man engaged in the revenge of its body's murder.

The ghost delivers at its first appearance a long speech on retribution, which, it says, inevitably overtakes every evil doer as certainly as the world "Stands by proportion." This in itself, leaving aside consideration of religion's inducement to mended ways, should suffice to make mankind good. As for its own mission:

> Up from the chaos of eternal night
> (To which the whole digestion of the world
> Is now returning) once more I ascend,
> And bide the cold damp of this piercing air,
> To urge the justice whose almighty word
> Measures the bloody acts of impious men
> With equal penance, who in th' act itself
> Includes th' infliction, which like chained shot
> Batter together still. . . . (V, i, 1)

It is of such divine justice administered by ghosts that Agrippa writes:

> For when the soul is separated from the body, the perturbations of the memory and sense remain. The Platonists say, that the souls, especially of them that are slain, stir up enemies, mans indignation not so much doing of it, as the divine Nemesis and Demon foreseeing, and permitting of it. So the spirit of Naboth (as the masters interpret it) because in the end of its life it went forth with a desire of revenge, was made to execute revenge, the spirit of a lye, and went forth, God permitting it, a lying spirit in the mouth of all the prophets. . . .[66]

This easy mingling of Platonism with scripture, and the relegation of revenge to a general nemesis operating through a vital instrument whose function is fore-ordained in the constitution of things, is in the very manner of Chapman's whole play and is a sufficient commentary, perhaps, upon the function of the ghost of Bussy. The function, like the ghost itself, is conceivable in Christian terms, but has undeniably that tang of paganism which Renaissance taste so relished.

A ghost in the conception of which paganism and Christianity are somewhat more puzzlingly mingled is that of the Lady in *The Second Maiden's Tragedy*. The concern of the Lady's soul over the fate of her body and the ghost's repeated reference to the body as "me" has a pagan taint, though her burial was in a cathedral.[67] The ghost proclaims: "My rest is lost." Reburial, the implication is, may restore its rest. Agrippa says that the early church called for burial in sanctified ground because the dust demon, Zazel, plagued the bodies and, presumably, the souls of those dead that were not especially fortified against him.[68] But the play has no hint of such a doctrine, nor indeed surely of any doctrine. Mr. Whitmore remarks that it would be interesting to know how the ghost is conceived,[69] and it would indeed be so; but pneumatology, though it could offer possibilities, finds nothing in the play to substantiate them. This is the only play ghost in which the motive of the ghost seems at a tangent to its providential function. Its function is unquestionably to bring about the downfall of the tyrant, and so far it serves that general nemesis of which Agrippa speaks; but the concern manifest in its words is for its disturbed rest.

Aside from the ghost of Montferrers, that of the Friar in *Bussy D'Ambois* is almost the only one in Elizabethan drama that notably seems to convey God's mercy rather than His wrath. Bussy says: "And now his restless spirit would forewarn me," and Tamyra: "O father, have my dumb woes wak'd your death?" But the ghost's assigned errand does not extend so far as the balking of justice to the sinful Bussy. His assassination is carried out, and it is only for the Friar to urge Christian reconciliation of slain with slayer, and husband with wife.

The only other reason for which ghosts appeared was one not admitted by the church: necromancy. The sole prominent instance of true necromancy in Elizabethan drama is in Greene's *Alphonsus of Arragon,*[70] a play too heterogeneous in its background to yield to any consistent rationale of its pneumatology.[71] Over the sleeping Amurack, the Great Turk, a sorceress, Medea, does "ceremonies belonging to conjuring," and she fetches the ghost of Calchas, "in a white surplice and a Cardinal's myter." Their colloquy seems to indicate the phantom indeed representative of the risen soul of the Greek seer, not of an impersonating devil. But the play is too uncertain in its general scheme for it to matter whether Greene intended *bona fide* necromancy or not. There is none of the care for consistency that in *Faustus* makes it clear that the "shades" of Alexander and his paramour are but phantasms managed by demons.

Bibliography

This bibliography is confined to titles cited in text or notes. For further bibliography in pneumatology see J. G. T. Grasse, *Bibliotheca magica et pneumatica,* Scribner and Armstrong's *Bibliotheca Diabolica,* Robert Yve-Plessis, *Essai d'une bibliographie de la sorcellerie,* and the *Short Title Catalogue* compiled by Harry Price for the National Laboratory of Psychical Research.

Primary Sources

Agrippa, Henry Cornelius von Nettesheim, *De incertitudine et vanitate scientiarum et artium,* Cologne, 1583.

—— *Of the Vanity and Uncertainty of Artes and Sciences.* Englished by Ia.San.gent., London, 1575.

—— *The Vanity of Arts and Sciences,* London, 1684.

—— *De occulta philosophia libri III,* Paris, 1567.

—— *Three Books of Occult Philosophy . . .* translated out of the Latin into the English Tongue by J. F. [riske], London, 1651.

Apuleius, *The Works* (*The Golden Ass, The God of Socrates, The Defense or Discourse on Magic, The Florida*), trans. in the Bohn Libraries, London, 1900.

—— *The Golden Asse,* translated out of Latin by William Adlington, London, 1566.

Aquinas, St. Thomas, *Summa Theologica,* trans. by the Fathers of the English Dominican Province, London, 1921.

Arbatel of Magick: or the Spiritual Wisdom of the Ancients . . . trans. by Robert Turner, London, 1655.

Augustine, S., *The City of God,* trans. by Marcus Dodd, Edinburgh, 1872.

Bacon, Francis, *The Advancement of Learning,* ed. by Joseph Devy, London, 1904.

Binsfield, Peter, *Tractat von bekantnuss der zauberer und hexen . . .* trans. by Heinrich Bock, Treves, 1590.

Bodin, Jean, *La Demonomanie des Sorciers,* Paris, 1598.

—— *Refutation des opinions de Iean Wier,* Paris, 1598.

Boguet, Henri, *An Examen of Witches* (*Discours des Sorciers,* Lyons, 1590) trans. by A. E. Ashwin, ed. by Rev. Montague Summers, London, 1929.

Bullinger, Heinrich, *The Decades,* trans. by H. I., ed. for the Parker Society by Rev. Thomas Harding, Cambridge, 1849.

Burton, Robert, *Anatomy of Melancholy,* ed. by Rev. A. R. Shilleto for Bohn's Libraries, London, 1912.

Calvin, John, *Institutes of the Christian Religion,* trans. by Henry Beveridge, Edinburgh, 1845.

—— *A Harmony upon the Three Evangelists,* trans. by E. P., London, 1584.

Cardan, Girolamo, *The Book of My Life* (*De vita propria liber*), trans. by Jean Stoner, New York, 1930.

Charles, R. H., Editor, *Apocrypha and Pseudepigraphia of the Old Testament,* Oxford, 1913.

Charron, Pierre, *Of Wisdome Three Books* (*De la sagesse,* 1601), trans. by Samson Lennard, London, c. 1612.

Cotta, John, *Infallible True and Assured Witch: or, The Second Edition of the Tryall of Witchcraft . . .* London, 1624.

D'Anania, Giovanni Lorenzo, *De natura daemonum,* Venice, 1589.

Daneau, Lambert, *A Dialogue of Witches* (*Les Sorcières*), anonymously trans., London, 1575.

Deacon, John and Walker, John, *A Dialogicall Discourse of Spirits and Devils,* London, 1601.

—— *A Summary Answere to all the Material Points in any of Master Darel his Books,* London, 1601.

Dee, John, *The Private Diary of Dr. John Dee, and the Catalogue of his Library of Manuscripts,* ed. by James Orchard Halliwell, London, 1842.

—— *A True and Faithful Relation of what Passed between Dr. John Dee . . . and Some Spirits,* London, 1659.

Delrio, Martin, *Disquisitionum magicarum libri sex,* Lyons, 1608.

—— *Controverses et recherches magiques,* Paris, 1611.

Erastus, Thomas, *Deux dialogues . . . touchant le pouvoir des sorcières,* appended to Johann Wier's *Illusions et impostures des diables,* Paris, 1579.

Examination and Confession of Certain Witches at Chensforde in the Countie of Essex, . . . 1566, as reprinted by H. Beigel for the Philobiblion Society, London, 1864–65.

Fairfax, Edward, *Daemonologia: a Discourse of Witchcraft as it was*

Acted in the Family of Mr. Edward Fairfax of Ferystone . . . 1621; ed. by W. Grainge, London, 1882.

The Famous Historie of Fryar Bacon . . . with the Lives and Deaths of the two Coniurers Bungye and Vandermast . . . London, n.d., as reprinted in *Miscellanea antiqua anglicana,* 1816, vol. I, pt. 7.

Faustus: *The Historie of the Damnable Life and Deserued Death of Doctor Iohn Faustus,* trans. by P. F., London, 1592, as reprinted by P. M. Palmer and R. P. More in *The Sources of the Faust Tradition,* New York, 1936.

The Second Report of Faustus, 1594, ed. by William Rose, London, 1926.

Historia von D. Johan Fausten . . . gedruckt zu Frankfurt am Mann durch Johann Spies, 1587, as reprinted for the Deutsche Bibliothek, ed. by Dr. Alfred Sternbeck.

Fludd, Robert, *Utriusque Cosmi Maioris scilicet et Minoris Metaphysica, Physica atque Technica Historia,* Oppenhemii, 1617–18.

Gifford, George, *A Dialogue Concerning Witches and Witchcraft,* London, 1593 (Shakespeare Association Facsimile I, with an introduction by Beatrice White, Oxford, 1931.)

Goulart, Simon, *Admirable and Memorable Histories Containing the Wonders of our Time . . . out of French into English by Ed. Grimestone . . .* London, 1607.

Guazzo, Francesco Maria, *Compendium Maleficarum,* 1608, as trans. by A. E. Ashwin and ed. by Rev. Montague Summers, London, 1929.

Hermes Trismegistos, *Hermetica,* ed. and trans. by Walter Scot, Oxford, 1924.

Hooker, Richard, *Of the Laws of Ecclesiastical Polity,* in *The Works,* with an account of his life and death by Isaac Walton, arranged by the Rev. John Keble, New York, 1890.

Iamblichus, *Mysteries of the Egyptians, Chaldeans, and Assyrians,* trans. by Thomas Taylor, London, 1885.

—— *Liber de mysteriis Aegyptiorum,* trans. by Marsilio Ficino, Aldine ed., 1516.

James I, *Demonologie,* 1597, as reprinted for Bodley Head Quartos, ed. by G. B. Harrison, London, 1924.

The Key of Solomon (*Clavicula Salomonis*) trans. and ed. by S. MacGregor Mathers, London, 1909.

Lancre, Pierre de, *Tableau de l'inconstance des mauvais anges et demons,* Paris, 1612.

Lavater, Lewes, *Of Ghosts and Spirits Walking by Nyght,* trans. from the Latin by R. H., London, 1572. (Shakespeare Association reprint, ed. by J. D. Wilson and May Yardley, Oxford, 1929.)

Le Loyer, Pierre, *Discours, et histoires des spectres, visions et appari-*

tions des esprit, anges, demons, et ames, se monstrans visible aux hommes . . . Paris, 1605.

—— *A Treatise of Specters or Strange Sights, Visions, and Apparitions Appearing sensibly unto men . . . Newly done out of French into English,* London, 1605.

Menghi, F. Hieronymi, *Flagellum daemonum, Fustis daemonum.* Printed together with other works in *Thesaurus exorcismorum atque conjurationum terrbilium* . . . Cologne, 1608.

Michaelis, Sebastien, *The Admirable History of the Possession and Conversion of a Penitent Woman, Seduced by a Magician that made her to become a witch* . . . translated into English by W. B., London, 1613. Volume II, *A Discourse of Spirits.*

Naudé, Gabriel, *Apologie pour les grandes hommes soupconnez de magie,* Paris, 1625.

—— *The History of Magic by way of Apology for all the Wise Men Who Have Unjustly been Reputed Magicians* . . . Englished by J. Davies, London, 1657.

Paracelsus, *The Hermetic and Alchemical Works of Aureolus Philippus Theophrastus Bombast,* trans. and ed. by A. E. Waite, London, 1894.

—— *Philosophy to the Athenians,* trans. by H. Pinnell, being tracts II, III, and IV of *Philosophy Reformed and Improved in Four Profound Tractates,* London, 1657.

Pereira, Bento, *De Magia, de observatione somniorum et de divinatione astrologica libri tres. Adversus Fallaces, et superstitiosas artes.* Cologne, 1612.

Perkins, William, *A Discourse of the Damned Art of Witchcraft,* in volume III of the *Works,* Cambridge, 1609.

—— *The Order of the Causes of Salvation and Damnation,* in volume I of the *Works,* Cambridge, 1609.

Peucer, Kaspar, *Les devins, ou commentaire des principales sortes de divinations . . . Nouuellement tourné en Francais par S.G.S.* [Simon Goulart, Senlisien], 1584.

Plotinus, *Complete Works,* trans. by K. S. Guthrie, London, 1918.

Pictorius, George, *A Discourse on the Nature of Spirits,* trans. from the Latin by Robert Turner, London, 1655.

—— *Einleitung in die Lehre von den sublunarischen Daemonen,* trans. from the Latin in volume XIV of *Geheime Wissenschaften: Eine Sammlung seltener alterer und neuerer Schriften über Alchemie, Magie, etc.* . . . Berlin, 1922.

Plutarch, *On the Daimon of Socrates,* in *Plutarch's Morals,* trans. from the Greek by several hands, corrected and revised by William Goodwin, Boston, 1870, volume II, p. 378 ff.

Primaudaye, Peter de la, *The French Academie fully Discoursed and Finished in foure Bookes* . . . London, 1618.

Proclus Diadochus, The Fragments that Remain of the Lost Writings of, trans. from the Greek by Thomas Taylor, London, 1825.

—— *Life, Hymns, and Works,* trans. from the Greek by K. S. Guthrie.

—— *Six Books on the Theology of Plato,* trans. from the Greek by Thomas Taylor, London, 1816.

Pseudo-Abano, Peter of, *Heptameron or Magical Elements,* trans. from the Latin by Robert Turner, London, 1655.

—— *Heptameron,* appended to *De occulta philosophia* of Agrippa, Paris, 1567.

Pseudo-Agrippa, Henry Cornelius von Nettesheim, *The Fourth Book of Occult Philosophy or Magical Ceremonies,* trans. by Robert Turner, London, 1655.

—— *Liber quartus de occulta philosophia, seu de ceremoniis magicis,* appended to the first three books, Paris, 1567.

Remy, Nicholas, *Daemonlatreiae libri tres,* 1595, trans. by A. E. Ashwin and ed. by Rev. Montague Summers, London, 1930.

Scot, Reginald, *The Discoverie of Witchcraft,* 1584, as reprinted under the editorship of Brinsley Nicholson, London, 1886.

—— *A Discourse of Devils and Spirits,* appended to the Nicholson edition of the *Discoverie.*

Sprenger, Jacob, and Institor, Henry, *Malleus Maleficarum,* 1487, trans. by A. E. Ashwin and ed. by Rev. Montague Summers, London, 1928.

Taillepied, Noel, *A Treatise of Spirits* (*Psichologie ou traité de l'apparition des esprit, 1588*), trans. by Rev. Montague Summers, London.

Vair, Leonard, *Trois livres des charmes, sorcelage, ou enchantmens* . . . Paris, 1583.

Wier, Johann, *De Praestigiis Daemonum, et incantationibus ac ueneficiis libri sex* . . . Basle, 1568.

—— *De Lamiis Liber* . . . Basle, 1577.

—— *Pseudomonarchia Daemonum,* p. 649 ff. in *Opera Omnia,* Amsterdam, 1660.

——*Histoires, disputes et discours des illusions et impostures des diables, des magiciens infames, sorcières et empoisonneurs* . . . Paris, 1579.

Wonderful Discoverie of the Witchcrafts of Margaret and Philip Flower . . . London, 1619, as reprinted in *A Collection of Rare and Curious Tracts Relating to Witchcraft,* London, 1838.

Secondary Sources

Alexander, Archibald, *Theories of the Will in the History of Philosophy,* New York, 1898.

Alexander, William M., *Demonic Possession in the New Testament,* Edinburgh, 1902.

Ankenbrand, Karl, *Die Figur des Geistes im Drama die Englishchen Renaissance,* Leipzig, 1906.

Burr, George, "The Literature of Witchcraft," *American Historical Association Papers,* IV, iii, p. 235.

Campbell, Lily Bess, *Shakespeare's Tragic Heroes: Slaves of Passion,* Cambridge, 1930.

—— "Theories of Revenge in Elizabethan England," *Mod. Phil.* XXVIII, 1930–31, p. 281.

Catholic Encyclopedia, ed. Michael Maher and Joseph Boland, New York, 1912.

Cauzons, Thomas de, *La magie et la sorcellerie en France,* Paris, 1910.

Conger, G. P., *Theories of Macrocosms and Microcosms in the History of Philosophy,* New York, 1922.

Craig, Hardin, *The Enchanted Glass,* Oxford, 1936.

Curry, W. C., *Shakespeare's Philosophical Patterns,* Baton Rouge, 1937.

Douglas, A. H., *The Philosophy of Pomponazzi,* Cambridge, 1910.

Ewen, C. L'Estrange, *Witchcraft and Demonianism: a Concise Account Derived from Sworn Depositions and Confessions Obtained in the Courts of England and Wales,* London, 1933.

—— *Witch Hunting and Witch Trials. The Indictments for Witchcraft from the Records of 1373 Assizes held for the Home Circuit A.D. 1559–1736,* New York, 1929.

Frazer, Sir James George, *The Golden Bough: The Magic Art,* New York, 1935.

Friedel, Egon, *A Cultural History of the Modern Age,* trans. from the German by Charles Francis Atkinson, New York, 1930.

Frost, Thomas, *The Lives of the Conjurors,* London, 1876.

Gaster, Moses, "The Sword of Moses," in volume I of *Studies and Texts in Folklore and Magic,* London, 1925–28.

Gayley, Charles Mills, "Critical Essay on Robert Greene," in *Representative English Comedies,* ed. by Charles Mills Gayley, New York, 1912.

Ginsburg, Christian, *The Kabbalah,* London, 1925.

Glover, T. R., *The Conflict of Religions in the Early Roman Empire,* London, 1919.

Graf, Arturo, *The Story of the Devil,* trans. by E. N. Stone, New York, 1931.

Grant, Enid, "Webster and Lavater," *Lond. Times Lit. Supp.*, April 11, 1936.

Gregg, W. W., "Hamlet's Hallucination," *Mod. Lang. Rev.*, Oct., 1917.

Green, Joseph C., *The Medieval Morality of Wisdom Who is Christ*, Nashville, 1937.

Hartman, Franz, *The Life of Philippus Theophrastus Bombast of Hohenheim, known by the name of Paracelsus, and the Substance of his Teachings* . . . London, 1887.

Hastings (James), *Encyclopedia of Religion and Ethics*, Edinburgh, 1908.

Hatch, Edwin, *The Influence of Greek Ideas and Usage upon the Christian Church*, London, 1888.

Herford, Charles H., *Studies in the Literary Relations of England and Germany in the Sixteenth Century*, Cambridge, 1886.

Herrington, H. W., "Witchcraft in the Elizabethan Drama," *Journal of American Folklore*, XXXII, 1919.

Inge, William Ralph, *The Philosophy of Plotinus*, London, 1929.

Kittredge, G. L., *Witchcraft in Old and New England*, Cambridge, 1928.

Lea, Henry Charles, *Materials Toward a History of Witchcraft*, arranged and ed. by Arthur C. Howland, with an introduction by G. L. Burr, Philadelphia, 1939.

Lecky, W. E. H., *History of the Rise and Influence of Rationalism in Europe*, New York, 1870.

Logeman, Henry, *Faustus Notes: A Supplement to the Commentaries on Marlowe's Tragical History of Dr. Faustus*, Gand, 1898.

Mannhart, W., *Zauberglaube und Geheimwissen im Spiegel der Jahrhunderte*, Leipzig, 1897.

McDougal, William, *Body and Mind; A History and a Defense of Animism*, London, 1923.

Mathiessen, F. O., "Toward our Understanding of Elizabethan Drama," *Southern Review*, IV, 1938, p. 398.

Moore, Clifford H., *Pagan Ideas of Immortality during the Early Roman Empire*, Cambridge, 1918.

—— *Ancient Beliefs in the Immortality of the Soul*, New York, 1931.

Morley, Henry, *The Life of Cornelius Agrippa*, London, 1856.

Murray, Margaret A., *The Witch Cult in Western Europe*, Oxford, 1921.

Oesterreich, T. K., *Possession, Demoniacal and Other*, New York, 1930.

Olliver, C. W., *An Analysis of Magic and Witchcraft*, London, 1928.

Palmer, P. M., and More, R. P., *The Sources of the Faust Tradition*, New York, 1936.

Potter, R. R., "Some Aspects of the Supernatural in English Comedy from the Origins to 1642," *University of North Carolina Record,* 1934–35.

Pratt, Sister Antoinette Marie, *The Attitude of the Catholic Church toward Witchcraft and the Allied Practices of Sorcery and Magic,* Washington, 1913.

Rudwin, Maximilian, *The Devil in Legend and Literature,* London, 1931.

Scheible, Johann (ed.), *Das Kloster, weltlich und geistlich; meist aus der altern deutschen volkswunder-, curiositaten-, und vorzugsweise komischen Literatur,* Stuttgart, 1845–49.

Schelling, F. E., *Shakespeare and Demi-Science,* Philadelphia, 1927.

Sheldon, Henry, *The History of Christian Doctrine,* New York, 1886.

Sinnett, A. P., *Esoteric Buddhism,* Boston and New York, 1884.

Smith, Winifred, "Anti-Catholic Propaganda in Elizabethan England," *Mod. Phil.,* 1930.

Spalding, T. A., *Elizabethan Demonology,* London, 1880.

Steiner, Rudolph, *The Mystics of the Renaissance,* London, 1911.

Stoll, Elmer Edgar, *John Webster: the Periods of his Work as Determined by the Drama of his Day,* Boston, 1905.

—— "The Objectivity of the Ghosts in Shakespeare," *PMLA,* XXII, 1907.

Summers, Montague, *The Geography of Witchcraft,* New York, 1927.

—— *A History of Witchcraft and Demonology,* London, 1926.

Svoboda, K., *La Demonologie de Michel Psellos,* Brno, 1927.

Symonds, John Addington, *Shakespeare's Predecessors in the English Drama,* London, 1924.

Taylor, A. E., "Marlowe's Dr. Faustus," *London Times Literary Supplement,* Dec. 6, 1917.

Taylor, H. O., *The Medieval Mind,* 2 vols., London, 1930.

—— *Thought and Expression in the Sixteenth Century,* 2 vols., New York, 1930.

Thorndike, Lynn, *The History of Magic and Experimental Science,* 2 vols., New York, 1929.

Waite, A. E., *The Book of Black Magic and of Pacts Including the Rites and Mysteries of Goetic Theurgy, Sorcery, and Infernal Necromancy,* London, 1889.

—— *The Doctrine and Literature of the Kabalah,* London, 1902.

Ward, Sir A. W., *A History of English Dramatic Literature, to the Death of Queen Anne,* 3 vols., London, 1899.

—— *Old English Drama,* (edition of *Faustus* and *Friar Bacon and Friar Bungay* with introduction and notes), Oxford, 1901.

Whitmore, Charles Edward, *The Supernatural in Tragedy,* Cambridge, 1915.

Whittaker, Thomas, *The Neo-Platonists: a Study in the History of Platonism,* Cambridge, 1901.

Wilson, J. Dover, *What Happens in Hamlet,* Cambridge, 1935.

Withington, E. T., "John Wier and the Witch Mania," in volume I of *Studies in the History and Methods of Science,* ed. by C. J. Singer, Oxford, 1917–21.

Zeller, E., *The Stoics, Epicureans, and Sceptics,* trans. by O. J. Reichel, London, 1892.

Zender, Rudolph, *Die Magie im Englischen Drama des Elizabethanischen Zeitalters . . .* Halle, 1907.

Zilboorg, Gregory, *The Medical Man and the Witch during the Renaissance,* Baltimore, 1935.

Dramatic Texts

Barnes, Barnabe, *The Devil's Charter,* ed. from the quarto of 1607 by R. B. McKerrow for W. Bang's *Materialen zur Kunde des älteren Englischen Dramas,* London, 1904.

Caesar: *The Tragedy of Caesar's Revenge* (Anonymous), Malone Society Reprints, 1911, prepared by F. S. Boas.

Chapman, George, The Plays and Poems of . . . : The Tragedies, ed. by Thomas Marc Parrott, London, 1910. *Bussy D'Ambois, The Revenge of Bussy D'Ambois, The Tragedy of Caesar and Pompey.*

—— *Bussy D'Ambois and the Revenge of Bussy,* ed. by F. S. Boas, London, 1905.

—— (attributed) *The Second Maiden's Tragedy,* Hazlitt's Dodsley, volume V.

Dekker, Thomas, The Dramatic Works of, 4 vols. (Pearson Reprints), London, 1873. *If this be not a good play, the Diuel is in it,* volume III.

—— *The Witch of Edmonton,* in the Mermaid Series, ed. by Ernest Rhys, London, 1874.

Greene, Robert, The Plays and Poems of, ed. by J. Churton Collins, 2 vols., Oxford, 1905. *Friar Bacon and Friar Bungay, James IV, Alphonsus of Arragon, Orlando Furioso.*

—— *The Honourable History of Friar Bacon and Friar Bungay,* ed. by Sir Adolphus William Ward, Oxford, 1901.

—— *The Honourable History of Friar Bacon and Friar Bungay,* prepared for reading by G. B. Harrison, London, 1928.

Haughton, William, *Grim, the Collier of Croydon or The Devil and his Dame,* volume VIII of Hazlitt's Dodsley, London, 1874.

Heywood, Thomas, The Dramatic Works of, 6 vols., (Pearson Reprints), London, 1874. *The Late Lancashire Witches* in volume IV. *The Iron Age* in volume III.

—— *The Wise Woman of Hogsden,* in the Mermaid Series, ed. by A. W. Verity, London, 1888.

Hughes, Thomas, *The Misfortunes of Arthur,* vol. IV of Hazlitt's Dodsley, London, 1874.

Jonson, Ben, ed. by C. H. Herford and Percy Simpson, 6 vols., Oxford, 1925. *The Alchemist* and *Catiline* in volume V, and *The Devil is an Ass* in volume VI.

—— *Works,* ed. by William Gifford, revised by P. Cunningham, 9 vols., London, 1875. *The Sad Shepherd* in volume VI; the *Masque of Queens* in volume VII.

Kyd, Thomas, *The Spanish Tragedy,* in the *Works,* ed. by F. S. Boas, Oxford, 1901.

Marlowe, Christopher, *The Tragical History of Dr. Faustus,* ed. by F. S. Boas, London, 1932.

—— *The Tragical History of Dr. Faustus,* ed. by Sir Adolphus William Ward, Oxford, 1901.

Marston, John, Works, ed. by A. H. Bullen, 3 vols., London, 1887. *The Second Part of Antonio and Mellida,* in volume I; *Sophonisba,* in volume II.

Massinger, Phillip, *The Roman Actor, The Virgin Martyr, The Unnatural Combat,* in the Mermaid Series, ed. by A. Symonds, 2 vols., London, 1887–89.

Merry Devil of Edmonton, The, in *The Shakespeare Apocrypha,* ed. by C. F. Tucker Brooke, Oxford, 1908.

Middleton, Thomas, Works, ed. by A. H. Bullen, 8 vols., London, 1885. *The Witch,* in volume 5; *The Changeling,* in volume 6.

Munday, Anthony, *John a Kent and John a Cumber,* Malone Society Reprint, 1923, prepared by Muriel St. Clare Byrne.

Peele, Robert, *The Old Wives Tale,* in *The English Drama, an Anthology, 900–1642,* ed. by Edd Winfield Parks and Richmond Croom Beatty, New York, 1935.

—— *The Battle of Alcazar,* Malone Society Reprint, 1907, prepared for the press by W. W. Gregg.

—— (attributed) *Locrine,* in *The Shakespeare Apocrypha,* ed. by C. F. Tucker Brooke, Oxford, 1908.

Rowley, William, *The Birth of Merlin,* in *The Shakespeare Apocrypha,* ed. by C. F. Tucker Brooke, Oxford, 1908.

Tourneur, Cyril, The Plays and Poems of, ed. by John Churton Collins, 2 vols., London, 1878. *The Atheist's Tragedy,* in volume I.

Webster, John, The Complete Works of, ed. by F. S. Lucas, 4 vols., London, 1927. *The White Devil,* in volume I; *The Duchess of Malfi,* in volume II.

Notes

Notes on Chapter I

[1] *Religio Medici,* Sect. xxx. My information on witch indictments in Essex in 1607 comes from the tables in *Witch Hunting and Witch Trials,* by C. L'Estrange Ewen, New York, 1929. Ben Jonson's magical manuscript was the famous *Liber Sacratus,* or *Sworn Book of Honorius.* My authority that Jonson once owned a manuscript of it is Professor Lynn Thorndike's *History of Magic and Experimental Science* II, 284. The work annotated by Bacon is the *De Lamiis* of Johannes Wier, Basle, 1577. The marked copy is in the Folger Library in Washington.

[2] Thus Edward Fairfax, translator of *Jerusalem Delivered,* published in 1621 *Daemonologia: a Discourse of Witchcraft as it was acted in the Family of Mr. Edward Fairfax. . . .* Yet more convincing are the facts that both Burton and Bacon, neither a daemonologist by inclination, find daemonology too important in the learning of their time to be overlooked in their great works. See "A Digression of Spirits" in part I of *Anatomy of Melancholy,* and *The Advancement of Learning,* III, ii.

[3] I use the words *animistic* and *animism* always in their broader sense. *Hastings' Encyclopedia of Religion and Ethics* says of animism: "From the point of view of the history of religions, the term is taken in a wider sense, to denote the belief in the existence of spiritual beings, some attached to bodies of which they constitute the real personality (souls), others without necessary connection with a determinate body (spirits)." I do not, of course, intend ever to refer to the animism of which Professor Tylor wrote, which Mr. McDougal preferred to designate *primitive animism.* See William McDougal, *Body and Mind; a History and a Defense of Animism,* London, 1923.

[4] I use the spelling *daemon* to indicate these non-human spirits without bias as to their moral condition, whether blessed or damned or, indeed, within the Christian scheme at all. By *demon* I shall mean the devil of Christianity. N.E.D. gives *daemon* as Latin, *demon* as Medieval Latin. This suits very well with my usage.

[5] The temporary sensible bodies representing daemons and ghosts were not regarded as "vitalized" in the manner that an organic body is vitalized by its soul. See *post,* p. 27.

John Cotta, an English writer of the early seventeenth century on witchcraft, has a passage illustrative of the division of the world into spirit and body. He says (*The Infallible True and Assured Witch,* London, 1624, iv, 23): "All created substances indowed with powers and vertue from God their Creator, are either bodily or corporall substances, or spirituall, or mixt and betweene both.

"Bodily and corporal . . . are the heavens, the celestial bodies of the Starres, of the Sunne, of the Moone; the bodies of the elements, and all elementarie substances from them derived and composed.

"Spirituall substances are either Angels, or Diuels, or souls of men after death, separated from their bodies.

"Mixed substances, partly spiritual, partly bodily, are mankinde compounded of a naturall body and understanding."

[6] For many writers of the time witchcraft and any other spirit magic were virtually synonomous. The Jesuit, Martin Delrio, for instance, classifies the kinds of magic as Natural, Artificial, and Demoniacal (Diabolical) to correspond to the classes which the occultist, Cornelius Agrippa, calls Natural, Mathematical, and Ceremonial. See Delrio's *Disquisitionum Magicarum,* Lyons, 1608, Bk. I, ch. ii, p. 2. For enlightening definitions and distinctions (by which, however, not all authorities by any means abide, and which I make no attempt to follow consistently) see C. W. Olliver, *An Analysis of Magic and Witchcraft,* London, 1928, pp. 15, 16.

[7] This is virtually the definition given by Jean Bodin in his *La Demonomanie.* On the resemblance of witchcraft and ceremonial magic and the distinctions between them, see *post,* chapter III.

[8] I use "orthodox" here to apply to the dogmatic interpretations made by both Protestant and Catholic theology. Though differing in some points, they had in common that they presented sober, authoritative pneumatology strictly conformed to general religious doctrine.

"Rationalistic" I apply to the newly arising mode of interpretation which was semi-empirical in its spirit. I intend to use the word *rationalism* in Lecky's sense. He says of rationalism that "It predisposes men, in history, to attribute all kinds of phenomena to natural rather than miraculous causes." (*History of Rationalism,* I, 17.) In this sense the truest rationalist of the sixteenth century on spirit matters was Montaigne, who scouted daemonology and seems to have disbelieved it on grounds of "antecedent probability." (See the essay on Cripples.) Wier, and even Reginald Scot, merely try to make a reduction of the dogma of spirits to its most impersonalized terms consistent with a literal interpretation of the Bible. The practical result of this was a severe abridgement of the domain of daemonology; but the point of view was still the point of view of that other and very rigorous kind of rationalism which based upon authority and which the orthodox daemonologists, Bodin, Delrio, and the rest exemplify.

By "occult" I mean the esoteric, half-mystical style of interpretation which, it has been said, contributed in its own way to the rise of science and the break up of the "rationalistic dogmatism" of the Middle Ages. The magician's approach to spirit lore allowed for imaginative conceptions and for an experimentation which proved productive, though not in the direction it was aimed. (See the *Encyclopedia Britannica* on *mysticism,* and Mr. Hardin Craig's *Enchanted Glass,* Oxford, 1936, p. 75.)

[9] I use this word as the only one known to me that covers speculations on unbodied souls as well as on daemons. That the speculation itself existed in the sixteenth century and Middle Ages there can, of course, be no question. Francis Bacon, for instance, classifies knowledge of spirits under Natural Theology and says of daemons that "the contemplation and knowledge of their nature, powers, and illusions appears from Scripture, reason, and experience, to be no small part of spiritual wisdom." (*Advancement of Learning,* III, ii, 122 of the edition by Joseph Devy, London, 1904.)

[10] There was, of course, a traditional spirit lore of folk legend that was easy, unanalytical, often local, and (the theologians held) superstitious, which did not by any means always conform to pneumatological theory, and certainly has its place in Elizabethan drama. My concern with it is only to point out occasionally where its echo in the plays parts with pneumatology.

[11] F. O. Mathiessen, "Towards our Understanding of Elizabethan Drama," *The Southern Review,* IV (1938) 414. "But where Wilson makes a crucial mistake is in assuming that the distinctions between the three schools of thought were as sharply marked to the Elizabethans as they are to him."

[12] Mathiessen, *op. cit.,* p. 415.

[13] Reginald Scot in *The Discoverie of Witchcraft* gives a list of two hundred and forty-seven authors he has used, of which two hundred and fourteen are "forren."

The English ministers Deacon and Walker, writing on demoniacal possession, give an equally extensive list of authorities. They include most of the contemporary polemical writers such as Scot, Daneau, Bodin, Lavater, *et cetera,* and the more general authors such as Erasmus, Scaliger, Pomponazzi, Bucer, and Ficino. But there is a much larger number of ancients such as Proclus, Pliny, Strabo, Plutarch, Hermes, *et cetera,* and yet more fathers of the church and their heretical opponents: Augustine, Montanus, Cyprian, Athanasius, Origen, Chrysostom, *et cetera.* There are also scholastics: Aquinas, Albertus, Malmesbury; besides two Jews, Ben-Sirah and Josephus, and an Arab, Avicenna.

[14] John Deacon and John Walker, *Dialogicall Discourses of Spirits and Devils,* 1601, V, 137. Mr. Lecky in the introduction to his *History of Rationalism* distinguishes lucidly between the perspective-conditioned outlook that arose near the end of the eighteenth century and the absolutism of conviction previous to that time. See also Craig, *op. cit.,* p. 212, on how the Elizabethans used ancient authority.

[15] The general popularity of such works is attested by such facts as that Ficino's translation of the Hermetic Books ran to no less than twenty-two editions between 1471 and 1641, and that English writers so different as Richard Hooker and Sir Walter Raleigh cite with approval moral passages from Hermes. Hooker, in his *Ecclesiastical Polity,* I, v, 3; vi, 3; VII, xxiv, 16, shows acquaintance with the Greek. Sir Walter's citations in the preface of his *History of the World* (see p. xxiii of the London edition of 1687) seem probably from Ficino's Latin.

[16] T. R. Glover, *The Conflict of Religions in the Early Roman Empire,* eighth ed., London, 1919, p. 230.

[17] This latter story, which is the older of the two versions of the fall of angels, is mentioned briefly, too, in Genesis vi, 1–4. It has a fuller treatment in the Book of Enoch. See chapters vii, viii, and lxix as edited by R. H. Charles in *The Apocrypha and Pseudepigraphia of the Old Testament,* II, pp. 193–4, 233. Josephus also mentions it. See *The Antiquities of the Jews,* I, iii, 1 in *The Works of Flavius Josephus,* translated by William Whiston, London, 1872.

[18] The "Pseudo-Clementine Literature," which was the core of the legend of Simon Magus, is often referred to in sixteenth century polemic on magic. As frequently cited are *The Conversion of St. Justina and St. Cyprian* and the perhaps yet older *Confession of St. Cyprian.* Calderon's *El Magico Prodigioso* is, of course, based on the legend.

[19] In his notes on patristic daemonology H. C. Lea says: "Aquinas' perpetual references to St. Augustin show how powerful was Augustin's influence on medieval thought. When his utterance could be quoted, nothing more was required." (See p. 92 of *Materials Toward a History of Witchcraft,* collected by Henry Charles Lea, arranged and edited by Arthur C. Howland, Philadelphia, 1939.) The Reformation, with constant Protestant appeal to the early church, increased rather than lessened Augustine's authority. On Aquinas Professor Lynn Thorndike says (*History of Magic and Experimental Science,* New York, 1929, II, 598) that on the subjects of magic, witchcraft, *et cetera,* Aquinas summed up Christian thought satisfactorily and was both "the most popular and the most moderate teacher of his own time," and that "his opinions upon these subjects remained for centuries acceptable and authoritative to the Roman Catholic Church."

[20] See the introductory essay by J. D. Wilson and the appendix on the ghost controversy by Miss May Yardley to the Shakespeare Association reprint of Lavater's *Of Ghosts and Spirits* for accounts of the popularity of pneumatological treatises.

In his diary entry for March 19, 1597, Dr. Dee mentions the lending to a Mr. Edward Hopwood of a work on witchcraft, *De Praestigiis Daemonum.* He had it back on April 15 and lent *Flagellum Daemonum* and *Fustis Daemonum.* On July 1 the same gentleman borrowed *Malleus Maleficarum* in an edition of 1517 "to use tyll new yere's tyde next."

[21] Lecky says (*op. cit.,* vol. I, p. 105) that Wier was the first to throw "into a systematic form" a good deal of "latent and undefined" "scepticism" in regard to the guilt of witches. Wier supplemented his *De Praestigiis* not only by a sixth book but by two subsidiary works, *De Lamiis* and *Pseudomonarchia Daemonum* which are appended to later editions.

Wier had many allies, most of whom took about the same line of argument that he did. Professor G. L. Burr considers that the opponents of the witch persecution were neither so few nor so feeble as Lecky intimates, since the persecutors never cease to complain of them. Professor Burr names several continental disciples of Wier. See "The Literature of Witchcraft" in *American Historical Association Papers,* vol. IV, pt. iii, p. 235.

[22] *Malleus Maleficarum Maleficas et earum haeresim, ut framea potentissima conterens per F. Henricum Institoris et Jacobum Sprengerum Ord. Praedic. Inquisitores.* There is an edition dated 1584, but the Rev. Montague Summers says that this can hardly be right. Professor Burr says that the earliest edition was probably 1486 or 1487. The work was translated into French as *Le Maillet des Sorcières.* There were many editions; the latest we need note was 1620. Most sixteenth century editions include besides the work of Sprenger and Institor the last book of Nider's *Formicarius* of 1437 and to this was added in the 1588 and subsequent editions the works of nine other divines, so that *Malleus Maleficarum* became the title for a great compilation of Catholic works on witchcraft.

Egon Friedell in his *Cultural History of the Modern Age* says (I, 282): "It was only towards the end of the fifteenth century that this witch-mania, beginning in the Northern lands, became a scourge of humanity. The decisive date is 1487, the year of publication by the two papal inquisitors Henry Institor and Jacob Sprenger of the notorious *Malleus Maleficarum* . . ."

[23] Nicholas Remy (Remigius), *Daemonlatreiae libri tres,* Lyons, 1595. Henri Boguet, *Discours des Sorciers,* Lyons, 1590; Pierre de Lancre, *Tableau de L'Inconstance des Mauvais Anges et Demons,* 1610. Of these works Remy's carried the most weight. Lea says (*op. cit.,* II, 104) that it superseded the *Malleus.*

[24] John Cotta (*op. cit.,* vii, 57) so cites Binsfield. The *De Confessionibus* was published in 1589 at Treves. I have seen a German translation by Heinrich Bock, Treves, 1590.

[25] Dozens of other titles might be mentioned. See the bibliography to Summer's *History of Witchcraft* for a selected list, and J. G. T. Grasse's *Bibliotheca Magica et pneumatica* for what was in its time considered an exhaustive bibliography, and Robert Yve-Plessis's *Essai d'une bibliographie de la sorcellerie* . . . for additional French titles. Of continental works which have the general argument of witchcraft as central theme, I will name here only two others to which I shall make later reference: *Compendium Maleficarum* of the Ambrosian, Francesco Maria Guazzo, Milan, 1608; and two dialogues of the Swiss physician, Thomas Erastus. Both authors were orthodox in their witch doctrine, insisting upon the reality and the culpability of witchcraft. The dialogues of Erastus, written in 1578, are in reply to some anonymous opponent. They were translated from the original into French and bound with a French edition of Wier's *De Praestigiis* in 1579 to give the reader, as the publisher said, insight into both sides of a vexed question. The Latin title of the dialogues: *Repetitio disputationis de lamiis seu strigibus,* Basle, 1578.

There were many subsidiary treatises on special phases of the witch question. George Pictorius (Mahlen) in his work translated into English by Robert Turner in 1655 as *A Discourse on the Nature of Spirits,* written sometime before the end of the sixteenth century; Giovanni D'Anania in *De Natura Daemonum,* 1589; Reginald Scot in his *Discourse of Devils and Spirits,* treat specially the fundamental ground of all witchcraft, devil doctrine. Leonard Vair writes of charms: *Trois Livres des Charmes, Sorcelage, ou enchantemens,* 1583; and Kaspar Peucer on divination: *Les Devins ou Commentaire des Principales Sortes de divinations* . . . 1584.

[26] There were Latin, German, and Italian translations of the *Demonomanie* in 1590, 1581, and 1587 respectively. There were also several French editions. I have used one of Paris, 1598. It contains, in addition to the four books of the regular work, seventy-five pages of *Refutation des Opinions de Iean Wier.* Bodin says that it is appended because his work was virtually complete before he saw Wier's *De Lamiis* and that he adds this in special refutation.

[27] *Daemonologie in form of a Dialogue, Diuided into three Books.* There are two London editions of 1603.

[28] George Gifford, *A Discourse of the Subtill Practises of Deuilles by Witches and Sorcerers,* 1587; *A Dialogue Concerning Witches and Witchcraftes,* 1593.

[29] It is included in the three volume *Workes* printed by Cantrell Legge for the University of Cambridge, 1609.

[30] A second edition of *The Tryall,* augmented and revised, appeared in 1624 as *Infallible true & Assured Witch . . . Shewing the right and true Method of the Discoverie with a Confutation of erroneous waies, carefully revised and more fully cleared and augmented.* Other English writers on witchcraft: Alex Roberts, *A Treatise of Witchcraft,* 1616; Thomas Cooper, *The Mystery of Witchcraft,* 1617; Henry Holland, *A Treatise against Witchcraft . . .* Cambridge, 1590.

[31] Delrio's work is, of course, primarily but another witchcraft polemic. It presents, however, in its early books, a specific attack on ceremonial magic. In this it is matched in extent and detail by Wier—whose attitude in this is much like that of Delrio in condemnation of magicians—and by Bento Pereira in his *De Magia,* 1591. Delrio's work was first published at Lyons in 1599. Another edition of the Latin is 1608 and there is a slightly condensed French translation, *Controverses et recherches magiques,* Paris, 1611.

[32] In the epistle to the 1537 edition (which is of the first book only, though titled *Three Books* and originally planned as of the entire work) Agrippa explains that since the work is abroad in an evil, corrupted form, it is proper, though he has ceased to hold many of the doctrines expounded, for him to present an alternative and authoritative edition which he is sure is less harmful than the pirated ones, may correct many hurtful impressions.

The first edition of the whole work appeared at Cologne, July, 1533. Within a century and a half of first publication, says Mr. Morley, Agrippa's biographer, the work was translated into most European languages, including English.

Publishers seem to have regarded it as in a sense the spearhead of literature on magic and frequently bound it with less worthy works on the same general subject. For instance, a Paris edition dated 1567 has the following title page: *Henry Cornelius Agrippae ab Nettesheym de occulta philosophia libri III. Quibus accesserunt, spurius Agrippae liber de ceremoniis magicis: Heptameron Petri de Albano; Ratio compendiaria magicae naturalis, ex Plinio desumpta; Disputatio de fascinationibus; Epistola de incantatione et adiuratione, collique suspensione; Iohannis Tritemii opuscula quaedam huius argumenti.*

For information about the conditions of composition and publication of Agrippa's work see Henry Morley's *Life of Agrippa,* London, 1856. The best English translation of the *Occult Philosophy* is that of 1651.

[33] Morley says that of this work there were several English translations made in the sixteenth and seventeenth centuries. I have used one of 1684 printed in London by R. E. for R. B. and another (less reliable, Morley indicates) of 1575 by Ia. San. gent., and checked both from the 1583 Cologne edition of the Latin. Extracts from the *De Vanitate* which seem to recant the *Occulta Philosophia* are bound with the 1567 edition of the latter referred to in note 32 *ante.* Translations of these same extracts are bound with the 1651 English translation of the *Occulta Philosophia.*

[34] Paracelsus' pneumatology has seemed to me so individualized that I have touched upon it very little. I have relied almost entirely upon Hartman's *Life* which translates a great number of extracts, and upon A. E. Waite's *The Hermetic and Alchemical Writings of Philippus Theophrastus Bombast of Hohenheim, called Paracelsus the Great,* London, 1894.

[35] Trithemius stoutly denied that the *Steganographie* contained anything illicit, but it is one of the chief works attacked by Wier as of the "magiciens infames." Some authorities say that the book is an elaborate anagram innocent of connection with the superstitious spirit doctrine normal to the times. See Rudolph Steiner's *The Mystics of the Renaissance,* London, 1911. Gabriel Naudé in his *Apologie pour les Grandes Hommes Soupconnés de Magie,* 1625, makes a similar defense for Trithemius. The Abbott wrote, however, several other works quite compatible with average demonological doctrine. One was a tract against witches, *Antipalus Maleficorum,* 1508.

[36] *De Arte Cabalistica,* 1517.

[37] His famous Nine Hundred Theses include twenty-six on magic and he has much to say of spirits. He is attacked by Bodin as one almost as reprehensible as Agrippa—saving his nobility.

[38] Both the *Fourth Book of Agrippa* and the *Heptameron* were printed with the first three books of *Occulta Philosophia* in the 1567 edition mentioned in note 32 *ante*. Professor Lynn Thorndike says (*op. cit.*, II, 925) that the *Heptameron* was printed with the *Occult Philosophy* in 1565 also. He is my authority, too, for the English translation of 1600. I have not seen any English translation earlier than Robert Turner's of 1655. Turner includes, besides the *Fourth Book of Agrippa* and the *Heptameron,* treatises by Agrippa and Gerard Cremonensis on Geomancy, Pictorius on daemons, and the famous ritual of transcendental magic, the *Arbatel.* Most of these rituals were in themselves probably new in the sixteenth century, though heavily indebted to others much older. See Moses Gaster's "The Sword of Moses," p. 288 ff., in volume I of his *Studies and Texts in Folklore and Magic. . . .* London, 1925–1928.

[39] For quotations and analysis see A. E. Waite, *Book of Black Magic and of Pacts,* London, 1898.

[40] Of the *Clavicula Salomonis* there are manuscripts, but none in any Hebrew that could have been Solomon's, thinks Mr. A. E. Waite. Mr. S. McGregor Mathers, editor of the only published edition in English, seems to disagree. The Mathers edition is London, 1909. In his *Book of Black Magic* Waite gives an epitome in translation of the *Lemegeton.* On the "practical" Cabala and its place see Waite, *Doctrine and Literature of the Kabalah,* London, 1902, Bks. VII and VIII.

[41] Of Lavater's work there was a second English edition in 1596. The first was titled: *Of Ghostes and Spirits Walking by Nyght.* The 1605 French edition of Le Loyer is called: *Discours, et histoires des spectres, visions et apparitions des esprit, anges, demons, et ames, se monstrans visible aux hommes . . .* Paris, 1605. It rearranges the matter of the earlier "IIII Livres" into eight. The English translation of Le Loyer is titled: *A Treatise of Spectres or Strange sights, visions and apparitions appearing sensibly unto men. . . . Newly done out of French into English.*

[42] The questions of the real presence and the intercession of saints were involved. Le Loyer argues that the Eucharist and the return of saints to their shrines proves the return of souls. The doctrine of purgatory was also concerned. See *post,* pp. 49, 50.

[43] John Deacon and John Walker, *A Dialogicall Discourse of Spirits and Devils,* 1601.

——— *A Summary Answere to all the Material Points in any of Master Darel his Books. . . .* London, 1601. These two books are bound together in the 1601 editions.

[44] In 1603 was published Harsnett's tract, *A Declaration of Egregious Popish Impostures* from which work Shakespeare is supposed to have taken devils' names for *Lear.* For a discussion of the English controversy on possession see Professor Kittredge's *Witchcraft in Old and New England,* Boston, 1929.

A Catholic authority on exorcism was Girolamo Menghi whose works, *Flagellum Daemonum* and *Fustis Daemonum,* were owned and circulated by Dr. Dee. (See note 20 *ante.*) A less technical work was that of Father Sebastian Michaelis which was translated into English in 1613 as *The Admirable History of the Possession and Conversion of a Penitent Woman.* The second volume of this book, which is mostly testimony to the Catholic faith, is *A Discourse of Spirits.* Father Michaelis seems to have compiled it in part from the statements of possessing devils constrained by exorcists.

Notes on Chapter II

[1] See G. P. Conger, *Theories of Macrocosms and Microcosms in the History of Philosophy,* New York, 1922.

[2] Agrippa in the first chapter of his *Occult Philosophy* says that he will recant whatever of it the church shall consider misguided. Jerome Cardan, half rationalist,

half occultist, professes himself (*De Vita Propria Liber,* xlviii, 244 of the translation by Jean Stoner, New York, 1930) willing in interpreting spirit communications to submit himself "in points where I can fall into error" to his "intellectual betters, that is, to the theologians." Among Protestant authors no one insists on his orthodoxy more than Reginald Scot.

[3] On Celsus and his attack on Christianity through doctrines of magic see the special chapters in Thorndike, *History of Magic and Experimental Science,* New York, 1929, and Glover, *The Conflict of Religions in the Early Roman Empire,* London, 1919.

[4] On the fall of angels see, for instance, Lactantius, *The Divine Institutes,* II, xv, as translated by William Fletcher in *The Ante-Nicene Christian Library,* I, 126–8; *The Clementine Homilies,* VIII, xii–xv, as translated by Thomas Smith in *Ante-Nicene Fathers,* VIII, 272–3; and similarly Athenagoras, Commodianus, Justin Martyr, *et cetera.* On angelic rank among fallen and unfallen angels, see John of Damascus, *Exposition of the Orthodox Faith,* II, iii, as translated by R. S. D. Salmond in *Nicene and Post Nicene Fathers,* second series, IX, 20; Cassian, *Conferences,* VIII, ii, as translated by E. C. S. Gibson in *Nicene and Post-Nicene Fathers,* second series, XI, 381; Gregory of Nyssa, *Against Eunomius,* VII, 5, as translated by William Moore and H. A. Wilson, *Nicene and Post-Nicene Fathers,* V, 199, *et cetera.* On possession see Minucius Felix, *The Octavius,* xxvii, as translated by R. E. Wallis, *Ante-Nicene Fathers,* IV, 289–90; *The Recognitions of Clement,* IV, xvi, as translated by Thomas Smith, *The Ante-Nicene Fathers,* VIII, p. 138; Cassian, *Conferences,* VII, xxv, as translated by E. C. S. Gibson, *Nicene and Post-Nicene Fathers,* XI, 371, *et cetera.* The possible citations are almost innumerable. For collected quotations on Hebrew and early Christian doctrine of the fall, possession, *et cetera,* and its historical connexity with medieval thought see H. C. Lea's *Materials Toward a History of Witchcraft,* Philadelphia, 1939, pp. 1–137.

[5] John Wier opens his *De Praestigiis Daemonum* by saying that he writes according to the gospel and Christianity, rejects the opinions of Aristotle and the Peripatetics that there are no spirits in nature; and Scot says repeatedly that he does not hold with Peripatetics and others who deny the existence of spirits. The full list of the schools of thought that departed from orthodoxy in spirit belief toward rationalism may be found in the *Discours et Histoires des Spectres* of Pierre Le Loyer. He devotes five long chapters to answering atheists, Sadducees, Epicureans, Peripatetics, Pomponatists, Averrohists, Sceptics, and "Naturalists," of which last he seems to hold Cardan the leader. See I, i–iv, vi, of the 1605 Paris edition.

It is true, of course, that Lucretius and Aristotle were widely known in the Renaissance and were approved for their views on other things than spirits, and it is even true too that the works of Lucian, scoffer at spirits and magic, were translated into English in 1565 and again in 1604. But the contribution of ancient sceptics and materialists to Elizabethan rationalism on spirits is probably to be thought indirect and rather one of attitude than of doctrine.

[6] On the reception of Wier's book see E. T. Withington's "Dr. John Weyer and the Witch Mania," in C. J. Singer's *Studies in the History and Method of Science,* Oxford, 1917. On Gifford, see *The Wonderful Discoverie of the Witchcraft of Margaret and Philip Flower . . .,* London, 1619, as reprinted in *A Collection of Rare and Curious Tracts Relating to Witchcraft . . .,* London, 1838.

[7] See Gregory Zilboorg, *The Medical Man and the Witch during the Renaissance,* Baltimore, 1935.

[8] There was also much talk of Peripatetical and Sadducaical atheists or pneumatomachie, persons denying the existence of spirits as essential beings, holding with *Pneumatomachus* of Deacon and Walker's dialogue that "spirits are none other matters at all, but the good or euill motions and affections arising in men: as also those your imagined angels, . . . nothing but the sensible signes or tokens of Gods unspeakable power." (See *A Dialogicall Discourse of Spirits and Devils,* by John Deacon and John Walker, London, 1610, I, 10.) But there is no real representative of such views among the authors I have read. Scot seems sometimes to incline to them (the pneumatomachie at whom he rails in the concluding chapter

to his *Discourse* he conceives as deniers of the Holy Spirit, not merely of finite spirits); but he was cautious, and there is no real ground for King James' assertion that Scot "mainteines the old errour of the Sadducees, in denying of spirits." (See the Epistle to the *Daemonologie.*) Scot seems for the most part to hold spirits proper creatures though separated from the world of sense. He says that Sadducees are "impious and fond" "which say that spirits & devils are but motions and affections, and that angels are but tokens of God's power." For his part, he "will not stick to say that they are living creatures ordained to serve the lord in their vocation and although they abode not in their first estate, yet that they are the Lords ministers and executioners of his wrath, to trie and tempt in this world, and to punish the reprobate in hell fier in the world to come." (See *The Discourse of Devils and Spirits,* xxxi, 453. All my citations in Scot are to the Nicholson edition.)

No doubt there were those, however, who utterly denied spirits; most of the authors with whom we deal seemed to feel it necessary to assert the essentiality of spirits as though there were sceptics. Thus the witchmonger Nicholas Remy: "Demons are not merely a debased mental condition in man, as was maintained by Democritus and Averroes and the whole Peripatetic School; but are essential spirits, if I may so put it, constant in their own nature." (See the *Demonolatry* as translated under the editorship of the Rev. Montague Summers, I, xxiii, 69.)

[9] Scot, (*Discoverie of Witchcraft,* VIII, i, 125); King James (*Daemonologie,* III, ii, 66); Deacon and Walker (*op. cit.,* To the Reader); William Perkins (*A Discourse of the Damned Art of Witchcraft* in vol. III of the *Works,* Cambridge, 1609, v. 648) all deny contemporary miracles and take the cessation as ground to abate credulity a little. But it must be said that except for Scot they, though Protestants, stood pretty solidly with the scholastics in most spirit doctrine.

[10] Scot derides this limited incredulity, saying that it shows merely that Protestants are superstitious on somewhat fewer matters, not less superstitious, than Catholics. (*Discourse of Devils and Spirits,* xxvii, 446–7.)

[11] John Cotta says (*Infallible, True and Assured Witch,* London, 1624, x, 88) that the devil works on man in two ways: (1) by tempting, and the issue should be called not devil's works, but devilish; (2) "in his own proper action as he is a spirit," *i.e.,* a superhuman agent handling material things. Scot acknowledged the first sort of work, denied the second.

[12] Scot, *Discoverie of Witchcraft,* VII, xv, 122; Lewes Lavater, *Of Ghostes and Spirits Walking by Nyght,* I, xii, 53 ff. For Lavater's work I have used exclusively the Shakespeare Association reprint edited by J. D. Wilson. On Lavater and his work see *ante,* p. 13. John Wier, *Histoires, Disputes et Discours des Illusions et Impostures des Diables . . .* (French translation of the *De Praestigiis*), Paris, 1579, III, v, 218, and Pierre Le Loyer, *Discours et Histoires des Spectres. . . .* Paris, 1605, II, i–iv, also have much to say on how feeble persons deceive themselves by false imaginings. But both hold also that such persons are merely the apter victims for real spectres. Le Loyer says explicitly that spirits appear also to persons in good health whose testimony should be accepted. (*Op. cit.,* III, i., 171.) See also Noel Taillepied *Psichologie,* Paris, 1588, as translated by Montague Summers, xv, 94.

[13] *Discourse,* xiii, 427. In the *Discoverie* Scot gives elaborate etymologies of Biblical key words.

[14] See, for instance, the explanations of the various meanings of the word *spirit* in Heinrich Bullinger's *Decades* as translated by H. I. and edited for the Parker Society by Rev. Thomas Harding, Cambridge, 1849. See the *Fourth Decade,* Sermon, vii, p. 298.

[15] See, for instance, the opening of Apuleius' brief work on the daemon of Socrates.

[16] Cotta, *op. cit.,* v, 27.

[17] *Malleus Maleficarum,* Pt. I, Q. 2, p. 2 of the English translation edited by Montague Summers. All my references are to this translation unless otherwise noted.

[18] Thomas de Cauzons says (*La Magie et la Sorcellerie en France,* Paris, 1910, vol. I, p. 118) that some theologians accepted the pagan scheme of daemons fiery, aerial,

etc., but that others held this imaginary and stuck to the simple principle of "les bons et les mauvais."

[19] For this etymology of the term daemon see William Alexander, *Demonic Possession in the New Testament,* appendix.

[20] See St. Augustine's *City of God,* I, 376, Bk. I, c. 19 of the Marcus Dodd translation, Edinburgh, 1872: ". . . never have we read in scripture of good demons."

[21] In book III of the *Occulta Philosophia* Agrippa opens chapter xvi, which is on the nature of intelligences, by saying: "By daemons I do not mean here those beings we call devils, but I understand thereby in the true meaning of the word spirits as it were wise, understanding, and sage." The English translation of 1651 which I have used when possible and to which most of my references are made, has here *angels,* but the Latin is *daemonis.* The subsequent discussion leaves it plain that Agrippa's conception was a mixture of Christian, Judaic, and Neo-Platonic ideas of heavenly intelligences, and that the Neo-Platonic predominated. In spite of his assertion that he does not mean devil by the term *daemon,* he frequently uses *daemon,* as do his contemporaries, for evil daemon, meaning fallen angel.

[22] Le Loyer, *op. cit.,* III, ii, 182; Bodin, *La Demonomanie,* Paris, 1598, I, i, 50, 51. George Pictorius in the treatise translated by Robert Turner in 1655 as *A Discourse of the Nature of Spirits,* on p. 156 cites Augustine and Eusebius against the Platonists that daemons are all bad. See the same treatise in German translation in *Geheime Wissenschaften,* Berlin, 1922, V, 30.

[23] Henri Boguet, *Discours des Sorciers,* v, 15. My references are all to the Summers translation (*An Examen of Witches*) of this exceedingly rare book. Remy, *op. cit.,* I, xx, 66. Aquinas subscribes in general to the order of good angels given by Pseudo-Dionysus and holds (*Summa Theologica,* Pt. I, Q. 109, A. 1) for a persistence of this order among fallen angels so far as it is one of nature and not of grace. The order of angels, he explains, is at once natural, *i.e.,* according to the varying native endowments of the classes, and gratuitous, *i.e.,* according to the special fitness bestowed by God for approach to the angelic goal, which is to love and know God. (Pt. I, Q. 108, A. 4.) Among good angels the two orders conform exactly to each other since God grants grace to angels according to their natural capacity. This order by grace did not endure among the fallen angels, for they receded from grace; but a precedence according to nature persisted and by such authority the actions of one demon are governed by another. (Pt. I, Q. 109, A. 2.)

Wier in his compendious treatment of demons in the *Discours des Diables* lists (I, xxiii, 99) the nine orders of demons as named by "some theologians": (1) False gods, (2) Lying spirits, (3) Vessels of iniquity, (4) Avengers of crime, (5) Impostors, (6) Powers of the air, (7) the Furies, (8) Accusers, (9) Tempters. In this he follows Agrippa's *Occult Philosophy,* III, xviii, sometimes word for word. Agrippa says that he also follows "the theologians," but does not name them. Robert Burton, Pt. I, sect. II, Mem. 1, Subs. 2, of the *Anatomy of Melancholy* cites the same classification as of "our School-men and other divines," and a footnote names "Agrippa, Zanchius, Pictorius, Pererius, Cicogna." For the classification according to Pictorius see *op. cit.,* p. 143 ff. The same classification is reproduced by Robert Fludd and by many other writers, occult and orthodox.

[24] See Burton, *loc. cit.* A. E. Waite says (*Book of Black Magic,* p. 55) that the "old book" of Burton's mention was the *Lemegeton* (*Lesser Key of Solomon*) known to Wier as *Liber Spirituum.* See also Wier's *Discours* on the organization of the demons according to the *Steganography* of Trithemius.

[25] *Daemonologie,* I, vi, 21.

[26] *Ibid.,* I, vi, 20.

[27] See K. Svoboda, *Demonologie de Michel Psellos.* Psellos had several slightly variant classifications of demons according to the elements.

[28] See the *Compendium Maleficarum,* I, xviii, 73 of the English translation edited by the Rev. Montague Summers. See also Bk. II, Q. 27, sect. ii, p. 284 of *Controverses et recherches magiques,* Paris, 1611, by Delrio whose exposition is virtually identical with Guazzo's, acknowledges Psellos.

[29] See Scot, *Discourse of Divells and Spirits,* iii, 415, and Wier, *op. cit.,* I, xxiii, 99 ff. Wier rejects also several other classifications, saying that he has no desire in

imitation of Psellos and other magicians to divide daemons according to the elements nor according to planets, or the signs of the Zodiac, nor into day and night, eastern, western, northern and southern demons, nor into any other farcical categories devised by magicians. His master, Agrippa, however, makes all these divisions and more. Wier himself evidently forgot his strictures before writing the *Pseudomonarchia* if his purpose there was serious. Many orthodox authors—Le Loyer for instance—give seriously all the classifications which Wier eschews in the *De Praestigiis* as superstitious.

[30] *Ibid.*, xii, 426.

[31] *Op. cit.*, Pt. I, Q. 3, p. 27.

[32] Bodin quotes (*op. cit.*, I, i, 61) from Apuleius' *Deo Socratus:* "Demones sunt genere animalia, ingenio rationabilia, animo passiua, corpore aërea, tempore aeterna . . ."

[33] For a brief, comprehensive statement of Renaissance theological opinion on angelic substance see Henry Sheldon, *History of Christian Doctrine,* New York, 1886, II, 100. H. O. Taylor says in his *Medieval Mind* (II, 487) that Aquinas had a large share "in perfecting the conception of the angelic nature as immaterial and essentially intellectual." Aquinas is usually the authority cited by the polemists as chief sponsor of the doctrine of pure spirituality. He says (*Summa,* Pt. I, Q. 50, A. 1 and 2) that angels are substances wholly intellectual as existing in grade between God and man, and that intelligence cannot be the act of a body, nor of any corporeal faculty. "It is, further, impossible for an intellectual substance to have any kind of matter. For the operation belonging to anything is according to the mode of its substance. Now to understand is an altogether immaterial operation, as appears from its object, whence any act receives its species and nature. For a thing is understood according to its degree of immateriality; because forms that exist in matter are individual forms which the intellect cannot apprehend as such. Hence it must be that every intellectual substance is altogether immaterial."

A few Protestants, reviving patristic views, expressed doubt that any being but God could be completely immaterial. The materiality they attributed to angels may probably be taken in the Aristotelian or Plotinean sense as of "intelligible matter" which is incorporeal, the substrate not of bodies, but of superior forms. (See *Enneads,* II, Bk. IV, 2 of the Guthrie translation of Plotinus, p. 198.) Plotinus says that though the being of demons is united with aerial or fiery "bodies," they are incorporeal, not animals possessing sensation. (*Enneads,* III, Bk. V, p. 1133.) On matter in the spiritual world according to Plotinus, see Dean Inge's *The Philosophy of Plotinus,* I, 139 ff. Aquinas notes the related supposition of Avicebron "that the universal matter of spiritual and corporeal things is the same; so that it must be understood that the form of incorporeal substance is impressed in the matter of spiritual things, in the same way as the form of quantity is impressed in the matter of corporeal things," and attempts to confute it (*Summa,* I, Q. 50, A. 2). My quotations from Aquinas are from the translation of the *Summa* by Fathers of the English Dominican Province, London, 1920.

Bodin treats of the substance of daemons in his preface, in the first chapter of book I, pp. 60, 61, and in *Refutation des Opinions de Iean Wier,* appended to the 1598 edition of *La Demonomanie,* pp. 548 and 549. On the quintessence as the substance of spirits, see Pierre Charron, *Of Wisdome Three Books,* the English translation (*c.* 1612) by Samson Lennard of *De la Sagesse,* p. 24–5; and Agrippa's *Occult Philosophy,* III, xiv, 33, which says that the quintessence is "a certain first thing" not from the four elements, but "having its being above, and besides them." See also Hardin Craig, *The Enchanted Glass,* Oxford Press, 1936, p. 2.

[34] Remy, *op. cit.,* I, xxix, 84. See also Perkins, *op. cit.,* i, 610; Guazzo, *op. cit.,* I, iii, 7. Aquinas explains (*Summa,* Pt. I, Q. 64, A. I) in what sense the fallen angels retain their angelic powers.

[35] Aquinas explains (*Summa,* Pt. I, Q. 110, A. 2 and 3) that though angels do not move bodies by their will alone, they move them by the natural conjunction which exists between local motion—the most perfect of all bodily motions, hence extending upward toward the spiritual realm—and the governing powers of spiritual agents. This is the *power* that spirits have in the world. It is thus that the soul moves the body and thus, though without the limitation of union, angels

control the local motion of whatever bodies they apply themselves to. On this very difficult matter, which was central to every contention of the witchmongers but which most preferred to pass with a hasty citation of patristic and medieval authorities, see also *Malleus Maleficarum,* Pt. I, Q. 1, p. 11.

Of the motion of angels Aquinas explains that they are superior to place so far as place is dimensional and that they contain it, as the soul does the body, rather than are contained in it. The contact of an angel with a place is a virtual one, not a commensurate one. "An angel is said to be in a corporeal place by application of the angelic power in any manner whatever to any place." Since this is so "it follows necessarily that the movement of an angel in a place is nothing else than the various contacts of various places successively." (*Summa,* Pt. I, Q. 52, A. 2; Q. 53, A. 3.)

The transfer of the angelic application from any place to another cannot be called instantaneous since there is a "before" and an "after" to it and "time is nothing else than the reckoning of before and after in movement." But the time which measures an angel's motion is not the time marked for corporeal things by the movement of the heavens since an angel's movements do not depend upon those of the heavens. Angels are not required in their transfer from spot to spot to pass through intervening space. Remy's remark that they were endowed with *speed* seems, therefore, quite justified. (*Summa,* Pt. I, Q. 53, A. 3, A. 2.)

Of the knowledge of angels, St. Thomas explains (*Summa,* Pt. I, Q. 57, A. 1) that as regards material things it is a knowledge essential in the angels in whom as superior beings all earthly species pre-exist intelligibly. The angelic concept of the species of created things is derived not from the creatures but from God (Pt I, Q. 55, A. 2). "Through the species imparted to them do the angels know things, not only as to their universal natures, but likewise in their individual conditions. . . ." (Pt. I, Q. 57, A. 2.)

[36] Remy, *op. cit.,* I, vii, 27. St. Thomas does not—though he uses the analogy of clouds, ridiculed by Scot (see *post,* p. 26)—touch on the physics of the assumption of airy bodies, saying simply that it is by a divine power of condensing air, "so far as is needful for forming the assumed body." (*Summa,* Pt. I, Q. 51, A. 2.) Le Loyer, who has a chapter on the dispute over assumption of bodies, follows Aquinas in general doctrine, gives a more or less systematic refutation of several arguments against assumption, elaborates to little purpose on the method of it. On the question of whether spirits take bodies see Le Loyer, *op. cit.,* I, v, 32; on how the assumed bodies are formed, see III, xiv, 260.

[37] Guazzo, *op. cit.,* I, xi, 30. See also Perkins, *op. cit.,* i, 610; Boguet, *op. cit.,* vii, 16, and so on through almost the whole list of the witchmongers. King James, *op. cit.,* II, vi, 52; Boguet, *op. cit.,* viii, 21; Remy, *op. cit.,* II, i, 86; Taillepied, *op. cit.,* xvi, 112; Guazzo, *op. cit.,* I, xi, 30; Le Loyer, *op. cit.,* I, v, 34 and III, x, 241 ff.; and many others say that demons can take also a dead body and animate it for a time. *Malleus Maleficarum* makes the distinction (Pt. II, Q. 1, ch. iv, p. 109) that when devils act through any natural body, as through Balaam's ass, it is not said to be *assumed,* as is said of an airy body, but *occupied.* Lavater (*op. cit.,* II, vii, 128 and xviii, 171) denies that devils can ever take the body of a dead person and reanimate it. King James (*op. cit.,* II, vi, 52) and Deacon and Walker (*Dialogicall Discourse of Spirits and Devils,* V, p. 143) mention that apparitions of demons are also sometimes hallucinatory, as demons may employ their power to control men's senses from within and present to them baseless images. This is a point in Wier's argument against the possibility of witchcraft. (See *post,* p. 37.)

Le Loyer sums up the whole doctrine of assumption and occupation of bodies in a chapter: "En quelles formes & façons se monstrent les Diables visibles aux hommes." See *op. cit.,* IV, xiii, 347.

[38] Boguet, *op. cit.,* x, 26 ff. See also Remy, *op. cit.,* I, viii, 30; Perkins, *op. cit.,* i, 612.

[39] Scot, *Discourse,* xvii, 433. Scot here neglects to emphasize a necessary distinction between the *assumed* bodies which Roman Catholic theologians admitted to spirits acting in the world, and the peculiar elementary bodies which Platonists such as Psellos ascribed to daemons as native and constant. No doubt the conceptions were amorphous and mingled in popular usage, and Scot was perhaps

justified from a practical polemical point of view, though not from a dialectical one. Remy makes the distinction, considering "the shapes and forms which they principally assume, not with reference to the quality and difference of the element in which they exist (which has been dealt with by Psellos, *cap. Quomodo Daemones occupent hominem*), but with reference to the demands and exigences of the particular work or task which they have in hand." (*Op. cit.*, I, xxiii, 69.)

On air as *corpus homogenium,* hence no substance for devils' bodies, see Deacon and Walker, *op. cit.*, III, 82.

Le Loyer on the Catholic side denies that spirits have peculiar bodies at all, insists on assumed ones. (*Op. cit.*, I, v, 32; III, i, 172–3.) Taillepied agrees and specifically rebukes Psellos. (*Op. cit.*, xvi, 111–2.)

[40] Scot, *Discoverie,* IV, x, 68; xi, 69. See also III, xix, 56. By "vitall spirits" Scot means, of course, the highly rarefied bodily liquors and vapors which Vesalius and other physiologists of the day held to be the physiological basis of corporeal animation. On Vesalius' doctrine of the bodily spirits see William McDougal, *Body and Mind,* London, 1923. For exposition of the general doctrine of the spirits and humors see Miss Lily Bess Campbell, *Shakespeare's Tragic Heroes,* Cambridge, 1930.

[41] Boguet, *op. cit.*, xi, 29.

[42] *Ibid.*, xiii, 36. See also Aquinas, *Summa,* Pt. I, Q. 51, A. 3, reply to Obj. 3; and for the opinion among Renaissance witchmongers: Guazzo, *op. cit.*, I, xi, 30; James, *op. cit.*, III, iii, 67; Remy, *op. cit.*, I, vi, 11; Bodin, *op. cit.*, II, vii, 276; *Malleus Maleficarum,* Pt. I, Q. 3, p. 26; and many others.

[43] *Malleus Maleficarum,* Pt. I, Q. 3, p. 27. Aquinas says (*Summa,* Pt. I, Q. 51, A. 3, reply to Obj. 2): "The body assumed is united to the angel not as its form, nor merely as its mover, but as its mover represented by the assumed movable body." This is in answer to the objection that if angels assumed bodies, all bodies moved by them would have to be said to be assumed. It is a nice question whether or not the incubus assumes as part of his body the semen he uses. It seems at the moment of the *actus* representative of, as well as controlled by, the demon, though genetically it is of the human male from whom it was taken.

[44] Aquinas explains that the assumed body is not what Scot calls an "organicall" body in construction and function, but only in appearance. The angels presenting such bodies "appear to be living men, although they really are not. For the bodies are merely assumed for this purpose, that the spiritual properties and works of the angels may be manifested by the properties of man and his works." "Vital functions can be performed in the assumed bodies of angels, as to that which is common in such operations [*i.e.*, in so far as walking is a thing in common with the local motions which angels can impart to bodies, speech a thing in common with sound]; but not as to that which is special to living subjects [*i.e.*, digestion, for example, a process peculiar to animal vitality]." (*Summa,* Pt. I, Q. 51, A. 3.)

See Taillepied, *op. cit.*, xv, 105, on demons' ability to take what forms they like and simulate the functions proper to those forms, though they have no sex or other natural affinity with those functions.

[45] *Discoverie,* IV, xi, 61.

[46] Wier, *op. cit.*, III, xix, 285; I, xxiv, 107.

[47] King James, *op. cit.*, III, iii, 69.

[48] Scot, *Discourse,* xiv, 430.

[49] See, for instance, Boguet, *op. cit.*, v, 10, 12; Le Loyer, *op. cit.*, IV, ix, 318.

[50] So, the Christian fathers Chrysostom and Origen allege, the prophesying spirit entered into the Pythoness at Delphi. See T. K. Oesterreich, *Possession, Demoniacal and Other,* New York, 1930, p. 315. This idea was, of course, familiar to the sixteenth century polemists. See for instance Bodin, *op. cit.*, II, iii, 209, 212.

[51] Perkins, *op. cit.*, i, 610.

[52] Deacon and Walker, *op. cit.*, II, 40, 41. They held that possession occurred only in Biblical times. Taillepied says, however (*op. cit.*, xvi, 112): "It is very certain spirits can insinuate themselves into the most material, compact and preponderable hyle; they can enter and possess the bodies of men dead or alive; and these they can move and energize, directing them and tormenting them, making such bodies perform unnatural and extraordinary feats."

[53] Deacon and Walker, *op. cit.,* II, 40.

[54] Deacon and Walker, *op. cit.,* VII, 226. This is vague language and leaves it uncertain whether obsession is simply the devil's concealed claw in all the ordinary afflictions of life, or whether he is overtly and actively creating special afflictions. The former interpretation would, perhaps, have been satisfactory to Scot, who cites (*Discourse,* xvi, 432) Calvin that the devil is "that power of wickednesse that standeth against the kingdom of justice." But Deacon and Walker seem certainly to have held the devil to be an essential spirit (see Dialogue I); whereas that Scot did so is not always apparent (see the *Discourse* xxxii, 453, 454) despite his explicit admission that devils are "living creatures." (See note 8 *ante.*)

[55] King James, *op. cit.,* III, i, 57, 62. Summers in his *History of Witchcraft,* p. 202, makes this distinction. See also p. 8 of *The Story of the Devil* by Arturo Graf, translated by E. N. Stone, New York, 1931.

[56] Wier, *op. cit.,* I, xx, 77. He says he follows St. Clement. See books II and IV of the *Recognitions.*

[57] Wier, *op. cit.,* III, viii, 226–9. Aquinas says that "Both a good and a bad angel by their own natural power can move the human imagination. This may be explained as follows. For it was said above [Pt. I, Q. 110, A. 3] that corporeal nature obeys the angels as regards local movement, so that whatever can be caused by the local movement of bodies is subject to the natural power of the angels. Now it is manifest that imaginative apparitions are sometimes caused in us by the local movement of animal spirits and humours. Hence Aristotle says (*De Insomniis,* iii) when assigning the cause of visions in dreams, that when an animal sleeps, the blood descends in abundance to the sensitive principle, and movements descend with it, that is, the impressions left from the movements of sensible things which movements are preserved in the animal spirits, and move the sensitive principle; so that a certain appearance ensues, as if the sensitive principle were being then changed by the external objects themselves. Indeed, the commotion of the spirits and humours may be so great that such appearances may even occur to those who are awake, as is seen in mad people, and the like. So, as this happens by a natural disturbance of the humours, and sometimes also by the will of man who voluntarily imagines what he previously experienced, so also the same may be done by the power of a good or a bad angel, sometimes with alienation from the bodily senses, sometimes without such alienation." (*Summa,* Pt. I, Q. 111, A. 3.)

[58] Cotta says (*op. cit.,* iv, 25) that all good angels are either "tutelar" or, as the name indicates, messengers. Le Loyer also makes this classification. He says (*op. cit.,* III, i, 172) of angels: "Ils ont en garde les hommes, & sont liez d'amitié auecques eux: non seulement, inuisible, ils ont defendu les hommes desquels ils ont la tutelle, ains souuent ont apparu visibles aux sainct personnages, . . . D'autre part les anges sont les ministres de Dieu, &, come Philon Iuif escrit, ses ambassadeurs: par lesquels il enuoye aux hommes ses saincts Edicts & ordonnances, arrestées en son conseil estroit."

[59] Le Loyer says (*op. cit.,* III, ix, 229): "Ie suis bien informé auecques l'Eglise, que le ministre des Anges est pour le plus inuisible, si est-ce que les Anges ne laissent pour tant quelquefois, mais rarement & par miracle, de se monstrer aux hommes."

[60] Lavater, *op. cit.,* II, xiv, 161.

[61] Scot, *Discoverie,* V, i, 125; King James, *op. cit.,* III, ii, 65. James says that spirits have testified that they are guardians, but that such spirits are lying devils. For such a testimony see *A True and Faithful Relation of What Passed between Dr. John Dee . . . and some spirits.* This record by Elizabeth's Dr. Dee was published in 1659.

[62] Scot, *Discourse,* x, 424. For Calvin's statement see the *Institutes,* I, xii, 196 of the Beveridge translation, 1845. On the Catholic side, Aquinas explains that the guardian assists man only so far as is consonant with free will. He helps his charge to avoid evil, to incline to good and to reason truly. (*Summa,* Pt. I, Q. 113, A. 1.)

[63] Lavater, *op. cit.,* II, xiv, 161. Le Loyer, too, says that every one has an angel assigned at birth to conduct and govern him until death and that, maugre St. John Chrysostom, even pagans have such helpers. (*Op. cit.,* III, viii, 220.)

[64] Agrippa cites indiscriminately Hermes, Iamblichus, and "the theologians",

i.e., fathers and scholastics. He says it is uncertain whether every man has only one guardian angel or more than one. "We think there are more. . . ." See the 1651 English translation of the *Occult Philosophy,* III, xx, 406. See also chapter xxi.

65 Agrippa, *op. cit.,* III, xxii, 410 ff.

66 See Rudolph Steiner's *The Mystics of the Renaissance,* London, 1911, for the view that Agrippa did not hold spirits to act in the world of sense, that by spirits he signified natural processes.

The evident affinity of Agrippa's conception of the guardian angel with the classical idea of the tutelary genius or personal daemon is not enlightening on this point. The Platonic daemon might be variously a personal being, an abstraction from human mentality, or an intelligible stage of emanation. The Stoic daemon was man's good reason. See Zeller's *The Stoics, Epicureans and Sceptics,* London, 1892, p. 351; the treatises of Plutarch and Apuleius on the daemon of Socrates; Olympiodorus' commentary on Plato's daemon as conscience; Plotinus on the daemon as the highest power of a man's soul, and Porphyry's *Letter to Anebo,* as translated by Thomas Taylor in his *Mysteries of the Egyptians,* London, 1885.

67 Augustine and other fathers developed this doctrine. Aquinas restates it, *Summa,* Pt. I, Q. 57, A. 3.

68 James, *op. cit.,* I, i, 5. See also Perkins, *op. cit.,* ii, 617.

69 Perkins, *op. cit.,* ii, 617; Remy, *op. cit.,* III, x.

70 See, for instance, Bodin, *op. cit.,* I, vi, vii.

71 Cotta, *op. cit.,* vi, 36. Aquinas says: ". . . if we take a miracle in the strict sense, the demons cannot work miracles, nor can any creature, but God alone: since in the strict sense a miracle is something done out the order of the entire created nature, under which order every power of a creature is contained. But sometimes miracles may be taken in a wide sense, for whatever exceeds the human power and experience. And thus demons can work miracles, that is, things which rouse man's astonishment, by reason of their being beyond his power and outside his sphere of knowledge. For even a man by doing what is beyond the power and knowledge of another leads him to marvel at what he has done, so that in a way he seems to that man to have worked a miracle." (*Summa,* Pt. I, Q. 114, A. 4.)

The Jesuit, Martin Delrio, is careful in his *Disquisitionum Magicarum* to call magic an art *non supernaturalem.* He does so, he says, to exclude from his definition true miracles, which are the work of God only. See Bk. I, ch. ii, p. 2 of the Lyons 1608 edition.

72 Perkins, *op. cit.,* i, 609, 610. See also Delrio, *op. cit.,* Bk. II, Q. 7, p. 63; James, *op. cit.,* I, vi, 22.

73 Boguet, *op. cit.,* Preface, p. xlii; Guazzo, *op. cit.,* I, iii, 7. Aquinas says: "As we have said above [see note 35 *ante*] corporeal matter does not obey either good or bad angels at their will, so that demons be able by their power to transmute matter from one form to another; but they can employ certain seeds that exist in the elements of the world, in order to produce these effects, as Augustine says (*De Trin.* iii, 8, 9). Therefore it must be admitted that all the transformations of corporeal things which can be produced by certain natural powers, to which we must assign the seeds above mentioned, can alike be produced by the operation of the demons, by the employment of these seeds; such as the transformation of certain things into serpents or frogs, which can be produced by putrefaction. On the contrary, those transformations which cannot be produced by the power of nature, cannot in reality be effected by the operation of the demons; for instance, that the human body be changed into the body of a beast, or that the body of a dead man return to life. And if at times something of this sort seems to be effected by the operation of demons, it is not real but a mere semblance of reality.

"Now this may happen in two ways. Firstly, from within; in this way a demon can work on man's imagination and even on his corporeal senses, so that something seems otherwise than it is, as explained above [see note 57 *ante*]. It is said indeed that this can be done sometimes by the power of certain bodies. Secondly, from without: for just as he can from the air form a body of any form and shape, and assume it so as to appear in it visibly: so, in the same way he can clothe any corporeal thing with any corporeal form, so as to appear therein." (*Summa,* Pt. I, Q. 114, A. 4.)

Delrio distinguished (*op. cit.,* Bk. II, Q. 6, p. 61 ff.) the three sorts of effects demonic magic could achieve: true, false and mixed, with examples of each.

[74] Perkins, *op. cit.,* i, 611. See also Guazzo, *op. cit.,* I, iii, 7; Wier, *op. cit.,* I, x, 30.

[75] Deacon and Walker, *op. cit.,* V, 143 ff. See also Wier, *op. cit.,* II, viii, 153; and *Malleus Maleficarum,* Pt. I, Q. 1, p. 8.

[76] Remy, *op. cit.,* III, xi, 175; Guazzo, *op. cit.,* I, iv, 9. See also Cotta, *op. cit.,* vi, 39, on miracles true to the eye though not in substance.

[77] See Guazzo, *op. cit.,* I, xiii, 51; Boguet, *op. cit.,* xlvii, 146; Remy, *op. cit.,* II, v, 112; Le Loyer, *op. cit.,* II, vii, 139 for these points.

[78] Bodin, *op. cit.,* II, vi, 260, 268.

[79] Scot, *Discoverie,* V, ii, 74.

[80] *Ibid.,* V, vi, 81. To this Deacon and Walker agree and cite Wier, *De Praestigiis, lib.* 4, *cap.* 23. But that this did not represent a unanimous or sure opinion among physicians is shown by the fact that Agrippa, Wier's master, seems to hold (*Vanity of the Arts and Sciences,* London 1684, xliv) that witches can effect metamorphoses by means inclining toward "the snares and Delusions of the Evil Spirits." He cites the transformation of Nebuchadnezzar, but it is not clear whether or not he held it veritable. Bodin triumphs in the same example (*op. cit.,* II, vi, 267), but King James says (*op. cit.,* III, i, 61) that Nebuchadnezzar's affliction was a mental illness, and Scot (*op. cit.,* V, vi, 81) rebukes Bodin for taking literally what is intended figuratively in scripture, or worse, for conferring upon demons a power which scripture seems to credit to God. Boguet (*op. cit.,* xlvii, 145) says that the monarch was not changed, but merely thought he was, and Le Loyer agrees (*op. cit.,* II, vii, 144).

[81] Wier, *op. cit.,* IV, xxiii, 436–7; IV, xxii, 432.

[82] *Ibid.,* IV, xxii, 432

[83] *Ibid.,* IV, xxv, 441.

[84] Remy says (*op. cit.,* II, v, 112) that lycanthropes attack and pull down cattle with their teeth. Perkins says (*op. cit.,* i, 610) that a possessing devil can work in the body of his victim "not only according to the principles of the nature thereof, but as far as the strength and abilitie of those principles will possibly reach and extend themselves."

Notes on Chapter III

[1] Thus Thomas Erastus in the second of his two dialogues on witchcraft says that magicians use books and diligence whereas witches do not. This would have been generally accepted though his previous statement that witches and magicians alike derive their power from devils would have been unacceptable to the Agrippa of the *Occult Philosophy,* and, of course, to the sceptics on devils. See Erastus, *Deux Dialogues,* appended to Wier, *op. cit.,* p. 821.

Malleus Maleficarum says (Pt. II, Q. 1, p. 95) that witchcraft is not taught in books, nor practiced by the learned, and has but one foundation [*i.e.,* the express compact]. Its use of the word witchcraft it seems to make depend entirely on this characteristic. But that it regards necromancy also as devil working is clear.

Le Loyer says (*op. cit.,* IV, viii, 309) that he can scarcely make any distinction between magicians and witches. Both serve the devil though the former do so in a somewhat less degraded manner than the latter.

[2] Scot says (*Discoverie,* XV, i, 313): "What will not couseners or witches take upon them to doo? Wherein will they professe ignorance? Aske them anie question, they will undertake to resolve you, even of that which none but God knoweth. And to bring their purposes the better to passe, as also to winne further credit unto the counterfet art which they professe, they procure confederates, whereby they worke wonders. And when they have either learning, eloquence, or nimblenesse of hands to accompanie their confederacie, or rather knaverie, then (forsooth) they passe the degree of witches, and intitle themselves to the name of conjurors. . . . These are

no small fools, they go not to worke with a baggage tode, or a cat, as witches doo; but with a kind of majestie, and with authoritie they call up by name, and have at their commandement seventie and nine principall and princelie divels, who have under them, as their ministers, a great multitude of legions of pettie divels. . . ."

In another place (*Ibid.*, XV, xxxi, 380) he says: "Thus you see that conjurors are no small fooles. For whereas witches being poore and needie, go from doore to doore for releefe, have they never so manie todes or cats at home, or never so much hogs doong or charvill about them, or never so manie charmes in store: these conjurors (I saie) have gotten them offices in the church of *Rome*, whereby they have obtained authoritie and great estimation."

[3] But Agrippa was one of the first successfully to defend a woman accused of witchcraft. In his letters detailing the case he ridicules and condemns the *Malleus Maleficarum*. See Henry Morley's *Life of Agrippa*, II, 60.

[4] Of this position Wier makes a general statement in the Preface where he outlines the organization of the entire work. Most of the particular points I have mentioned are covered in detail in the third book. Wier leaves it somewhat uncertain how far he believed a magician actually and detachedly able to coerce spirits and how far reliant on a tacit compact which his charms established and on the spirit's complaisance. Bodin points out (*Refutation des opinions de Jean Wier*, appended to *La Denomomanie*, p. 539) that Wier himself seems to agree that effective pacts can be made with the devil. Bodin cites chapters iv, viii, xxxiv of book II, chapter xiv of book IV, and chapter ix of book V from *De Praestigiis*.

[5] King James recognized the contention that the Biblical pronouncements turned against witches were originally intended to apply only to the *magicien infame*, in a chapter in which, he says, it is *Proued by Scripture that such a thing* [*as witchcraft*] *can be*. He makes little answer to Wier's argument except to assert a contrary belief. See the *Daemonologie*, II, i, 27.

[6] Wier, *op. cit.*, III, iii, 209 ff.

[7] *Ibid.*, III, v, 218.

[8] *Ibid.*, III, vi, 220.

[9] *Ibid.*, III, xi, 236 ff.

[10] Among English writers on witchcraft George Gifford takes almost the same line as Wier. Like Wier he exculpates the old women ordinarily accused of *Maleficium*, by casting the blame on the machinations of devils who of themselves perform the injurious deeds which they try to fasten on innocent villagers. Like Wier, Gifford insists that the Biblical injunctions against witches are aimed at a class of professional conjurors, "wise women" and "wise men," who profess to do good by good means, to counteract *maleficia*, but are really tools and accomplices of the devil who achieves a tacit compact with, hence a claim to the souls of, all who resort to them.

As Miss Beatrice White points out in the preface to the Shakespeare Association facsimile of Gifford's *Dialogue Concerning Witches*, Gifford's work is homely and insular in its particulars, for its whole argument is to rustics. But in general doctrine it is certainly in the main stream of European demonology.

[11] "My question [says Scot, p. xvii of his Epistle to the *Discoverie*] is not (as manie fondlie suppose) whether there be witches or naie: but whether they can doo such miraculous works as are imputed to them."

This ironical distinction has, it seems to me, been widely misinterpreted. Professor F. E. Schelling in a paragraph devoted to establishing the credulity of the learned in the sixteenth century, says condoningly: "Excellent Reginald Scot, although he humanely wrote a very long book to display the shallowness of the evidence on which witches were convicted, did not venture to deny the existence of witchcraft. . . ." (See *Shakespeare and Demi-Science*, p. 159.) Similarly Professor A. W. Ward in the Introduction to his *Faustus* (p. xlix, 4th edition) says that Scot "did not venture to assert that witchcraft was a fiction." The Rev. Montague Summers in the introduction to his edition of the *Discoverie* says (p. xxix) that Scot cries "ingenuously" that he does not deny witches, then expends five hundred odd pages denying them.

Scot did not deny witches because he held the term properly applicable to poisoners and impostors; that witches existed in the sense that the *Malleus,* for instance, put upon the word he did, of course, spend his pages denying.

[12] Scot, *Discoverie,* VI, i, 89.

[13] *Ibid.,* VI, ii, 93.

[14] *Ibid.,* XVI, ii, 397.

[15] Cotta mentions (*op. cit.,* ix, 70) in a footnote that Scot erroneously takes witches and impostors to be one. King James in his preface calls Scot a Sadducee and devotes half a page to refuting the claim that witches are melancholy persons, *i.e.,* persons of diseased imagination. (*Op. cit.,* II, i, 30.)

[16] Bodin, *op. cit.,* I, i, 49; Perkins, *op. cit.,* v, 636.

[17] Bodin, *op. cit.,* I, vi, 140; Perkins, *op. cit.,* ii, 614 ff.

[18] Bodin, *op. cit.,* II, iv, 218.

[19] Guazzo, *op. cit.,* I, vi, 17. He cites Trithemius on the point. Perkins explains (*op. cit.,* vii, 640) that since the covenant with Satan is an "unlawful league" there need not be a "mutual bond."

[20] Remy, *op. cit.,* II, vi, 114; II, ix, 120. See also *Malleus Maleficarum,* Pt. I, Q. 2, p. 12. Gifford in his preface, *op. cit.,* gives a concise statement to the same effect.

[21] Boguet says (*op. cit.,* ix, 24) that the witch renounces her baptism and receives a devilish one. De Lancre, *Tableau de l'Inconstance de Mauvais Anges,* Paris, 1612, II, i, 74, says that a neophyte witch was bidden to renounce her Savior, the Virgin, the saints and baptism. Remy and James touch incidentally the point of the renunciation of baptism. James says explicitly (*op. cit.,* II, ii, 33) that it is renounced, and Remy seems to hold a similar view (*op. cit.,* I, v, 9). None of the witchmongers meet Wier's contention that the benefit of baptism could not be escaped. The witchmongers held the contract veritable as a sin, whatever its status as a bargain.

[22] That this was true in England as well as on the continent—in the theory, at least—is shown by such asseverations as this from an English witch tract: "Therefore though it were so, that neither Witch nor Diuell could doe these things [*maleficia*] yet *Let not a Witch liue,* saith God, and *Let them dye,* (saith the law of England) that haue conversation with Spirits, and presume to blaspheme the name of God with spells and incantations." See p. 26 of *The Wonderful Discoverie of the Witchcrafts of Margaret and Philip Flower . . . ,* London, 1619, as reprinted in *A Collection of Rare and Curious Tracts Relating to Witchcraft . . . ,* London, 1838. See, too, p. xli of Professor G. L. Burr's introduction to H. C. Lea's *Materials toward a History of Witchcraft,* Philadelphia, 1939.

[23] Bodin, *op. cit.,* II, ii, iii, iv.

[24] Delrio says (*op. cit.,* I, ii, 2) that as to final cause magic is good if the intentions of the operator are good and his means lawful, as natural and artifical (mathematical) magic are. But other magic is by tacit pact with demons and thus is idolatry. Kaspar Peucer, Melancthon's son-in-law, says (*Les Devins, ou Commentaires des Principales Sortes de Divination. . . .* Paris, 1584, V, iii, 211) that some have distinguished magic from "Sorcellerie" as that which deals with good daemons, not with evil. His further comment makes it clear that he himself, even though he treats of the two separately, considers them at bottom one, save that magic is more pretentious in its means.

[25] James, *op. cit.,* I, ii, 7.

[26] *Ibid.,* I, v, 15.

[27] Erastus says that no magician can perform anything out of nature except he give himself to the devil; at least he must have the aid of devils, even though there is no explicit bargain. Magicians may think that they work by an art Solomon used and that it is of God; but witches know that their power is from hell. (*Second Dialogue,* p. 819–21.) Le Loyer says that theurgy, or white magic, is as much prohibited by God as is Necromancy, and that in theurgy also devils "se presentent sous le nom de Dieu, Anges, sainctes ames & Heros." (*Op. cit.,* VII, v, 721.)

[28] Quoted from Morley's *Life of Agrippa,* Book I, p. 217 ff. Agrippa's letters to Trithemius and others on the *Occult Philosophy* are published in most of the sixteenth century editions of the work and in the English translation of 1651.

[29] Bodin, *op. cit.,* I, iii, 89, 90–2; v, 129–30; II, i, 160–2, *et cetera.*

[30] Almost all authors on theory of magic use it, and even Bodin appeals to it

respectfully. (*Op. cit.,* III, iii, 83.) He mentions, too, that there had been made at Rome a more nearly complete translation than Ficino's.

[31] Delrio notes (*op. cit.,* Bk. II, Q. 2, p. 53) this distinction of magic by the Neo-Platonists into *Albam* and *Nigram,* or *Theurgia* and *Goetia.* Most of the orthodox writers comment on the distinction as a false one. Many say that in primeval times magic was a true and lawful thing, but that "the giants" or Zoroaster corrupted it.

Mr. Hardin Craig says (*The Enchanted Glass,* p. 5) that "white" magic was "natural" magic. The divisions of the *Occult Philosophy* and distinctions made in many another sixteenth century work indicate that this needs some qualifying. Into the magic which Agrippa sought to justify as "white," religion entered as the vivifying element. It is definitely a supernatural thing. Agrippa's "natural" magic is subsidiary to and a part of his ceremonial magic and it is for the latter that he claims consideration, for it was only this, the magic dealing with spirits, that orthodoxy attacked vigorously.

[32] Thomas Whittaker says (*The Neo-Platonists,* Cambridge, 1901, p. 113) in a footnote on a passage of Porphyry's *Sententiae:* "All changes, even in bodies, have their true cause in immaterial being. Material approach or contact is not an efficient cause, but accompanies as its 'accident' the real order of metaphysical causation." *The Mysteries of the Egyptians* explains that the superior genera are not in bodies but rule them. (See Taylor's translation, I, viii, 39.) On magic by the sympathies of the universe see Plotinus, *Enneads* IV, 4, 40 in Guthrie's translation. Proclus in the fragments of his *Ten Doubts Concerning Providence* says: "That the Gods, with an exempt transcendency, extend their providence to all things, but that daemons, dividing their superessential subsistence, receive the guardianship of different herds of animals, distributing the providence of the Gods, as Plato says, as far as the ultimate division." Quoted from a footnote in Taylor's translation of the *Mysteries,* p. 364.

[33] *Mysteries,* III, xxviii, 191 ff.; xxxi, 200 ff.; IV, x, 217.

[34] ". . . the perfect efficacy of ineffable works, which are divinely performed in a way surpassing all intelligence, and the power of inexplicable symbols, which are known only to the gods, impart theurgic union." (See the *Mysteries,* II, xi, 109.)

[35] *Occult Philosophy,* I, i.

[36] "Of things which are perpetually effected in sacred rites, some have a certain arcane cause, and which is more excellent than reason; others are consecrated from eternity to the superior genera as symbols; others preserve a certain other image, just as nature, which is effective of invisible reasons, expresses certain visible formations; others are adduced for the sake of honour, or have for their end some kind of similitude, or familiarity and alliance; and some procure what is useful to us, or in a certain respect purify and liberate our human passions, or avert some other of those dire circumstances which happen to us." (*Mysteries,* I, xi, 51–2.)

[37] "For the illumination which takes place through invocations, is spontaneously visible and self-perfect; is very remote from all downward attraction; proceeds into visibility through divine energy and perfection, and as much surpasses our voluntary motion as the divine will of the good transcends a deliberately chosen life. Through this will, therefore, the Gods being benevolent and propitious, impart their light to theurgists in unenvying abundance, calling upwards their souls to themselves, and accustoming them, while they are yet in body, to be separated from bodies and to be led round to their eternal and intelligible principle.

"But it is evident, from the effects themselves, that what we now say is the salvation of the soul. For the soul in contemplating blessed spectacles, acquires another life, energizes according to another energy, and is then rightly considered as no longer ranking in the order of man." (*Mysteries,* I, xii, 55.)

It was possible to conceive the rites of theurgy, performed by a mortal, as initiating a kind of upward sweep in which the gods themselves, though willingly and according to their divine natures, were caught. Theurgical operations are not, however, a matter of intellection, though intellect leads a man toward them. ". . . neither are divine causes precedaneously called into energy by our intellectation; but it is requisite to consider these, and all the best dispositions of the soul, and also the purity pertaining to us, as certain concauses; the things which properly excite the divine will being divine synthemata [the inexplicable theurgic symbols or signs] themselves." (*Ibid.*, II, xi, 110.)

[38] *Occult Philosophy,* I, xxxviii, 75. Agrippa is here elucidating a phase of "Natural Magic"; that is, of the attraction of superior powers by the arcane juxtaposition to them of material things. The principle is the same for ceremonial attraction by means of anagogic utterances, ritually consecrated materials and figures, *et cetera.* Indeed, as appears in Book III, the inferior branches of magic—the natural and the mathematical—are drawn to the service of ceremonial magic. See Book III, xxxiii, on the three sorts of bonds for spirits.

[39] *Ibid.,* III, iii, 350; lxii, 540, and elsewhere.

[40] *Ibid.,* III, iv. Agrippa cites among superstitions which have a large measure of truth, hence a potency in magic, Judaism. Le Loyer devotes a chapter (*op. cit.,* IV, iv, 281 ff.) on superstition as an attraction to demons, largely to Jews and Jewish magicians.

[41] Bodin, *op. cit.,* I, iii, 89–92.

[42] *Ibid.,* II, i, 161. In a similar vein Le Loyer slights magicians' claims, though he admits some of their terminology. He says that sortilege, predictions, enchantments, divination, *et cetera* are called *Magie,* and the search for things sublime is theurgy or white magic, representing the devil-born persuasion of magicians that they can evoke angels or souls of the blessed dead. (*Op. cit.,* IV, xv, 364.) Delrio, as already noted (note 31 *ante*) remarks this distinction of magic into black and white, saying that the Platonists call magic by good angels white, but that such angels do not participate in magic. (*Op. cit.,* Bk. II, Q. 2, p. 53.)

[43] Bodin, *op. cit.,* II, i, 160, 162.

[44] Magicians did not ordinarily confess that their ceremonies to spirits amounted to worship of the spirits, though they were aware of the charge. Scot cites from the magicians a charm for binding Bealpheares *without prayer or sacrifice to him.* (*Discoverie,* XV, xix, 350.) In the *Mysteries of the Egyptians* the observances paid to every rank of spirits seem to have been conceived as worship though not in the Christian sense of complete prostration. Agrippa says that prayer may legitimately be said to heavenly beings other than God, who are entrusted by God with administration of particular services of which the officiant stands in need. (*Op. cit.,* III, lviii, 530; lxi, 539.) This is based on the ceremonial adorations recommended by Proclus and other sacerdotal mages of the Neo-Platonists, and confirmed to Agrippa by the Catholic distinction that angels may be worshipped to the degree of the inferior honor called *dulia. Latria* is reserved for God alone. On the worship of the spirits of the stars as sanctioned by Aquinas see Agrippa, *op. cit.,* III, xv, 389.

[45] Augustine says that the miracles of Christianity "were wrought by simple confidence and devout faith, not by incantation and spells compounded by an art of depraved curiosity." (Quoted from Thorndike, *History of Magic and Experimental Science,* I, 505, where the citation is *De civitate Dei,* X, 9; PL vol. 41.)

[46] Aquinas quotes from Augustine: "When magicians do what holy men do, they do it for a different end and by a different right. The former do it for their own glory: the latter for the glory of God: the former, by certain private compacts: the latter by the evident assistance and command of God, to whom every creature is subject." (*Summa,* Pt. I, Q. 114, A. 5.)

[47] Perhaps the entire strife between the church and magicians rooted in a fundamental opposition between the principles of magic and those of religion. Frazer points out that religion "clearly assumes that the course of nature is to some extent elastic or variable, and that we can persuade or induce the mighty beings who control it to deflect for our benefit the current of events from the channel in which they would otherwise flow." Magic, on the other hand, he says, even spirit magic, necessarily assumes the order of nature rigid and invariable so that a cause produces arbitrarily a specific effect. Religion acts with prayer and submission, magic by compulsion. Frazer says that when magic deals with spirits, "personal agents of the kind assumed by religion," it "treats them exactly in the same fashion as it treats inanimate agents, that is, it constrains or coerces instead of conciliating or propitiating them as religion would do. Thus it assumes that all personal beings, whether human or divine, are in the last resort subject to those impersonal forces which

control all things, but which nevertheless can be turned to account by any one who knows how to manipulate them by appropriate ceremonies and spells."

Frazer says further that magic which works by spirits is alloyed with religion, *i.e.,* its ceremonies are tinged with worship. This is especially so of magic under Christianity; it is precisely this alloyed magic—or contaminated religion—which the church so constantly fought. Under the Christian scheme of the universe the fundamental assumption of magic by spirits as stated by Frazer could never be warrantable, for in the Christian scheme the ultimate "forces which control all things" are not "impersonal," but are comprised in a supreme volition, an infinite spirit, who cannot, properly conceived, be "turned to account" by manipulation. The will of God, the church could insist, is exempt; all natural order in His universe is subordinate, subject to infringement at His caprice—though caprice cannot be ascribed to God. Such a spirit can be the object of worship only, and a worship whose earthly purpose is devotion, life to the glory of God. With this any form of magic is incompatible since the end of magic is the enhancement of the personality in itself. (See *The Golden Bough,* I, 220–5.)

[48] Plotinus says in the course of a discussion of providence: "Although I am able to make any desired decision, nevertheless my decision enters into the plan of the universe, because my nature has not been introduced into this plan subsequently; but it includes me and my character." (*Enneads,* II, 3, 3, in Guthrie's translation, p. 1079.)

[49] Proclus in his treatise, *Ten Doubts Concerning Providence,* says in discussion of the third doubt: "Moreover sublunary affairs demonstrate the existence of a particular Providence, inasmuch as every one of them somewhat affects the whole universe, inasmuch as nothing is superfluous, even though we might not be able to define every one of its causes. Further, the power of Providence is affected by the characteristics of certain souls, which must be as influential as any other factors." (Guthrie's translation, p. 23.)

[50] Whittaker says (*op. cit.,* p. 56) that in the universe as conceived by Plotinus "All the producing causes and their effects in every grade always existed and always will exist. The production by the higher causes has the undeviating character of natural necessity, and is not by voluntary choice and discursive reason, which are secondary resultants within the world of particulars." The theurgist realized in himself these non-temporal causes. Proclus in the last of his *Ten Doubts* says: ". . . the providential energies of souls do not consist in reasonings conjectural of futurity, like those of political human characters, but in the God-derived soul's illumination in the unifier. Hence being surrounded with the transcendently united splendour of deity, they see the temporal untemporally, that which is divisible indivisibly, and everything local unlocally; and they function not from themselves, but from the powers by which they are illuminated." (See Guthrie's translation, p. 54.)

[51] Both Neo-Platonism and Christianity conceived the administration of providence as largely resident in the activity of spirits intermediate in nature and office between man and supreme deity. There was this difference, however: Neo-Platonism regarded such activity as the usual—if not the entire—process of causality in the sublunary world, as arranged according to a graduated scheme of motivation or stimulation from superessential gods down through irrational daemons; whereas Christianity regarded such activity of spirits as conveying the extraordinary oversight of God who usually administered only specially by spirits, governed ordinarily by "natural" means. See, for instance, *Malleus Maleficarum* Pt. II, Q. 1, pp. 92, 93 on how God's grace is usually shed through the stars, sometimes by special angelic activity. See also *Occult Philosophy,* III, xii, 379.

There was a further difference in the conception of the spirits themselves. Neo-Platonists called the intermediate spirits generally daemons—including gods, archons, heroes, and other ranks of beings—and held them good or evil according to station, *i.e.,* according as they were free from or submerged in matter; held them to vary widely in powers and functions and substance. Christianity, on the other hand, held that spirits were of a single created essence, that they were, like man, responsible moral beings some of whom had rebelled, been eternally dismissed from God's presence, devoted themselves to fostering evil in the world.

Since paganism thus identified its gods with daemons, Christianity was quick to identify daemons with fallen angels, *i.e.*, devils. To the church, consequently, all magical working by daemons which Neo-Platonists professed, meant working by devils. This added a manifest impiety for Christian magicians, who so far as they were operating according to Neo-Platonic theory of evocation were certainly calling spirits which Christianity labelled evil. Bodin notes (*op. cit.*, II, i, 158) that the Neo-Platonists are careful to define magic as the invocation of *good* spirits, but says that such claims are unwarranted though very insidious.

[52] Various Protestant authors charge this against the Roman church, and also against Puritan clergymen who believed in exorcism. See, for instance, Perkins, *op. cit.*, v, 648.

[53] Agrippa, *op. cit.*, III, xxxii, 447 ff.

[54] Bodin, *op. cit.*, II, i, 167; ii, 180–1. King James, also, says that such procedure is blasphemous and that there is no power inherent in it except that by it the devil recognizes a likely victim. Agrippa seems conscious that the magician must avoid the appearance of binding the Deity by His own holiness and the letter of His promise, that to constrain spirits with the name of God at the will of the utterer seems almost to constrain God. He emphasizes the necessity for prayer, and says that it will not win from God what is unjust. (*Op. cit.*, III, lviii, 529 ff.) The *Arbatel of Magic* says with confidence that God will not deny a true worshipper.

[55] Professor Kittredge says (*History of Witchcraft in Old and New England*, p. 145): "Throughout the middle ages, and in modern times as well, the Christian Church has had to struggle against the abuse of its sacraments, ordinances, ceremonies and holy things for profane purposes, particularly by would-be sorcerers, but also at the hands of well-meaning but ignorant persons who cannot distinguish between a prayer and a spell and who insist on misapplying religious rites and on employing holy objects in unauthorized ways. . . ." Bodin (*op. cit.*, III, v, 508) attacks priests who have fallen into sorcery, saying that they are worse than other witches, deserve the most extreme punishments. See also his arguments against Wier, p. 524–5.

[56] I borrow this phrase, 'priesthood of all believers,' from Professor Vernon Parrington's *Main Currents in American Thought*.

[57] See Egon Friedell's *Cultural History of the Modern Age*, I, 120, 208, 282–3.

[58] Scot, *Discoverie*, XV, xxii, 365.

[59] Perkins says (*op. cit.*, v, 648): "The most learned Papists of this age doe teach and avouche that there is in Gods Church an ordinarie gift and power, whereby some men may cast out deuils and help annoyances that come by Witches. The Protestant is of a contrarie iudgment, and holdeth according to truth, that there is no such ordinarie gift left to the church of God, since the daies of the Apostles." God, he adds, gave abnormal powers to the Apostles to confirm the doctrine, retracted them later in order not to shake the sufficiency of their ministry. Use by Catholics of the name of Jesus, the sign of the cross, and other symbols, Perkins condemns as superstitious.

[60] Lavater, *op. cit.*, II, vi, 124.

[61] *Ibid.*, II, vii, viii, ix, 127 ff.

[62] *Ibid.*, II, x, 145 ff.

[63] *Ibid.*, II, 146.

[64] *Ibid.*, II, v, 119, 121, 122, citing Athanasius and Chrysostom. But Taillepied reverses the argument (*op. cit.*, xix, 130): "Almighty God can and does permit the souls of the dead to return and appear, not very often, indeed, but at any rate not altogether infrequently, when it pleaseth Him to use an extraordinary course, chiefly (it seems) that the evil angel, the prince of darkness, transforming himself into an angel of light, may not wholly deceive simple folk by feigning to be the Spirit of such an one who has passed away. . . . If, then, the devil pretends to be the soul of one departed, it follows that the dead may return; for he is too cunning to pretend an impossibility, since he would be at once found out and his malice exposed."

This reasoning is as good as Lavater's; but in the next chapter Taillepied shows its sophistry when he uses Lavater's very argument to oppose the occult claim that souls linger near graves: "S. Athanasius . . . says that were it the case departed spirits not unseldom appeared near the graves, the demons would seize the opportunity to manifest themselves in the guise and shape of those recently dead, and familiars would pretend they were raised from the dead whereby they would be able to impress upon those who are given to these superstitions all kinds of false doctrines and heresies. . . ." (*Op. cit.*, xx, 137.)

[65] Lavater, *op. cit.*, II, v, 118.

[66] *Ibid.*, II, v, 122; vi, 126; III, vii, 197 ff.

[67] *Ibid.*, II, ii, 103–4; iv, 114; v, 118; xiii, 155.

[68] Bullinger, *op. cit.*, Fourth Decade, Sermon X, p. 100.

[69] Lavater, *op. cit.*, II, xiii, 155 ff. In II, iii, 110, he echoes Bullinger that it is on "those apparitions of spirits, as on a sure foundation their Purgatory is builded." See also II, v, 118.

[70] *Ibid.*, II, iii, 111; ix, 142; xv, 164; III, vi, 194.

[71] See H. O. Taylor's *Thought and Expression in the Sixteenth Century,* II, 54 ff. on the controversy in England on purgatory.

[72] Lavater, *op. cit.*, I, vii, viii, ix, 27 ff.; II, iii, 111.

[73] *Ibid.*, II, ix, 140 ff.; v, 120; xiv, 160; xv, 163; I, xvi, 72. He cites Chrysostom at length. King James says (*op. cit.*, III, i, 57) and the Protestant authors in general subscribe, that nearly all apparitions are of demons though there may come an occasional good angel.

[74] Lavater, *op. cit.*, II, xi, 148.

[75] See Le Loyer, *A Treatise of Specters* (the 1605 English translation of the first book of the *Histoires des Spectres*), i, 5. In his insistence that ghosts are wholly supernatural he follows Aquinas; most Catholic pneumatologists concur in the doctrine. The supplement of Aquinas' *Summa* Pt. III, Q. 69, A. 3, has: "There are two ways of understanding a person to leave hell or heaven. First, that he goes from thence simply, so that heaven or hell be no longer his place: and in this way no one who is finally consigned to hell or heaven can go from thence, as we shall state further on (Q. 71, A. 5, *ad* 5). Secondly, they may be understood to go forth for a time: and here we must distinguish what befits them according to the order of nature, and what according to the order of Divine providence; for as Augustine says (*De Cura pro Mort.* xvi): 'Human affairs have their limits other than have the wonders of the Divine power, nature's works differ from those which are done miraculously.' Consequently, according to the natural course the separated souls consigned to their respective abodes are utterly cut off from communication with the living. For according to the course of nature men living in mortal bodies are not immediately united to separate substances, since their entire knowledge arises from the senses: nor would it be fitting for them to leave their abode for any other purpose other than to take part in the affairs of the living. Nevertheless, according to the disposition of Divine Providence separated souls sometimes come forth from their abode and appear to men, as Augustine, in the book quoted above relates of the martyr Felix who appeared visibly to the people of Nola when they were besieged by the barbarians. It is also credible that this may occur sometimes to the damned, and that for man's instruction and intimidation they be permitted to appear to the living; or again in order to seek our suffrages, as to those who are detained in purgatory, as evidenced by many instances related in the fourth book of the *Dialogues*. There is, however, this difference between the saints and the damned, that the saints can appear when they will to the living, but not the damned; for even as the saints while living in the flesh are able to work wonders, which can only be done miraculously by the Divine power, and cannot be done by those who lack this gift, so it is not unfitting for the souls of the saints to be endowed with a power in virtue of their glory, so that they are able to appear wondrously to the living, when they will: while the others are unable to do so unless they be sometimes permitted."

[76] See Aquinas, *Summa,* Pt. III, Q. 69, A. 3.

[77] I have dealt only briefly with this controversy over the appearance of ghosts because it seems epitomized in Lavater and Le Loyer, and of their clash there exists already Miss Yardley's full and excellent summary in the Appendix to the Shakespeare Association's Lavater.

[78] Le Loyer, *Histoires des Spectres,* Paris, 1605, V, vi, 510 ff.

[79] The strictly orthodox Taillepied says: "When the subject of the appearance of Spirits and ghosts is being discussed in company of agnostics and unbelievers it is sometimes well to adduce certain examples from profane writers as well as from Holy Writ, for to such a height of impudence are we arrived that men who question the Word of God actually dare to say, Ah yes, if that is in Plutarch, I will believe it; or, If Cicero says so, such is assuredly the case. It would seem as if we were only to accept the statements of the Bible in so far as they coincide with the premonitions of these fellows, and I take leave to doubt whether many such have any faith in apparitions. But in order to satisfy and abash their sleeveless effrontery I will now adduce some instances from profane historians." (*Op. cit.*, ix, 43.) On the apocryphal nature of Agrippa's sources see his biographer, Morley.

[80] Aquinas says souls may come from hell also (see note 75 *ante*), but Le Loyer declares the damned confined forever without interim (*op. cit.*, VI, vii, 590). Taillepied seems of two minds, citing (*op. cit.*, xii, 73) a story of a damned soul which returned to warn others, and again (*op. cit.*, xv, 101) a story of a lady who "knew that Spirits do not thus return from perdition."

[81] See Agrippa, *op. cit.*, III, xli, 475 ff.

[82] Le Loyer, *op. cit.*, V, vi.

[83] Scot, *Discourse*, xxvii, 446–7.

[84] Remy, *op. cit.*, II, i, 88. He says that tomb haunters are demons. With this King James agrees. (*Op. cit.*, III, i, 57.)

[85] Lavater denies this. "But it can never be proued by the testimony of holy Scriptures that as good & euil angels, so soules take some shapes upon them." (*Op. cit.*, II, xii, 155.) Agrippa says (III, xli, 476) that the soul enters into the *umbra* (*i.e.*, vestigial shape, astral body) as into an "Aerial body" (*aereu corpus*), and in another place (*cap. cit.*, 480) that the "impure soul of a man who in this life contracted too great a habit to its body doth by a certain inward affection of the elementall body frame another body to it self of the vapours of the elements. . . ." For the orthodox Romanists, Taillepied says (*op. cit.*, xvi, 115) that "if Almighty God allows a soul to appear to living men that soul will take such a body as the Angels employ when they manifest themselves."

[86] Agrippa, *op. cit.*, III, xli, 476.

[87] *Ibid.*, III, xlii, the chapter on necromancy. This doctrine of earth-bound spirits comes, of course, from antiquity. Lavater mentions the same doctrine (*op. cit.*, II, i, 99; III, iv, 187–8). See also *The Hermetic and Alchemical Works of Paracelsus* in Waite's translation, II, 303; Hartman's *Paracelsus*, first edition, pp. 87, 88. Orthodox authors, either Protestant or Catholic, did not, of course, grant the possibility of a true necromancy, mention the practice only to condemn it. They held that operators fetched only devils. Lavater cites (*op. cit.*, II, v, 118) the opinion of Tertullian and of Chrysostom that deceiving demons answer the invocations of necromancers. See also II, vii, 128. Also Le Loyer, *op. cit.*, V, vi, 510; Taillepied, *op. cit.*, xi, 64, xix, 129.

[88] Agrippa, *op. cit.*, III, xli, 481.

Notes on Chapter IV

[1] This is the term of H. W. Herrington in his article "Witchcraft and Magic in the Elizabethan Drama," *Journal of American Folklore*, xxxii, (1919), pp. 447–486. See p. 458.

[2] Charles Edward Whitmore in his *The Supernatural in Tragedy*, Cambridge, 1915. See pp. 217–219.

[3] Quoted from the Rev. Montague Summers' introduction to his edition of Reginald Scot's *Discoverie of Witchcraft*, p. xxviii.

[4] Herrington, *op. cit.*, p. 461.

[5] *Ibid.*, pp. 465–6.

[6] Most witch plays, however, are not tragic, for the witch is seldom a principal character. Further, most witch plays emphasize *maleficia* rather than the devil

dealing which was the efficient means of it. The reason for this was, no doubt, the prevailing use of the devil as a comic figure.

[7] Among the exceptions to this are Chapman's unacted tragedy, *Caesar and Pompey,* and the tragi-comedies, *The Virgin Martyr* by Dekker and Massinger, and *The Birth of Merlin* by Rowley.

Here I exclude fairies. Most sixteenth century pneumatologists recognize fairies on principle as daemons, but they belong exclusively to the folklore branch which is left largely unrationalized by pneumatologists. In view of the many extant works on Elizabethan fairies I have decided not to treat them.

As Professor W. C. Curry demonstrates in his *Shakespeare's Philosophical Patterns,* Baton Rouge, 1937, the witches of *Macbeth* may be regarded as demons, though in common acceptance since Spalding mere hags or, as Shadwell said, creatures wholly out of Shakespeare's imagination.

[8] See "Some Aspects of the Supernatural in English Comedy from the Origins to 1642," by R. R. Potter, pp. 42–45 in the *University of North Carolina Record,* 1934–35.

[9] Herrington says (*op. cit.,* p. 450) that the Merlin fantasy play was never to English taste.

[10] This is Whitmore's term. See the introduction to his *The Supernatural in Tragedy,* Cambridge, 1915.

[11] On the scenes cited above see *post,* pp. 75 ff., 90 ff.

[12] On the scene in *Bussy* see *post,* pp. 75, 90, 113, 115, 122, 134. On *Macbeth,* T. A. Spalding, *Elizabethan Daemonology,* London, 1880, and W. C. Curry, *Shakespeare's Philosophical Patterns.*

[13] For example of such disagreement among the characters of a play consider *Hamlet* as analysed by J. D. Wilson in his essay, "The Ghost-scenes in *Hamlet* in the Light of Elizabethan Spiritualism," originally the introduction to the Shakespeare Association's reprint of Lavater's *Of Ghostes and Spirites,* now incorporated with some changes in Mr. Wilson's *What Happens in Hamlet.*

Notes on Chapter V

[1] E. E. Stoll, "The Objectivity of the Ghosts in Shakespeare," *PMLA,* xxii (1907) 201.

[2] In his notes on *Bacon and Bungay* Mr. Churton Collins says that this name may exist somewhere in "the wilderness of magical literature" and "is hardly likely to have been coined by Greene." Mr. Fleay, he notes, has pointed out an evident relation to the place-name *Baal-Zephon* (Vulgate: Beelsephon), Exodus xiv. 2, Numbers xxxiii. 7. I have not found the name in any manual of magic, but *Beelzephon* as the name of a place and of a pagan god, *i.e.,* demon, is mentioned by Le Loyer in his chapter: *Les Dieux Gentils que l'Escriture saincte prend ordinairement pour Demons.* See the *Discours et histoires des spectres,* 1605, III, vii, 214. The reference is to "l'Idole Beelzephon" as of the place Beelzephon, as mentioned in Exodus.

Greene's Demogorgon, "master of the Fates," appears in that capacity in the infernal cabinet according to Wier. (See Maximilian Rudwin, *The Devil in Legend and Literature,* London, 1931, p. 80). Asmenoth, "ruler of the north" in Greene's play, I do not find. Agrippa, Wier, Scot, the *Grimoire of Honorius,* the *Lemegeton, The Key of Solomon,* all have their kings of the four directions, but none name Asmenoth.

[3] Belphegor is named in Wier's list of the great devils as Ambassador to France. (See Waite, *Book of Black Magic and of Pacts,* p. 156.) Wier mentions him from the Biblical references (Deut. 3.4.; Josuah 22) as 'Moabitarum deus' (*De Praestigiis Daemonum,* Basle, 1568, I, iv, 41). Akercocke is the 'Auerhan' of the Wagner books.

[4] Renaissance daemonology accepted these and other names from classical mythology as readily as it accepted Lucifer, Satan, *et cetera,* from scripture, and Astaroth, Belial, and the rest from eastern cults via scripture. Wier names Pluto

as Prince of Fire (see Waite, *loc. cit.*). Proserpine is in the same list. Le Loyer names Pluto, Dis, *etc.*, among devils. See *A Treatise of Specters,* ii, 11.

[5] On the assumed bodies of daemons as *representative* see *ante,* ch. ii, p. 25, especially note 37, and p. 27, notes 43 and 44.

[6] ". . . there are three degrees, according to the doctrine of Great S. Denis followed of all, that is, we must consider in spiritual creatures three things: *Essence, Facultie, Operation:* By the latter which is the action, we know the facultie and by it the essence." Quoted from *Of Wisdome Three Bookes . . .* by Peter Charron, I, vii, 27.

[7] Waite notes this usage in the *Grimoires* of the seventeenth and eighteenth centuries. I find its earliest occurrence in Fludd, *Utriusque Cosmi Maioris Scilicet et Minoris Metaphysica, Physica atque Technica Historia,* Oppenheimii, 1618, Tract. I, Tom. I, Lib. IV, cap. VII, p. 116 unless the Kabbalistic fragment which McGregor Mathers quotes from Eliphas Levi in an appendix to *The Key of Solomon* be accepted as earlier.

[8] *Occult Philosophy,* III, xxiv, 414.

[9] *Ibid.,* III, xxvii, 432.

[10] *Ibid.,* III, xviii, 397–8.

[11] See Bodin, *La Demonomanie,* Paris, 1598, I, iii, 80; Remy, *Demonolatry* (Summers translation), I, xxiii, 71.

[12] *Malleus Maleficarum,* (Summers translation) Pt. I, Q. 4, p. 30.

[13] Bodin, *op. cit.,* I, i, 50, 52; III, i, 308.

[14] *Occult Philosophy,* III, xviii, 399.

[15] Gifford, *A Dialogue Concerning Witches and Witchcraft,* 1593, C1. I have used the Shakespeare Association Facsimile, Oxford, 1931.

[16] For Agrippa see *ante,* p. 69. *The Arbatel,* aphorism 18: "There are other names of the Olympick spirits delivered by others; but they only are effectual, which are delivered to any one, by the Spirit the revealer, visible or invisible: and they are delivered to every one as they are predestinated: therefore they are called Constellations; and they seldome have any efficacy above 40 years." (P. 234 of Turner's translation, 1655.)

[17] Wier, who follows the *Lemegeton* or some common source in his catalogue of demons, gives a perhaps drolly intended resume of the political organization of hell—an organization modelled, apparently, on a German court. Beelzebub is Supreme Chief of the Infernal Empire, founder of the order of the fly. Satan is leader of the opposition; Astaroth, Grand Treasurer; Lucifer, Lord Chief Justice; and Behemoth merely Grand Cup-Bearer. Whether or not this is intended as foolery, it obviously taxes the demonic names with a bit more than they will bear. It is by no means unique, however. See Scheible's *Kloster,* XI, 350, for an account of a similar ranking of demons somewhat more in accord than Wier's with the ranks as given in *Faustus.*

[18] See Professor A. W. Ward's comment on the etymology of the name in his notes on the *dramatis personae* in his edition of *Faustus.*

[19] See V, ii, 99. All my references on *Faustus* are to Boas' edition.

[20] See his letter: "Marlowe's *Dr. Faustus,*" *Times Literary Supplement,* Dec. 6, 1917.

[21] Scheible's *Kloster* XI, 350, mentions a book printed in 1612, *Praxis Cabulae nigrae Doctoris Johannis Faustii,* which gives Lucifer and Beelzebub as but different names of a single spirit: "Lucifer ist der herrscher oder Kaiser des hollischen Reiches; er heisst auch Beelzebub, Nadannael oder Bludohn (*sic,* Pluto)." On this work see, too, W. Mannhart's *Zauberglaube, und Geheimwissen im Spiegel der Jahrhundert,* Leipzig, 1897.

King James' orthodox *Daemonologie* says (III, v, 76) that we see from Scriptures that Satan and Beelzebub are different names for one spirit, the prince of devils, and that Lucifer is an allegorical term for the same creature.

[22] Gifford says (*op. cit.,* C1): "Moreouer, the deuils be spirits, they haue no bodily shape or likenesse but yet can make an appearance of a shape, as appeareth by the inchanters before Pharao, when their rods were turned into serpents in shew. Exod. 7. And then one deuill can seem to be foure or fiue, and foure or

fiue can seeme to be one: It is therefore but the craft of Satan, to make shewe of more or lesse."

[23] See *post,* p. 82.

[24] A situation parallel to the one in *Faustus* occurs in Dekker's *If this be not a good play, the diuel is in it* when Friar Rush, who is the devil Shackle-soule, is assaulting the steadfast Subprior. A stage direction says: "Enter Shackle-soule, or some other Spirit." The dialogue for the fiend is under the rubric Shackle-soule.

[25] See the *Faust Book* of 1592, ch. 12, p. 150 of Palmer and More's reprint, for Mephistophilis' statement to Faustus that Lucifer ruled in the *Orient.*

[26] Agrippa (*op. cit.,* III, xxiv, 417) gives Urieus as king of the East. Scot, who follows Wier or the *Lemegeton,* gives Amaymon as king of the East (*Discoverie,* XV, iii, 327). But in Agrippa Amaymon is called king of the South, in the *Grimoire of Honorius,* king of the North, and Magoa is king of the East. (See Waite, *op. cit.,* p. 247.) There are many other versions of the distribution of daemonic kings to the points of the compass.

[27] Mr. Boas for his edition of *Bussy* was "unable to find any precedent for Chapman's application of this name. . . ." Professor Parrott in his edition cites Scot's mention of the name, but the quotation is not illuminating. To this citation I can add references to the writings of Bodin (see *ante,* p. 70), Sprenger (*Malleus Maleficarum,* Pt. I, Q. 4, p. 30), Agrippa (*Occult Philosophy* III, xxviii, 437), George Pictorius of Villingen (see p. 156 of Turner's translation of his *Discourse on the Nature of Spirits* bound with the 1655 translation of Agrippa's *Fourth Book* and Abano's *Heptameron*), Pierre Le Loyer (*Discours et Histoires des Spectres,* IV, xiv, 356 of the 1605 edition), Boguet (*An Examen of Witches,* preface, p. xlii), *et cetera.* But though these references demonstrate that Chapman took no liberty, they do not add much clarity to his figure called *Behemoth.*

Mr. Boas says that the *Astaroth* of the *Bussy* incantation is apparently the plural of Ashtoreth, the Phoenician moon goddess, and is here used mistakenly for the name of a male spirit. But there was no mistake on Chapman's part; at least his usage was not out of keeping with the daemonology of his time. Authorities made no distinction of sex in daemons, and the Phoenician moon goddess was conceived to have been, since the overthrow of her religion, but another among infernal rulers, and considered male or female at the whim of the author. The name *Astaroth* is well known to daemonology. See *Paradise Lost,* Bk. I, ll. 422–4.

[28] *Malleus Maleficarum,* Pt. I, Q. 4, p. 29. For a Protestant, homely, and English statement of the same doctrine see p. 25 of *The Wonderful Discoverie of the Witchcrafts of Margaret and Philip Flower . . .,* London, 1619, as reprinted in *A Collection of Rare and Curious Tracts Relating to Witchcraft . . .,* London, 1838.

[29] Waite (*op. cit.,* p. 164) specifically notes this characteristic of the rituals, saying that the shape of the apparition is always "a subject of apprehension, and a peaceable manifestation is always earnestly bargained for."

[30] Pictorius, *op. cit.,* p. 134, expounds the orthodox opinion that sublunary spirits are "the apostate spirits spread abroad from the bounds and borders of the Moon, unto us under the domination of their Prince Beelzebub, which before the fall of Lucifer had pure clarified bodies; and now, like unto the former do wander up and down, after their transgression, in the form of an airy quallity." In Greene's *Friar Bacon and Friar Bungay* the German magician Vandermast refers to the fallen spirits as "All subject under Luna's continent."

[31] See Parrott's note in his edition of Chapman's tragedies on the theogony of Pherecides in which appears the serpent-god, Ophiuneus.

[32] All my quotations and references to Chapman's works are from Parrott's edition.

[33] Bodin, *op. cit.,* I, i, 51; Agrippa, *op. cit.,* III, xviii, 399. Le Loyer makes a similar reference, saying that the devil is "that very Ophioneus or Serpent, the sworne enemie of God; which as Pherecides said, did contend and fight with Saturne." See ii, 11 of *A Treatise of Spectres,* the 1605 English translation of the first book of the *Discours.*

[34] My references for this play are from the version in *The Shakespeare Apocrypha* edited by Tucker Brooke.

[35] *Op. cit.,* III, xviii, 400. Agrippa's testimony is confused in the translation where he is made to say that the goddess is powerful in air, water, and earth; then to render the verse from Hesiod as attributing to her power in earth, *fire* and air. The first is correct according to Hesiod who says she rules the heavens, earth and sea.

[36] In *Grim, the Collier of Croydon,* for instance, devils' names are Pluto, Minos, *etc.* Dante and Milton, of course, exhibit the same usage. See note 20 *ante* for the use of Pluto as synonymous with Lucifer and Beelzebub. See also Le Loyer, *op. cit.,* ii, 11, for *Pluto* and *Dis* among devils' names.

[37] Aquinas, Pt. I, Q. 109, A. 2 of the *Summa* says: "The demons are not equal in nature; and so among them there exists a natural precedence; which is not the case with men, who are naturally equal. That the inferior are subject to the superior, is not for the benefit of the superior, but rather to their detriment; because since to do evil belongs to a pre-eminent degree to unhappiness, it follows that to preside in evil is to be more unhappy." In *Paradise Lost* Satan's speech when assuming the throne is reminiscent of this.

In *Friar Bacon and Friar Bungay* the German magician, Vandermast, disputing for the primacy of fiery spirits, voices one of the occult subtleties which orthodox authorities did not incline to respect. He says:

For when proud Lucifer fell from the heavens,
The spirits and angels that did sin with him,
Retain'd their local essence as their faults,
All subject under Luna's continent.
They which offended less hung in the fire,
And second faults did rest within the air;
But Lucifer and his proud-hearted fiends
Were thrown down into the centre of the earth,
Having less understanding than the rest,
As having greater sin and lesser grace. (sc. ix)

[38] In the *Heptameron* of Peter of Abano, acknowledged source of the conjuring scenes of *The Devil's Charter, Varcan Rex* appears as a daemon's name inscribed in the magician's circle for conjuration during the first hour on Sunday in Spring. In the "Considerations" for this operation Varcan is listed as king of the angels of the air ruling on Sunday in the Spring. Astaroth is not mentioned in the *Heptameron,* but the *Lemegeton* and the *Grimoire of Honorius* are magical manuals which give the name as that of a daemonic ruler. (See Waite, *op. cit.,* p. 251.) Scot, *op. cit.,* XV, ii, following Wier and the *Lemegeton,* calls Astoroth "a strong duke." In a more generally received classification Astaroth is mentioned by Agrippa, Wier, Burton, as prince of the Accusers. See *ante,* chapter II, note 23.

[39] *Daemonologie,* I, vi, 21.

[40] The syntax of this passage is susceptible of various constructions. I take *diuilish order* as object of the preposition *of,* modifying *voyd.* Perhaps *order* may be taken with *region* as compound subject of *requires,* though this construction seems to me to make less satisfactory sense than the former.

[41] *Malleus Maleficarum,* Pt. I, Q. 4, p. 30.

[42] If, as Astaroth's special prominence in the scene and his words "I the first" may be taken to indicate, there is still precedence among these fiends it is not of nature but of punishment. Such rank as existed in hell was simply the distinction between those deputed to torment the damned and those not so deputed. They boast the tortues they will inflict:

Belcher. And I with poysoned toads will stop his mouth,
Whose heart was never satisfied with lust.
Astaroth. And I with snakes and stinging Scorpions
Will scourge him from his pride and insolence.
Varca. And I with force of fiends will hall his limnes,
And pull them till he stretch an acre length.

Malleus Maleficarum says (Pt. I, Q. 4, p. 30): "It may be said that even in Hell there will be among them a gradation of power, and of the affliction of punishments, inasmuch as some, and not others, will be deputed to torment the souls.

But this gradation will come rather from God than from themselves, as will also their torments."

[43] See Waite, *op. cit.*, p. 194.

[44] Pt. II, Q. 1, chapter 15, p. 147; Pt. I, Q. 1, p. 23. See, too, Taillepied, *A Treatise of Ghosts,* xvii, 116.

Aquinas (*Summa,* Pt. I, Q. 64, A. 4) on the question *Whether our atmosphere is the demons' place of punishment,* says that as angels serve in the divine Providence to encourage man to good, so devils exercise him by temptation. "Consequently a two-fold place of punishment is due to the demons: one, by reason of their sin, and this is hell; and another, in order that they may tempt men, and thus the darksome atmosphere is their due place of punishment.

"Now the procuring of men's salvation is prolonged even to the judgment day: consequently, the ministry of the angels and wrestling with the demons endure until then. Hence until then the good angels are sent to us here; and the demons are in this dark atmosphere for our trial; although some of them are even now in hell, to torment those whom they have led astray; just as some of the good angels are with the holy souls in heaven. But after the judgment day all the wicked, both men and angels, will be in hell, and the good in heaven." He says further (reply to Objection three): ". . . although the demons are not actually bound within the fires of hell while they are in this dark atmosphere, nevertheless their punishment is none the less; because they know that such confinement is their due. Hence it is said in a gloss upon Jas. iii. 6: They carry the fire of hell with them wherever they go."

[45] Aquinas and the scholastics in general seem to have thought hell to have place locally. See the *Summa,* Pt. III (supplement) Q. 69, and the *Catholic Encyclopedia* on Hell. Better agreeing with *Faustus* as to the nature of hell, perhaps, is the doctrine of Jacob Brenz and the Ubiquists who held it not local place, but a state of suffering. At his second visit to Faustus, Mephistophilis says:

Hell hath no limits, nor is circumscribed
In one self place; for where we are is hell,
And where hell is there must we ever be.

He also says, however, that he "must back to hell" if Faustus won't pledge his soul; *i.e.,* must subside into the local hell if there is no work for him in "lower mists." I have thought it better on a question on which theology is so uncertain as on the nature of hell to go for a general explanation of the *Faustus* passages to that doctrine which was most widespread and basic, since it seems, too, to fit the situation in that it holds that for practical purposes hell is everywhere for the damned.

The rest of Mephistophilis' answer to Faustus' question as to the whereabouts of hell—that it is "within the bowels of these elements, Where we are tortured and remain forever"—seems to signify the demons' rejection from the empyrean (to which they belong by nature) and their confinement to the sub-lunar region, to the elementary world. It does not signify the demons' materiality, but their finity as opposed to the infinity of God. See *ante,* p. 24 and *post,* ch. VI, note 1, on the substance of demons.

Many critics have extolled Marlowe's spiritualized conception of hell, and justly. Mr. Whitmore (*The Supernatural in Tragedy,* p. 231) says that in *Faustus* "the conception of Hell has passed from the medieval grotesqueness, with its mingled crudity and terror, to a great imaginative height." This is undeniably true; but it is not as though Marlowe had made it all up. The spiritualized conception belonged to the medieval theologians first. Marlowe's good taste used the doctrine well, eschewed the morality play exhibition on the stage which his revisers added to *Faustus.* But it is not necessarily to be thought that a hell shown on the stage is really *conceived* more crudely than the one to which Mephistophilis' much admired exposition is directed, though the dramaturgy is certainly cruder.

[46] Pt. I, Q. 4, p. 29.

[47] Taillepied, *op. cit.,* xviii, 123, says: ". . . and there can be no doubt at all that if we live a spiritual life, walking with God and utterly despising this world, our Guardian Angels will visibly manifest themselves to us, just as, conversely, their dark familiars appear to and consort with warlocks and magicians."

[48] For references to the practice, see Act I, scene ii of Middleton's *Witch*.

[49] This is from the last scene of Act V. My citations from this play are made from the Pearson 1874 reprint, which gives acts but not scenes. I will, therefore, cite the act and the page number, which for the above quotation is 259.

[50] Pt. I, Q. 4, p. 29. "From which [discussion on the rank of demons] it is concluded that since the practice of these abominations [of coitus] is for the most part foreign to the nobility of the angelic nature, so also in human actions the foulest and beastliest acts are to be considered by themselves, and not in relation to the duty of human nature and procreation.

"Finally, since some are believed to have fallen from every order, it is not unsuitable to maintain that those devils who fell from the lowest choir, and even in that held the lowest rank, are deputed to and perform these and other abominations."

Notes on Chapter VI

[1] Cotta, *Infallible Witch,* says (iv, 24) that it is clear that ". . . all knowledge exceeding the knowledge of man, must needs issue from the knowledge of spirits, and also that all works exceeding and transcending, aboue the power and nature of corporall substances, must necessarily be the force of spirits." Wier says (*Impostures des diables,* I, x, 30) that it is no wonder if devils have extraordinary powers: "Car estans subtil en leur substance, il peuuent & entendent plusieurs choses, en partie par le permission de dieu, & en partie fallacieusement au moyen de leur tenureté, subtilité, vitesse incroyable, vigeur de sense, & de la lumiere naturelle, beaucoup plus claire & excellente en eux, qu'en tout autres corps terrestres et tardis en leurs sens." Further (I, xii, 37): the devil's "essence angelique n'est perie, mais est seulement corrompue par les effets de sa propre volonté: et pour autant aussi que par si long laps de temps, il a acquis une grand conoissance et une usage merueilleux des choses."

The only real index to the substance of play daemons is in the general cast of the rationale of the animistic material. Since the plays, with only one or two exceptions, seem orthodox in general pneumatological scheme, it is likely that either the Thomistic conception of pure spirituality, or the Protestant one of quintessential substance may best be read into them. A possible exception is *The Birth of Merlin* which has a daemon substantial enough to propagate truly and to be enclosed in a rock. These capacities seem to indicate an elementary body according to the conception of Psellos, who attributed to daemons the power to reproduce. It was by a similar daemon that Sycorax conceived Caliban; Ariel, fixed in the cloven pine, was of the element, air. See W. C. Curry's exposition of the matter in *Shakespeare's Philosophical Patterns,* p. 184–7. On the powers of daemons, see *ante,* p. 25 ff.

[2] See *Malleus Maleficarum,* Pt. II, Q. 1, ch. iv, p. 109 on the spirit's means of taking a body, though never truly acting through it.

[3] My references to *The Witch of Edmonton* are to the Mermaid edition of Dekker's works.

[4] *An Examen of Witches,* x, 26. For particulars on daemonic methods of speech, hearing, *et cetera,* see *Malleus Maleficarum,* Pt. II, Q. 1, chapter iv, p. 110.

[5] Or perhaps Faustus fears that the sound of the emperor's voice will break his charm. Agrippa says that in invocation of spirits the "prating of a companion hindreth the effect." (*Occult Philosophy,* III, ii, 349). There is a parallel passage in *The Tempest.* Prospero bids Miranda and Ferdinand "be mute, Or else our spell is marr'd." (IV, i, 125.)

[6] *Op. cit.,* III, xxiii, 413.

[7] Remy, *Demonolatry* I, vii, 28; I, viii, 30.

[8] For this play I have used the Herford and Simpson edition.

[9] See also *The Witch of Edmonton* V, i, where the demon dog says to Cuddy of the bodies devils get which are none of their own:

The old cadaver of some self-strangled wretch
We sometimes borrow, and appear human;
The carcass of some disease-slain strumpet
We varnish fresh, and wear as her first beauty.

On the devil's means of taking such bodies see *Malleus Maleficarum* Pt. II, Q. 1, ch. iv, p. 110.

[10] John a Kent in Munday's comedy says that "a sillie dazzling mist" is the cover for the deceptions he practices. See *ante,* p. 33 for Remy's explanation. See also *Malleus Maleficarum* Pt. I, Q. 9, p. 58 ff. Scot, of course, ridicules the whole theory. See the *Discoverie* XV, xxi, 364–5.

[11] Mr. Boas in a note on this scene says: "The characters [Monsieur, *et al.*] are supposed to be far off, but rendered visible and audible to Tamyra and D'Ambois by Behemoth's power." Mr. Boas overlooks the lines numbered 103 and 104 in his edition:

Bussy: May we not heare them?
Friar: No, be still and see.

Of course if Bussy had overhead the conspirator's plot against him the action would have been blocked. Professor Parrott's note: "The characters [Monsieur *et al.*] enter on the balcony. Although they speak and act in the following lines, they are not supposed to be really present, but only made visible and audible to Bussy and Tamyra by the Friar's art."

[12] Bacon says: "Stand here and look directly in the glass." Then comes the stage direction: "Enter Margaret and Friar Bungay." The modern stage directions added in the edition prepared by Mr. G. B. Harrison seem to assume the figures to be in the glass.

The general orthodox opinion was that the revelatory figures which conjurors showed in glasses to their patrons were managed by devils and were less in the glass than in the imaginations of the beholders. Greene's source, however, *The Famous History,* says (ch. vi, p. 19–21 of the *Miscellanea Antiqua Anglicana* reprint) that Bacon's glass was a "perspective," a product, therefore, of natural and mathematical knowledge, and a genuine reflector—though perhaps demons aided in its construction. Agrippa mentions such glasses in the *Occult Philosophy* II, i, 168; xxiii, 255.

[13] So Charles Mills Gayley seems to take it, calling it a "scene beside a scene." See his "Critical Essay on Robert Greene," p. 426, in his *Representative English Comedies,* New York, 1912.

[14] *Op. cit.,* III, xxxiv, 453. Whether Agrippa states this as true is uncertain. Half a page further on he seems to disavow such things as but "follies of the Gentiles." Whether the disavowal includes the statement on Merlin there is no way to tell.

[15] Gabriel Naudé, *The History of Magic by Way of Apology for all the Wise Men who Have Unjustly been Reputed Magicians. . . .* Englished by J. Davies, London, 1657. See chapter xvi, p. 203. This is the translation of *Apologie pour les Grand Hommes . . . ,* written by Naudé in his youth, published in 1625.

[16] See *ante,* pp. 26, 27 on how demons copulate. *Malleus Maleficarum* says (Pt. II, Q. 1, ch. iv, p. 112) that Aquinas concedes the offspring of incubi to be stronger than other men since devils know how to collect the best semen. But the child does not possess in himself supernatural powers.

[17] Though Agrippa says that the animastical orders, *i.e.,* heroes, demi-gods, have no less power in ruling terrestrial things than full spirits. *Op. cit.,* III, xxxiv, 454.

[18] Devils foretold often what they later themselves brought to pass. (See *ante,* p. 31.) Absolute foreknowledge of the sort that was God's they of course lacked. In Dekker's *If this be not a good play, the devil is in it* Shackle-soule tries to lead the virtuous Subprior into despair by prophesying his death. But the good man, bucklered by virtue against bodily attacks, successfully challenges the demon's knowledge.

In Rowley's play the "antic spirit" could not be supposed to know the Clown's thoughts by "reading them in the intellect," for in this way, says *Malleus Maleficarum,* only God can know the thoughts. But he might know them by seeing their effects in the man's expression, and for reading such a book a daemon has far more keenness than any human being. See *Malleus,* Pt. I, Q. 7, p. 53; Pt. II, Q. 1, ch. ii, p. 103; King James' *Daemonologie* I, ii, 8. Of the devil's throwing stones there are many tales. See for instance *Malleus Maleficarum,* Pt. II, Q. 1, ch. xi, p. 135.

[19] Another anomalous figure in the plays is the Erichtho of Marston's *Sophonisba.* Modelled from the figure of the same name in Lucan's *Pharsalia,* she seems best conceived as the classical witch or goetist such as appear in Apuleius' *Golden Ass.* (See *post,* p. 160.) Yet, like the witches in *Macbeth* (see W. C. Curry's *Philosophical Patterns,* chapter iii) she seems almost a supernatural creature, and her usage of Syphax is certainly the thing daemonologists declared characteristic of the succubus demon. It may be noteworthy, too, that another occurrence of the name Erichtho in Elizabethan drama is in *The Birth of Merlin* where the incubus devil invokes infernal gifts for his son Merlin. He calls on "Squint-eyed Erichtho, midnight Incubus, . . ." Whether the two terms are used in apposition I do not know.

William Gifford in his notes to Dyce's edition of Ford seems to have taken the episode in *Sophonisba* as a passage between Syphax and a succubus. In a note on the following lines in *The Witch of Edmonton:* "The carcass of some disease-slain strumpet We varnish fresh, and wear as her first beauty," he says: "Enough of this is to be found in Delrio, Remigius, and other superstitious and credulous writers; but the immediate allusion in this place is, I conceive, to the *Sophonisba* of Marston, where a loathsome scene of this kind takes place between Syphax and Erichtho."

[20] Bodin says (*op. cit.* II, ii, 183) that the devil seeks only the corruption and dissolution of creatures as God seeks generation. *Malleus Maleficarum* declares that demons work to keep people out of the kingdom of heaven, so delay the Last Judgment when all demons will be imprisoned in hell forever. (See Pt. II, Q. 1, ch. xiii, p. 141.)

[21] *Op. cit.* III, xx, 405. See, too, *Malleus Maleficarum* Pt. II, Q. 1, p. 92.

[22] *A Dialogue Concerning Witches and Witchcraft,* 1593. See The Epistle. Yet Bodin notes that several sorcerers who, having sworn alliance with Satan, then wished to forsake him, were maltreated unless they mustered true penitence. *Op. cit.,* II, iii, 215. Over his minion the devil gained power.

[23] *Histoires . . . des illusions et impostures des diables,* 1579. See I, xxiv, 106; xx, 77. Almost all authorities insist that daemonic powers are drastically limited by God's consent. See for instance Bodin, *op. cit.,* I, i, 60; II, iii, 212, 216.

[24] *Malleus Maleficarum* says that the devil can do most against the lustful (Pt. I, Q. 8, p. 55) and against sinners in general and those subject to infirmities of appetite (Pt. II, Q. 1, ch. vii, p. 120) but little against those in a state of grace, except occasionally to try them. To saintly men he is subject. (Pt. II, Q. 2, p. 156.) Calvin resolutely denies the devil's power to vex those in grace: "I deny that believers can ever be oppressed or vanquished by him [the Devil] . . . whereas they [devils] hold the wicked in thralldom, exercise dominion over their minds and bodies, and employ them as bond-slaves in all kinds of iniquity." *Institutes* I, xiv, 207, of the Beveridge translation, 1845.

[25] The demon can, however, touch Banks' fields and cattle. *Malleus Maleficarum* says that demons can by the permission of God injure even "the good in their fortunes, that is, in such exterior things as riches, fame, and bodily health," as is clear from the instance of Job. See Pt. II, Q. 1, ch. vii, p. 121.

[26] *Malleus Maleficarum* says (Pt. II, Q. 1, p. 90): "For the aforesaid Doctor affirms that witches have borne witness that it is a fact of their own experience that, merely because they have been taken by officials of public justice, they have immediately lost all their power of witchcraft." See also King James' *Daemonologie* II, vi, 50.

[27] *Malleus Maleficarum* says (Pt. I, Q. xviii, p. 85) that the devil is continually held in check by good angels so that he may not do all the harm he would like. See also Pt. II, Q. 1, p. 89 ff. Agrippa concurs, *op. cit.,* III, xx, 405.

[28] For a demon dog who at the sending of a witch touched her enemy so that he died, see, for instance, *The Examination and Confession of Certain wytches at Chensforde . . . ,* 1556. Whether the scene in the play is to be conceived as technically obsession or possession as Deacon and Walker distinguish them (see *ante,* p. 28) is uncertain. At any rate it is surely the derangement of the woman's

faculties by application of the demonic power. Similar, though not so violent, is Old Banks' ridiculous infatuation for his cow. See *post,* p. 152.

[29] *Malleus Maleficarum* says (Pt. I, Q. 7, p. 48 ff.) that only God can rule the will of a man, though an angel can influence the understanding by its sources. A demon can use his powers over a man's imagination subtly to instigate evil appetites and to suggest sinful deeds. See also Pt. II, Q. 1, pp. 92, 95, and Cotta, *Infallible Witch,* vi, 33, who cites the authority of Binsfield; and Agrippa, *op. cit.,* III, xxxvi, 458; and Vair, *Trois Livres des Charms. . . .* Paris, 1583, III, lx, 497.

[30] The *English Faust Book* says (chapter xiv): "Yea (quoth Mephistophilis) why should not we help the forwards: for so soone as we saw thy heart, how thou didst despise thy degree taken in Diuinitie, and study to search and know the secrets of our kingdom; euen then did we enter into thee, giuing thee diuers foule and filthy cogitations, pricking thee forward in thine intent and perswading thee that thou couldst neuer attaine to thy desire, untill thou hast the help of some diuell: and when thou was delighted with this, then tooke we roote in thee; & so firmely, that thou gauest thy selfe unto us, both body and soule the which thou (Faustus) canst not denie."

[31] The *Faust Book* says (ch. iv): "Dr. Faustus gaue him this answere, though faintly (for his soules sake) That his request was none other but to become a Diuel, or at the least a limne of him, and that the Spirit should agree unto these Articles as followeth.

"1. That he might be a Spirite in shape and qualitie." The play reproduces this article almost word for word.

[32] The action of the play indicates that Faustus did not become a spirit in the sense that his body was refined away to impalpability, the thing for which he perhaps bargained; nor were the daemonic powers of swiftness and control over local motion which belonged to separated spirit—*Malleus Maleficarum* says (Pt. II, Q. 1, ch. iii, p. 106) and Agrippa agrees (*op. cit.,* III, xlii, 490) that the separated soul has them equally with daemons—conferred on him directly. For these things he was dependent entirely on Mephistophilis. When he would be invisible he must ask Mephistophilis to make him so by art, and to traverse distances at speed he rides upon a demonic mount. At the end, the shreds of his body are found strewn in the corridors, relics of the fiend's seizure of that part of him which was spirit before any bargain with them. All this is in agreement with one of the most firmly and generally held articles of pneumatology: that daemons could not transmute, much less transubstantiate, any created thing. (See Vair, *op. cit.,* II, xii, 318; *Malleus Maleficarum* Pt. I, Q. 10, pp. 62, 64; Pt. II, Q. 1, ch. viii, p. 123; Wier, *op. cit.,* I, xxv, 109.) If, then, Faustus became spirit in form and substance it must have been in some sense not literal in the words of the compact.

One interpretation which might in the sixteenth century be placed on the words of the compact is indicated in *The Second Report of Faustus,* 1594: ". . . he [Wagner] remembered (for as then he had lately read it) how that one Article to which his Master had bound Mephistophilis was, that after his death he should be a Spirit in nature and essence as others were." (See p. 222 of *The Second Report* as edited with the *Faust Book* by William Rose, London, 1926.) This idea that the souls of the dead became daemons is to be found in Plotinus, Plutarch, Apuleius and other ancient writers. Occultists of the sixteenth century toyed with it as far as they dared; but orthodox writers uniformly and resolutely rejected it, though noting that devils often tempted witches with the promise of it. See, for instance, Taillepied, *A Treatise of Ghosts,* 1588, xx, 132; Delrio, *Controverses et recherches magiques,* 1611, Bk. II, Q. 4, p. 123; *Malleus Maleficarum,* Pt. I, Q. 8, p. 57; Guazzo, *Compendium Maleficarum,* 1608, II, xiii, 132.

[33] Pt. I, Q. 17, p. 82.

[34] Aquinas says (*Summa,* Pt. I, Q. 64, A. 2) on the question "Whether the will of the demons is obstinate in evil?" that because stability is necessary to true beatitude it is certain that the will of good angels cannot be inclined to evil, and that conversely the will of devils is obstinate in evil. "We must seek for the cause of this obstinacy, not in the gravity of the sin, but in the condition of their nature or state. For as Damascene says (*De Fid. Orth.* ii), death is to men, what the fall is to the angels. Now it is clear that all the mortal sins of men, grave or

less grave, are pardonable before death; whereas after death they are without remission, and endure forever.

"To find the cause, then, of this obstinacy, it must be borne in mind that the appetitive power is in all things proportioned to the apprehensive, whereby it is moved, as the movable by its mover. For the sensitive appetite seeks a particular good; while the will seeks the universal good, as was said above (Q. LIX, A. 1); as also the sense apprehends particular objects, while the intellect considers universals. Now the angel's apprehension differs from man's in this respect, that the angel by his intellect apprehends immovably, as we apprehend immovably first principles which are the object of the habit of intelligence; whereas man by his reason apprehends movably, passing from one consideration to another; and having the way open by which he may proceed to either of two opposites. Consequently man's will adheres to a thing movably, and with the power of forsaking it and of clinging to the opposite; whereas the angel's will adheres fixedly and immovably. Therefore, if his will be considered before its adhesion, it can freely adhere either to this or to its opposite (namely, in such things as he does not will naturally); but after he has once adhered he clings immovably. So it is customary to say that man's free-will is flexible to the opposite before and after choice; but the angel's free-will is flexible to either opposite before the choice, but not after. Therefore the good angels who adhered to justice, were confirmed therein; whereas the wicked ones, sinning, are obstinate in sin. Later on we shall treat of the obstinacy of men who are damned. (Suppl., Q. XCVIII.)

[35] I have followed Mr. Boas' edition in attributing the above speech to Faustus to whom, as Mr. H. T. Baker points out (*Mod. Lang. Notes,* xxi, p. 86–7) it seems clearly to belong. I do not, however, concur with Mr. Boas' interpretation in a footnote that "Faustus' realization that for the second time (cf. II, ii, 85–6) he had called upon his Saviour, contrary to his vow, would account for his agonized cry, 'what hast thou done?' and for Mephistophilis' offer of a dagger wherewith he may kill himself." This is, of course, in itself acceptable enough; but theologically the explanation is, I believe, rather as I say. The offer of a dagger or other means of suicide to a despairing witch was a recognized trick of the devil's to insure possession of her soul. On an earlier occasion Faustus says that when he names salvation echoes thunder:

> 'Faustus, thou art damn'd!' Then swords, and knives,
> Poison, guns, halters, and envenom'd steel
> Are laid before me to despatch myself.

This, says Professor Ward, is to be distinguished from the later incident as merely imaginary temptation to suicide. This may be, but the difference amounts to little since both surely are Mephistophilis' doing, the motive to get Faustus' soul.

For parallel incidents in drama see *The Virgin Martyr,* IV, ii, 357; *If this be not a good play, the devil is in it.* On how devils tempt witches to suicide see Remy, *op. cit.,* III, vi, 161; Guazzo, *op. cit.,* II, xiii, 129 and xiv, 132; Boguet, *op. cit.,* xlv, 131.

[36] This transformation, needless to say, was only by glamor, not actual. See *ante,* p. 33 and *post,* p. 156 on the theory of lycanthropy and on some instances from the plays. *Malleus Maleficarum* (Pt. I, Q. 10, p. 62) quotes St. Augustine "that the transmutations of men into brute animals, said to be done by the art of devils, are not actual but only apparent."

Logeman says in his *Faustus Notes* that in trying to elucidate the text of the Robin conjuring scenes, A and B, he was "inclined to suggest that after 1.1006 [Wagner's text], Faustus should come in, setting 'squibs at their backs' and that only afterwards 'Enters to them Mephastophilis.' This, as was pointed out to me, derives a certain degree of plausibility from the fact that Robin says (A. 1.1012 seq. cf. A. 1.940): 'Ile neuer rob thy Library more.' That Robin addresses the person that has just come (*i.e.,* Faustus on this supposition) as 'Good diuel,' just as he reports in the B text, 1.1610 seq., 'one of (Faustus') deuils turn'd me into the likenesse of an Apes face,' seems an objection. Could it be explained on the supposition that Faustus had dressed up as a devil? Or could it be that Faustus, having done some conjuring tricks—such as might be expected of a devil—should hence be called a devil here?"

Obviously speculation on these points can be only rather naively literal. Perhaps the contradictions Professor Logeman discusses are best ignored as unimportant products of careless dramaturgy. The possibility may be suggested, nevertheless, that rather than Faustus dressing like a devil, Mephistophilis assumed in the first scene the likeness of Faustus. *Malleus Maleficarum* says (Pt. II, Q. 1, p. 92) that devils might and often did so take the likeness of their masters. See, too, the parallel episode in Goethe where Mephistophiles cozens the young student.

Of course Professor Logeman's speculation is directed at visualizing rather the staging than the situation within the play world. But this does not in itself invalidate the conjecture that Mephistophilis appeared as a near, evil counterpart of Faustus, as Faustus' worser nature incarnate.

37 Scot (*Discourse of Devils and Spirits,* xiii, 427) says that often the Bible thus calls a man a devil. In drama the usage is most prominent in the title *The Merry Devil of Edmonton*—Peter Fabell, a conjuror, being the devil in question. There are, of course, innumerable instances in plays of persons quite human, being called devils. So, Generous in *The Late Lancashire Witches* (IV, 226) on discovering his wife a witch:

And hath that Serpent twin'd me so about
That I must lye so often and so long
With a Divell in my bosome!

In *The Witch of Edmonton,* Old Banks calls Mother Sawyer "the grumbling Devil" (IV, i), and the Duchess of Malfi similarly characterizes Ferdinand in Webster's play (III, v, 192).

38 *Occult Philosophy,* III, xx, 406; III, xxviii, 437. Taillepied comments (*op. cit.,* xx, 133) on the passage of Scripture from which Agrippa takes his references to Judas: "Our Lord said [John viii, 44] to the Jews: Ye are of your father the devil; and in chapter vi, 71, He said: Have I not chosen you twelve; and one of you is a devil? Not a devil by nature, but a devil in that the traitor so closely imitated Satan."

39 *Op. cit.,* III, xx, 406.

40 For a complete analysis of a very similar tragic process in *Macbeth* see Curry, *op. cit.,* chapter iv, "Macbeth's Changing Character."

41 "The Objectivity of the Ghosts in Shakespeare," *PMLA,* xxii, (1907), p. 232.

42 *La Demonomanie,* 1598, II, i, 160; I, v, 112.

43 See *post,* ch. IX.

44 *Op. cit.,* p. 63. In this comment on scene vi, Wagner's edition, Professor Logeman says further that Mephistophilis does not, of course, notice the Angels because, since they are subjective, "their voices cannot be supposed to be heard by Mephistophilis." But that Mephistophilis thus ignores them is no proof of the Angels' purely figurative status. As has been explained above, Mephistophilis may be conceived even as actually being one of the Angels.

45 Unless we take literally the Old Man's cry: "I see an angel hover o'er thy head, etc." (V, i.)

46 See *ante,* p. 88 on the speech of angels.

47 My citations are from Lucas' edition.

48 On this point see the chapter, "Those who see Spirits" in Miss Lily Bess Campbell's *Shakespeare's Tragic Heroes.*

49 Miss Enid Grant ("Webster and Lavater," *London Times Literary Supplement,* Apr. 11, 1936, p. 316) has already pointed out a parallel episode from ancient history as remarked upon by Lavater, *Of Ghostes and Spirits* . . . 1572, I, xii, 61. Taillepied, *op. cit.,* ix, 49, retails a similar episode.

50 The substance of this passage seems to come directly from Simon Goulart's *Histoires Admirables,* 1600, translated by Grimestone, 1607. See Lucas' citation of the passage in his edition of Webster. Goulart gives the medical and not the pneumatological description of lycanthropy. But this, since the passage in the play is in the mouth of the doctor, does not afford a certain presumption of the rationale for the action in the play world. The doctor is notably unsuccessful in his dealing with the patient. On the controversy over possession as disease or diabolic see *ante,* p. 34.

51 On the demonic influences abroad on the night of Duncan's murder and their

manifestation in storm, see Curry, *op. cit.*, p. 80 in his exposition of "The Daemonic Metaphysics of *Macbeth*."

[52] Lavater, *op. cit.*, I, xi, 50, and Taillepied, *op. cit.*, vii, 37, retail from Cardan, *De Subtilitate*, xviii, a tale of an echo taken for the voice of a fiend. Both tell it preliminary to other stories of veritable supernatural occurrences, and urge caution in scorning stories of daemonic voices.

In his *John Webster* Professor Stoll says (in a footnote, p. 121) of the Echo in *The Duchess of Malfi* that there is much evidence (which he recites) to indicate that the Echo takes precisely the same place in *The Duchess of Malfi* that is taken by Brachiano's ghost in *The White Devil*. "Indeed, the stage-direction (in the oldest copies) *from the Duchess' grave*, and Antonio's remark and the Echo's reply—' 'Tis very like my wife's voice,' 'Ay, wife's voice'—would give us to understand that the Echo is but the ghost of the Duchess." Whether it be taken as ghost or daemon, there is a strong presumption, though no certainty, that the Echo is supernaturally managed.

[53] Critics have noted the same kind of thing in Hawthorne and other writers. It is not my purpose to go into the manner of it in Webster other than to indicate that the uncertainty which he achieves reproduces an uncertainty which lies back of all the thinking of his time about the distinction between the natural and the supernatural.

[54] On these plays see *post*, ch. VIII.

Notes on Chapter VII

[1] Herford and Simpson in their discussion of Jonson's *Devil is an Ass* remark that devil plays are of two classes: (1) that in which "the action is provoked, as in Dr. Faustus and Peter Fabel, by the ambition or curiosity of a man"; (2) that in which the action originates in "the enterprise of the infernal world," *cf. The Devil is an Ass, Grim, the Collier of Croydon, If this be not a good play, the devil is in it.* It is with the first kind of plays, of course, that this chapter deals.

[2] On sixteenth century distinctions between magicians and witches see *ante*, p. 35 ff.

[3] It was the contention of the church, of course, that its office of exorcism and the miracles of its saints were not of the will of the officiating man, but of his faith and prostration freely answered by God; whereas the magician acted wilfully, even though acknowledging (as most magicians did copiously) the omnipotence of God and the necessity of faith. Agrippa says (*Occult Philosophy*, III, xxxii, 447–8) that evil spirits are coerced by the names of the Creator and by the service of the good spirits who are themselves very difficult to bind except by prayer and the signs of "Divine vertues" which appeal to them by similitude. In another place (III, xxxvi, 460) he says that man "hath power on all, even on God himselfe, by knowing and loving him. . . ." For evil spirits there was also (solely said the orthodox) the commercial method, the link by bargain. (See *Malleus Maleficarum* Pt. II, Q. 2, ch. v, p. 177 ff.)

[4] For a classification of Elizabethan play magicians according to their methods, but with little reference to daemonology, see Rudolph Zender, *Die Magie im englischen drama des Elisabethanischen zeitalters . . .*, Halle, 1907. In chapter ii, pp. 19, 20, Herr Zender says that the play magicians fall into two principal classes: *Beschworer*, who require the help of spirits, and *Zauberkunstler*, such as the enchanter in Peele's *Old Wives' Tale*, "die nichts auf die Hilfe der Geister angewiesen sind, sondern eine personliche Zaubergewalt besitzen über des Menschen und die Natur." The former class, by far the more populous, is subdivided into (1) those who rule spirits by sheer knowledge and art, (2) those who make a compact with the prince of hell. In the first group Herr Zender puts Bacon, Bungay, Vandermast, in *Friar Bacon and Friar Bungay;* Proximus and Merlin in *The Birth of Merlin;* and Prospero in *The Tempest*. In the second group are Alexander of Barnes' *Devil's Charter*, and Faustus. Herr Zender does not touch upon sixteenth century theory of magic save in an occasional passing reference.

[5] Agrippa says (*op. cit.,* III, vi, 357) that through religion man's soul is purified: "Hence it comes to pass that though we are framed a natural body, yet we sometimes predominate over nature, and cause wonderfull, sodain and difficult operations, as that the evil spirits obey us, the stars are disordered, the heavenly powers compelled, the Elements made obedient. . . ." But these things, he later indicates, are by the majority of practitioners, effected through mediate means, by sacrifices and oblations. "And these are (as Orpheus calls them) keys which open the gate of the elements and the heavens, that by them a man may ascend to the supercelestials; and the intelligences of the heavens, and the demons of the elements may descend to him." (III, lix, 536) Nevertheless, "men that are perfect, and truly Religious need them not, but only they, who (saith Trismegistus) being fallen into disorder, are made the servants of the heavens and creatures; who because they are subjected to the heavens, therefore think they may be corroborated by the favour of the celestial vertue, untill they flying higher be acquitted from their presidency and become more sublime than they." (III, lix, 537)

The prophets and the Apostles, Agrippa says (III, vi, 358) "were famous by the wonderfull power of God" directly applied. *Malleus Maleficarum* avers that the power of the Keys and all miracle "necessarily presupposes a condition of grace in him who performs that act of grace, since both these powers proceed from grace granted to men who are in a state of grace." (See Pt. II, Q. 2, ch. i, p. 167.)

[6] *The Arbatel of Magic* says that some wonders are brought about by invocation of God alone, but that another kind of magic operates by good angels and another through the chiefs of the evil angels. See the thirty-eighth Aphorism in Turner's 1651 translation.

[7] On the use of superstition and how it gives power in magic to votaries of false religion see *Occult Philosophy,* III, iv, 352 ff. and see *ante,* p. 43, and *post,* p. 116. On Christian miracle and magic and on compact see Aquinas, *Summa* I, 110, 4 and also *ante,* pp. 44, 46. *Malleus Maleficarum,* citing Augustine and Aquinas, says (Pt. I, Q. 5, p. 39): "Magicians [witches] do miracles by private contract, good Christians by public justice, and bad Christians by the signs of public justice. And all this is explained as follows. For there is a Divine justice in the whole universe, just as there is a public law in the State. But the virtue of any creature has to do with the universe, as that of the private individual has to do with the State. Therefore inasmuch as good Christians work miracles by Divine justice, they are said to work them by public justice. But the Magician, since he works through a pact entered into with the devil, is said to work by private contract; for he works by means of the devil, who by his natural power can do things outside the order of created nature as known to us, through the virtue of a creature unknown to us; and it will be for us a miracle, although not actually so, since he cannot work outside the order of the whole of created nature, and through all the virtues of creatures unknown to us. For in this way only God is said to work miracles. As it is said: Thou art God who alone workest great marvels. But bad Christians work through the signs of public justice, as by invoking the Name of Christ, or by exhibiting certain sacraments."

[8] All authorities are agreed that God alone can sway the will (see *ante,* p. 97) and that magic which is by His direct favor is at His instigation.

[9] *Op. cit.,* III, vi, 358.

[10] See *Malleus Maleficarum,* Pt. II, Q. 1, ch. ix, p. 126.

[11] See chapter xlv, p. 116 of the 1684 translation.

[12] See note 7 *ante* on how bad Christians work by the signs of public justice. Most of the sixteenth and seventeenth century rituals of magic fall under Agrippa's strictures, as indeed he makes clear by the authors he names as authorities of these magicians: Honorius, Robert of York, Bacon, Apponus, *etc.* See *Occult Philosophy,* III, xxxii, 448 on how evil men may to a limited extent use sanctified means.

[13] *Op. cit.,* III, iii, 350–1.

[14] *Ibid.,* III, iii, 351.

[15] *Ibid.,* III, lxii, 540. The 1651 translation says 'imitation' and Waite quotes it so. But the Latin of the edition dated Paris, 1567, which I have used has *initiationem. The Fourth Book of Agrippa* (p. 63 of the Turner translation) in a passage which is a virtual paraphrase of the place cited in Bk. III, says "initiation."

The Friar, as a churchman, had, of course, a power of consecration which was considered valuable in magic; but as a magician he needed 'initiation,' instruction in special rites of consecration.

[16] *Op. cit.,* III, vii, 358.

[17] *Ibid.,* III, iv, 354.

[18] *Demonolatry,* dedication, p. vi.

[19] This is an acknowledgement that black magic did not often make expressly, though it is tacit in many of the rites in the manuals. That it does not amount to the witch's express pact is clear from Mephistophilis' further exaction. It is not the utter renunciation of God's power, but simply the having of another God before Him, *i.e.,* one in a more special and accessible standing.

[20] King James says (*Daemonologie,* I, v, 18) that the ceremonies of magic are very laborious and that magicians so tire of them that they become willing to make the witch's pact, which supersedes all ceremony.

[21] "Books" were of considerable importance in magic (see Zender, *op. cit.,* chapter iii, on magical books in Elizabethan drama) and were of two sorts. First, there were the handbooks of the art, such as the *Heptameron,* which Barnes undoubtedly used for much of the ceremony in *The Devil's Charter;* second, there were books which were given by the spirits themselves after they had, by proper ceremonies, been summoned and bound according to the occult scheme of things. Alexander's book seems of the latter sort, but cannot be considered, in the light of his orthodox world, to have been truly effective according to occult claims. It was but one of the deceptions which his wilful blindness made him accept from his demons.

[22] So Bodin relates (*La Demonomanie,* II, iii, 216) a tale of a witch he knew whose devil never gave him anything he wanted or told him anything of worth, but continually urged him to revenge on his enemies. And so Mother Sawyer's devil said he would run to evil at her command, but could do no good.

[23] Chapter xv (p. 42 of the reprint in *Miscellanea Antiqua Anglicana,* 1816, I, vii) of *The Famous History of Friar Bacon* tells how Miles one day found his master's study open with conjuring materials lying about, and undertook to conjure for money. But by reason of his inexpertness, the fiend got the upper hand and Miles was forced to jump out the window. There is a similar story of a student of Agrippa's who was killed by the devil he inadvertently unloosed. See Thomas Frost, *The Lives of the Conjurors.* Compare also the lines in *Bussy D'Ambois* which call Bussy like "a spirit raised without a circle, Endangering him that ignorantly raised him." (III, ii, 42.)

[24] *The Fourth Book of Agrippa* says (p. 70 of Turner's translation): "There is extant amongst those magicians (who do most use the ministry of evil spirits) a certain rite of invocating spirits by a book to be Consecrated before to that purpose; which is properly called A Book of Spirits; whereof we shall now speak a few words. For this book is to be Consecrated; a book of evil spirits, ceremoniously to be composed in their name and order: whereunto they bind with a certain holy oath, the ready and present obedience of the spirit therein written." Then follow careful instructions for the compiling and consecrating of the book.

The Key of Solomon (II, xxi, 117 of the Mathers translation) gives similar explanation and instructions, and various other rituals mention similar books. The occultists, of course, held such volumes to be wrung from the spirits, whereas Faustus and Alexander received them as gifts, toys to keep them amused. So did the orthodox interpretation diminish the part of ceremony and the real powers of the operator.

[25] To erect a textual hypothesis upon such a foundation is to assume that the rationales of the scenes are surely detectable. This is an assumption difficult to warrant by correlation of the action with contemporary theory of magic. Mr. Percy Simpson considers the Robin scene proved not Marlowe's by the "contradiction" and by the vacuity of its buffoonery as contrasted with "Marlowe's method of raising the devil, [which] involved repudiation of the Trinity and devout prayer to Lucifer." (See *Essays and Studies by Members of the English Association,* Oxford, 1929, XIV, pp. 32, 33.) The difference in merit of the scenes can certainly be acknowledged, but there is no great inconsistency in the conjuring methods.

Faustus' renunciation of the Trinity and his prayer to Lucifer were both qualified in many ways considered important by occultists. (See *post,* p. 129 ff.) If Robin's conjuring seems the less terrible, it can be laid to his clownishness contrasted with Faustus' seriousness and knowledge of what he was about, not to any special abominations in the theory of Faustus' method. Simply, Faustus got the thing straight, Robin bungled it; Faustus had that awareness of guilt that is essential to mortal sin, the ignorant Robin did not have it.

[26] Zender notes (*op. cit.,* p. 20) that Bacon's magic seems to come in a class of efficient art distinct from the covenant magic of Faustus and Alexander. See *ante,* note 4.

[27] On the theurgic art of Prospero see Curry, *Philsophical Patterns,* p. 165 ff. The rationale of Prospero's art and world was an antique one which allowed for the elemental spirit, Ariel, in a manner intolerable to Renaissance orthodoxy but quite acceptable to Agrippa, who found no difficulty in classing the nature spirits of Neo-Platonism as good angels deputed to earth, and letting it go at that. See *Occult Philosophy,* III, xvi.

[28] *Op. cit.,* III, iii, 352.

[29] It was supposed that even the most innocent recitation of the words of invocation might bring a devil, *per accidens,* to see what could be had of the invocateurs. Scot ridicules Bodin for saying that he feared to read over the incantations in Wier's book. See the *Discoverie,* XV, xxvi, 374. See, too, "Anti-Catholic Propaganda in Elizabethan England," by Miss Winifred Smith, *Mod. Phil.,* 1930, on how stage devils led the audience to believe in the manifestation on the boards of real devils.

[30] See the introduction to R. B. McKerrow's edition of *The Devil's Charter* for Bang's *Materialen.*

[31] Ward in his note on 'Albanus' mentions the coupling of the names by Agrippa. See xliv, 117 of the 1684 translation of *The Vanity.* Perhaps it may be mentioned in support of the counter theory that holds the *Faustus* text should read 'Albertus,' that this name occurs also in *The Vanity* in the same list with Bacon and Apponus, though not contiguous as they are.

[32] Agrippa explains (*Occ. Phil.,* III, lxiv, 549) the general theory of perfume and sacrifice: "Further, perfumes, sacrifice, and unction penetrate all things, and open the gates of the Elements and of the Heavens, that through them a man can see the secrets of God, heavenly things, those things which are above the Heavens, and also those which descend from the Heavens, as Angels, and spirits of deep pits, and profound places, apparitions of desert places, and doth make them to come to you, to appear visibly, and obey you; and they pacify all spirits and attract them as the Loadstone Iron, and joyn them with the elements, and cause the spirits to assume bodies: so truly the spirituall body is very much incrassated by them, and made more gross: for it liveth by vapours, perfumes and the odours of sacrifices. . . ."

A conjuration of the *Key of Solomon* (I, vii, 39) contains these words to the spirits: "If ye come promptly and voluntarily, ye shall inhale our perfumes, and our suffumigations of pleasant odour, which will be both agreeable and delightful unto ye." Later directions on the suffumigation (II, x, 101) say that perfumes of good odor are for the good spirits and those of an evil are for the evil spirits. Whether the unpleasant odors are a penalty or a delight to the evil spirits is not made clear. The general conception was that bad odors were a weapon in the hand of the operator. The example of Asmodeus harried by the odor of burning fish is often triumphantly cited in proof. See Agrippa's special chapter xliii on perfumes in Book I on natural magic in *Occult Philosophy.*

Waite explains (*Book of Black Magic,* p. 141) that every operation undertaken in magic "assumed a religious aspect" so that almost every preparation had in part the aspect of a sacrifice to the spirits concerned. *The Fourth Book of Agrippa* says (p. 84 of Turner's translation): "Furthermore, he [the magician] is to be provided of lights, perfumes, unguents and medicines compounded according to the nature of the planet and spirit: which do partly agree with the spirit, by reason of their natural and coelestial virtue; and partly are exhibited to the spirit for religious and superstitious worship."

[33] *The Heptameron* gives (p. 97 of Turner's translation) *Festativi* as "the name of the earth in summer," and the angels of this season as Gargatel, Tariel, and Gaviel whom Alexander names in 1.62 of the scene in the play. His incense, "Red Sandall," is given as "Red Sanders" in the English translation of *The Heptameron* and is the perfume for conjuration on Sunday under the king Varca whom presently Alexander invokes with his ministers, Tus and Cynaball.

[34] See Agrippa, *op. cit.,* I, xxiii–xxx on how minerals are distributed to the planets, and the following chapters on how celestial affinities are signs of higher occult connections. See, too, *The Key of Solomon,* II, viii, 96, on the preparation of the knife, the sword, the poniard, the dagger and the lance of the art; and also I, xviii, 63, on how the medals and pentacles of the art should be "made of the metal the most suitable to the nature of the Planet" with the subsequent attribution of metals to planets.

[35] I construe the second line of this quotation to mean: He who reads only mathematic rules, *i.e.,* applies himself with exclusive diligence to mastering magic. If it be taken to mean: He who reads merely mathematic rules, in distinction from him who goes further in magic and takes up forbidden ceremony, then the sense of the entire passage is, of course, considerably altered. The succeeding speech by Burden seems to sustain the first conjecture, but it is not impossible that Mason means to say that even the man who stops with natural and mathematical magic, which are legitimate, and does not venture on to commerce with spirits can do much: how much more, then, may be expected of Bacon who has professed mastery of fiends.

It should be remembered that the Bacon of history was scientist rather than necromancer. Even the Bacon of the romance on which Greene levied for his play is in many of his feats—the perspective glass, the burning glass, the brazen head—a natural and mathematical magician rather than a necromancer.

The legend, of course, is little bound by the historical personage, nor the play too closely by the legend. Besides, the distinction between the three kinds of magic was a wavering one, since spirits entered into nature and were moved by natural and mathematical things so to enter.

There was, nevertheless, a budding conception of natural science, a feeling that man might shape things with his own hands and brain to do wonders. *The Famous History of Friar Bacon* says (ch. v, p. 13, of the *Miscellanea Antiqua Anglicana* reprint, 1816) that Bacon and Bungay "with great study and paines so framed a head of brasse that in the inward parts thereof there was all things like as in a naturall man's head." Apparently they were their own artisans. Only afterwards did they resort to a devil to know how to give their head the motion it required for speech. In the play, Bacon says he made Belcephon hammer out the brass for him; but he, apparently, had "contrived" it by his own knowledge.

Bacon's Brazen Head, therefore, is probably not to be conceived to be, like the head in Greene's *Alphonsus,* merely the mouthpiece of a fiend, but a head of such artful interior convolutions, so keyed to the stars, as to possess in itself the knowledge Bacon boasts for it.

In the matter of such heads Agrippa says in his *Vanity of the Arts* (xliii, 112): "There are . . . many . . . imitators of Nature, wise inquirers into hidden things, who without help of natural Virtues and Efficacies confidently undertake, onely by Mathematical learning, and the help of Celestial influences, to produce many miraculous Works, as walking and speaking Bodies, which notwithstanding are not the real animal: such was the wooden Dove of Archytas, which flew; the Statues of Mercury, that talk'd; and the Brazen Head made by Albertus Magnus, which is said to have spoken."

See, too, *Occult Philosophy,* II, i, 170.

[36] On this see *Occult Philosophy,* II, xxviii, 277.

[37] Bacon, too, uses "the latest night" for his operation. Night was, of course, the principal time for conjuring. *The Key of Solomon* says (II, i, 80) that "when neither hours nor time of operation or invocation is specified, it is then much better to perform these experiments at night, seeing that it is more easy to the spirits to appear in the peaceful silence of night than during the day." Bodin mentions (*op. cit.,* II, iii, 206) a magical book known in his father's day and called

"le Grimoire," used at night and full of secrets of damnable necromancy. This is probably not to be thought identical with any of the later grimoires, the oldest of which, says Waite, probably does not much antedate the beginning of the seventeenth century, but was no doubt of a similar cast.

38 Wheeler's note, quoted from Boas' edition of *Faustus*.

39 *Op. cit.,* II, xxiii, 253. The orthodox Catholic, Sebastien Michaelis, however, says (*A Discourse of Spirits,* London, 1613, p. 134) that magicians use a circle because it is the figure remotest from the cross. On the principles of numerology and what Agrippa means when he says that "the number ten being heaped together returns into a unity" see C. W. Olliver, *An analysis of Magic and Witchcraft,* p. 33 ff.

40 *Op. cit.,* III, xxxiii, 452.

41 "The human understanding is the only effecter of all wonderful works, so that it may be joined to any Spirit; and being joined she produceth what she will," says *The Arbatel of Magic,* Aphorism 35. See Turner's translation.

See also Agrippa's chapters on man as microcosm: *op. cit.,* III, xxxvi and xxxviii. The latter chapter Agrippa concludes (p. 468): "Therefore all those do labour in vain, who trusting only on the course of nature, and the power and favour of inferior things, do think to attain to divine things; and those who faining to have a foot in the heavens, to endeavour to receive those things from the favour of the heavens, which ought to be received from God alone; for these inferiours have, I mean animals, Herbs, stones, metals, their power subservient to the heaven; but from the Intelligences; but these from God, in whom all things pre-exist in the greatest power; as in man the little world there is not a member which hath not correspondence with some element, plant, intelligence, and with some measure and numeration in the Archetype: as we have shown before."

42 Thus, as Waite says (see *ante,* note 32), every operation in magic acquired a worshipful character. So in rituals the benediction and consecration of every item used is stipulated, as for instance *The Heptameron* directs (p. 98 of the Turner translation) the pious exorcism of the perfume that its odor may not be merely natural and so attract demons without controlling them, nor seem so unhallowed a sacrifice as to give the operator into the hands of the demons as a devotee.

Agrippa says (*Occ. Phil.,* III, lix, 535): "Moreover the Magicians when they made any confection either natural, or artificial, belonging to any star, this did they afterward religiously offer, and sacrifice to the same star, receiving not so much a natural vertue from the influence thereof being opportunely received, as by that religious oblation receiving it divinely confirmed and stronger. For the oblation of anything, when it is offered to God after a right manner, that thing is sanctified by God by the oblation as is a sacrifice, and is made part thereof."

43 The *Lemegeton* prescribes a hazel wand (see Waite, *op. cit.,* p. 169). *The Key of Solomon* also stipulates hazel wood, and says further that it must be "virgin," *i.e.,* of but one year's growth. See II, viii, 97.

44 *Occ. Phil.* has (III, lxii, 540): "Consecration is a lifting up of experiments, by which a spiritual soul, being drawn by proportion and conformity, is infused into the matter of our works according to the tradition of Magicall art rightly and lawfully prepared, and our work is vivified by the spirit of understanding. The efficacy of consecrations is perfected by two things especially, viz. the vertue of the person himself consecrating, and the vertue of the prayer itself. In the person himself is required holiness of life, and a power to consecrate; the former nature and desert perform: the latter is acquired by initiation and dignification, of which we have spoken elsewhere. . . . Now what things are required by prayer, are these. There is also a certain power of sanctifying placed in it by God, as if it be so ordained of God for this or that very thing . . . or instituted to this or that thing, by the vertue of the holy ghost, according to the ordination of the Church, of which sort are many every where extant: or this holiness is in the prayer itselfe, not by virtue of institution, but of the commemoration of sacred things, as of sacred letters, histories, miracles, works, effects, favours, promises, sacraments and such sacramentall things which shall seem to cohere with the thing to be conse-

crated, either properly, or improperly or analogically." *The Fourth Book* has a paraphrase of this passage on p. 63 of the Turner translation.

On the orthodox Catholic theory of consecration as a precaution against the devil's ordinary power in natural things see *Malleus Maleficarum,* Pt. II, Q. 2, ch. vi, p. 182.

[45] See *ante,* footnote 7, on how bad Christians were said to work miracles by "the signs of public justice."

[46] "Then he must be furnished with holy and consecrated things, necessary as well for the defence of the invocant, and his fellows, as also serving for bonds to bind and constrain the spirits. . . ." *Fourth Book of Agrippa,* p. 84 of Turner's translation.

[47] Waite says (*op. cit.,* p. 67) that *The Heptameron* presupposes a priest as operator or confederate. The cooperation of a priest is, for instance, necessary or at least desirable for the procuring of the stipulated robe and holy water, the consecration of the pentacle by the saying over it of a Holy Ghost mass, and various other items of procedure.

[48] The contention was a commonplace among occultists, and a favorite point of attack for the orthodox. Bodin (*op. cit.,* II, i, 166) taxes Pico della Mirandola with it: "Et mesme Iean Pic de la Mirande escript que les mots barbares & non entendus, ont plus de puissance en la Magie, que ceux qui sont entendus." See, too, Boguet, *An Examen of Witches,* xxvi, 80. The contention of the magicians rested in part upon the idea that Hebrew was the original language of mankind and its words especially ordained by heaven to innate correspondency with things, so that even a corrupt pronunciation of a Hebrew word would have more occult power than any possible rendering into another language; and partly upon the inheritance of divers other corrupted forms in magic formulae. The situation was as ancient as traditional ritual. Porphyry's *Letter to Anebo* criticizes it much in Bodin's spirit. Agrippa says, however, that not only "barbarous" words but uncorrupt Hebrew, Latin, Greek and words of other languages are effective. (*Occ. Phil.* III, lxiii, 546.) See, too, Thorndike's *History of Magic and Experimental Science,* I, 438, on Celsus' strictures against barbarous words in Christian magic.

[49] See *ante,* ch. III, note 44. Agrippa says further (*op. cit.,* III, lix, 536): "For they say that these sacrifices are certain natural Mediums betwixt the gods and men; which Aristotle affirming saith, that to sacrifice to God is in a man naturally. They are therefore they say, Mediums which savour of the nature of both, and represent divine things analogically, and have with the deity to whom they are offered certain convenient analogies, but so occult that a mans understanding can scarce conceive of them, which God, and the deities require in particular for our expiation with which the celestial vertues are pleased, and withhold themselves from execution of the punishment which our sins deserve." Protestants, of course, ridicule the distinction between *dulia* and *latria.* See Calvin, *Institutes,* I, xii, 140, the Beveridge translation, Edinburg, 1845.

[50] For a pronouncement on this see Waite *op. cit.,* p. 113: "To do evil because it is pleasing to the Prince of Evil did not enter into the conception of sorcery."

[51] *The Key of Solomon,* II, xxii, 119, Mathers' translation.

[52] *Ibid., loc. cit.* Agrippa mentions the same distinction between sacrifices for evil and for good spirits. *Op. cit.,* III, lix, 535.

[53] On the "Numerations" or "Attributes" of God and the names that signify them and by a divine analogy convey them into the world, see *Occ. Phil.* III, x, xi. "The Mecubales of the Hebrews from a certain text of Exodus, derive seventy-two names, both of the Angels and of God, which they call the name of seventy-two letters, and Schemhamphores, that is, the expository." On the Schemhammaphorash or Mirific word, see Morley's *Life of Agrippa;* Waite, *The Doctrine and Literature of the Kabalah;* Christian Ginsburg, *The Kabbalah;* Olliver, *An Analysis of Magic and Witchcraft.*

[54] Pt. I, Q. 17, p. 82.

[55] See A. E. Taylor, "Marlowe's Dr. Faustus," in *Times Literary Supplement,* 6 Dec., 1917.

[56] Waite says (*Book of Black Magic,* p. 202) that the long and tiresome conjurations of the *Lemegeton* are in Wier replaced by "one general form of citation,

in the name of the Christian Trinity." For the usage in Scot (who leans largely on Wier and on a common source with Wier) see *Discoverie of Witchcraft,* XV, iv, x, xii, xiii, xiv, xvi, xix, pp. 327, 338, 341, 342, 350, 354 of the Nicholson edition. The *Grimoire of Honorius* also has conjurations by the Trinity. See Waite, *op. cit.,* pp. 248, 257.

[57] On the use of holy water see *Malleus Maleficarum* Pt. II, Q. I, p. 91; King James *Daemonologie* I, v, 17; *The Fourth Book of Agrippa,* p. 64 of the Turner translation.

[58] This classification of the realms of the universe was, of course, general in the sixteenth century though there were others. For a particular expression of it see Primaudaye, *The French Academie,* II, xiv, 670, of the 1618 translation.

[59] Agrippa says (*op. cit.,* III, xi, 373) : "Therefore sacred words have not their power in magicall operations, from themselves, as they are words, but from the occult Divine powers working by them in the minds of those who by faith adhere to them; by which words the secret power of God as it were through Conduite pipes, is transmitted into them, who have ears purged by faith, and by most pure conversation and invocation of the divine names are made the habitations of God, and capable of these divine influences; whosoever therefore useth rightly these words or names of God with that purity of mind, in that manner and order, as they were delivered, shall both obtain and do many wonderfull things. . . ." In another place (III, xii, 381) : "Hence is it that seeing every creature feareth and reverenceth the name of him who hath made it, sometimes even wicked and ungodly men, if so be they believe the invocation of Divine names of this kind, do bind devils, and operate certain other great things." See also III, xiii, 382; xxxvi, 463.

[60] Yet it should be noted that most of Acts III and IV deal with Faustus as, outwardly at least, a magician. The emphasis in these acts is on his feats of wonder, the "shadows" which make "all Europe honour him," and he speaks again of his "art" by which he'll revenge himself on Benvolio. Only occasionally (as in IV, Aii, 101–4) is his witchcraft recalled to us, and "the restless course That time doth run with calm and silent foot Shortening my days and thread of vital life Calls for the payment of my latest years."

[61] Professor Ward says (and Collins follows him) that this passage "Strictly speaking . . . ought to be 'three-fold' or 'four-fold'; . . . but perhaps Greene had the virtues of the pentagramma in his mind, and in any case it is impossible to bring order into his loose references to magical lore." It may, perhaps, be admitted that Greene's references are loose; certainly they are made but in passing. Possibly it should be recalled, however, that in many ways "magical lore" was about as "loose" as Greene's references—or at any rate so variable in use of terms like that under discussion that within certain limits almost any allusion may be accommodated tentatively. Though Professor Ward's conjecture is no doubt acceptable, it seems to me that mine is a somewhat closer accommodation of the matter as it stands, though by no means apodictic. For the rationale of the play the important thing is that Bacon seems to have coerced devils by the powers of heaven and not by any affinity with hell.

For Agrippa's scale of the number five, see *Occ. Phil.,* II, viii, 190. On the souls of celestial bodies and their place in magic see III, xiv, xv. On Heroes or blessed souls see III, xxxiv, where Agrippa for once boldly denounces the "follies of the Gentiles," who held Apollonius of Tyana, Aesculapius, and others to be demi-gods, and declares the only true 'heroes' to be the Christian saints, who "enjoy a peculiar gift of working."

[62] All these names except *Manoth* are cited in the Solomonic rituals and in Agrippa. *Tetragrammaton* was probably the one most generally known among the non-initiate. Heinrich Bullinger, the father-in-law of Lewes Lavater, has left a somewhat misleading sermon on the name. See the *Decades* (translated into English in 1587) Fourth Decade, Sermon III, p. 131 of the Parker Society edition.

[63] See p. 84 of Turner's translation.

[64] This is Parrott's translation of the Latin incantation.

[65] *Op. cit.,* III, xxxii, 447. The passage of Apuleius is in *The Golden Ass,* Book II, the Third Episode, the Story of Telephron, the Student. Here the invocation is a plea addressed not to spirits but to a priest.

Notes on Chapter VIII

[1] Thus the Theophilus legend, a forerunner of the Faust legend, has the penitent sinner redeemed by the intercession of the Virgin. See the translation of the Latin version of Paulus Diaconus in P. M. Palmer and R. P. More's *The Sources of the Faust Tradition,* New York, 1936. For a condensation of this and many kindred tales see chapters viii and xii of Arturo Graf's *The Story of the Devil* (translated by E. N. Stone) New York, 1931; and Maximilian Rudwin's *The Devil in Legend and Literature,* London, 1931. In Elizabethan drama Peter Fabell in the Induction to *The Merry Devil of Edmonton* evades by a ruse the consequences of his compact, and there is mention in Munday's *John a Kent and John a Cumber* that John a Cumber has foiled the devil.

[2] Remy says (*Daemonolatry,* III, viii, 166): "Here the question arises whether it is possible for a witch, against the will of the Demon, to break her compact with him, or whether she is not rather compelled to keep it for as long as she lives. If a lawyer were asked for his opinion, no doubt he would say that a contract which contains a dishonourable clause is not binding. But here there is no question of legality: the point is whether, just as a military deserter is denied the right of postliminy, in the same way those who have once deserted from God to the enemy of the human race are cut off from every approach to God's mercy, so that they may never return from the side to which they have fled."

It was the opinion of the English Protestant, Perkins, that some witches were redeemed—for instance, those who were of the elect. This, however, was entirely by the grace of God, and took no account of the covenant as such. See Perkins' *Discourse of the Damned Art of Witchcraft,* vii, 645.

[3] King James, Daemonologie, I, ii, 7.

[4] *Malleus Maleficarum* (Pt. I, Q. V, p. 38) says that man sins from a malice which is either habitual or actual. The first produces the sin of wickedness in one who knows the good but, because of a weakness of habit, does not achieve it. The second produces the perverse and deliberate choice of evil "which is called the sin against the Holy Ghost." It was for the sake of expressing and fixing this perversity that devils exacted explicit covenant. The moment at which a person fell irretrievably into damnation cannot, of course, be certainly marked; indeed no one was held either damned or saved in any meaning compatible with temporality until death. But obviously Faustus might have retreated from hell before his compact, found it humanly impossible to do so after. St. Augustine's definition of the sin against the Holy Ghost (*Lib. de Correp. et Gratia,* cap. xii), that it is obstinate perverseness, with distrust of pardon, *continued until death,* meets Faustus' situation. Even before his compact he distrusted the promise of God, and he continued to distrust it to the end. The growth of that distrust is his tragedy. Yet before the end he was not damned.

[5] See chapters iii and iv in the Palmer and More reprint of the *English Faust Book* of 1592.

[6] *An Examen of Witches,* ix, 24.

[7] John Addington Symonds says of this passage: "Thus a devil speaks the naked truth to Faustus, who perforce must cringe before him, slinking back into obedience." (See p. 515 of *Shakespeare's Predecessors in the English Drama,* London, 1924.) On the contrary, it is not the truth which subdues Faustus here or anywhere, but the devil's plausible twisting of it.

[8] *Op. cit.,* III, viii, 166. The *Faust Book* says (chapter xv): "Doctor Faustus parted from his Spirit very pensiue and sorrowful, layd him on his bed, altogether doubtful of the grace and fauor of God, wherefore he fell into fantasticall cogitations: faine he would haue had his soule at liberty again, but the diuel had so blinded him, and taken such deepe roote in his heart, that he could neuer think

to craue Gods mercy, or if by chance hee had any good motion, straightwaies the diuel would thrust him a fayre lady into his chamber, which fell to kissing and dalliance with him, through which means, he threw his goodly motions in the wind, going forward still in his wicked practices to the utter ruine both of his body and soule."

[9] *Institutes,* III, iii, 179 of the Beveridge translation, Edinburgh, 1845.

[10] Calvin, of course, did deny free will in the sense that man could will what was good, for he denied that man after original sin could know good without God's special mercy. Man might choose freely among those acts which appealed to his judgment; but the good was not among them. According to Calvin "original sin necessarily determines the will to evil, but this necessity acts upon the will, not against the will. Grace determines the will to good, but this again is necessary determination, and not involuntary nor coercive." (Quoted from *Theories of the Will in the History of Philosophy* by Archibald Alexander, New York, 1898. See p. 148.)

[11] Perkins in his *Order of the Causes of Salvation and Damnation* says that the assaults of Satan are three-fold: first, the devil blindfolds a man's eyes and hardens his heart that the word of God may not "worke in him to saluation"; second, the devil inspires doubts of God's mercy; third, the devil provokes to sin, "according to the disposition of every man, and as occasion shall offer itselfe." In this last Satan extentuates the sins by urging the eventual accessibility of God's mercy and by hiding the punishment. The flesh and the world are his helpers. When the man falls, Satan aggravates the offence in his mind and enlarges on God's wrath. (See chapters xli, xlii, xliii, p. 86 ff., volume I of the three volume *Workes,* Cambridge, 1609.) Unquestionably all of these causes contributed in the eyes of sixteenth century audiences to Faustus' damnation.

[12] *Op. cit.,* III, iii, 178.

[13] Graf, *op. cit.,* chapter xii.

[14] From Act IV, p. 225 of Pearson's 1874 reprint, which does not indicate scenes.

[15] *Discoverie,* XV, xxxi, 380.

[16] *Op. cit.,* I, vi, 19, 21.

[17] *Ibid.,* II, ii, 32. See also Guazzo, *Compendium Maleficarum,* I, vi, 17.

[18] Many authorities held that threatening and beating witches was the best way to remove their spells. See, for example, Remy, *op. cit.,* III, iii, 143; Guazzo, *op. cit.,* II, xii, 124. The principal anxiety of orthodox authorities in seeking remedies for bewitchments was to avoid superstitious means, which might themselves be taxed as witchcraft. Boguet says (*op. cit.* xxxvii, 115) that even the beating of a witch savors of resort to Satan since it compels her to go to him for remedy, and is not, therefore, a thing to be used. But he adds that he has no objection to a man's bearing himself always proudly and fiercely toward a witch as a deterrent.

[19] Perkins says (*Discourse of Witchcraft,* v, 637): ". . . [the thing] that maketh a Witch to be a Witch: The yeelding of consent upon covenant." This he takes to exempt from witchcraft all who are "through weaknesse of the brain deluded by the deuill. For these, though they may be said after a sort to haue societie with Satan, or rather he with them, yet they cannot giue their consent to use his aide truly, but only in imagination; with the true witch it is far otherwise." This certainly contains the germ of Wier's humane sentiment, but Perkins goes on to insist upon the verity and the guilt of witchcraft, though without a real basis for distinguishing the apparent from the real witchcraft.

[20] But Perkins says (*op. cit.,* vii, 640) that since the covenant with Satan is an "unlawful league" there need not be a "mutual bond," that it is immaterial that the human party is always cheated. Since the compact is not binding as such, it is only the consent that matters. In another place (*The Order of the Causes of Salvation and Damnation,* xxi, 40) he says "They which spread abroad by their writings or otherwise that Witches are nothing else, but melancholike doting women, who through the diuels delusion, suppose that they themselves doe that, which indeed the diuell doth alone: albeit they endeauour cunningly to cloake this sinne, yet by the same meanes they may defend murther, adultery, and what other sinne soeuer."

[21] Gifford, *Dialogue Concerning Witches* . . . H4.

[22] See Remy, *op. cit.*, III, viii, 164; Guazzo, *op. cit.*, II, xiv, 132. Perkins says (*Discourse*, vii, 645) that some witches the devil protects because they have contracted for a term of years, and others that they may spread evil. Perkins agrees with Gifford, however, that since Satan intends only the witches' utter confusion he often gives them up to justice, either that he may the sooner acquire them for hell or that they may be cut short in whatever enjoyment they may derive from his service.

[23] C. E. Whitmore says (page 268 ff. of his *The Supernatural in Tragedy*) that *The Late Lancashire Witches* exploits simple sensationalism and that the witch material in Middleton's play is incidental, whereas *The Witch of Edmonton* is the "real tragedy of witchcraft." These are obvious truths of dramatic treatment that take their rise in part from the point of view the plays assume toward pneumatology.

[24] For an exposition of this see Delrio, *Controverses Magique*, Bk. III, Pt. I, Q. 8, p. 443 ff.; Remy, *op. cit.*, II, vi, 114 and ix, 120. In discussing the sin of the witch, *Malleus Maleficarum* says that so far as her acts are concerned the witch is doubly guilty in that her *maleficia* are evil in two ways: inherently, and in being expressly forbidden of God. Pt. I, Q. 14, p. 74.

[25] This was the final cause with respect to the devil, not, of course, with respect to God's providence. For explanation of why God permitted *maleficia*—to punish the guilty, try the good, generally serve His glory—see Delrio, *op. cit.*, Bk. III, Pt. I, Q. 6, 7.

[26] These are the trivial works of Jonson's Pug, scorned by Lucifer as not damning enough to keep pace with man's developing inclinations. They are the tricks, nevertheless, which got most notice for English witches. The continental prosecutors detail more awesome deeds such as those boasted by Middleton's Hecate.

[27] Gifford, *op. cit.*, L4.

[28] *Ibid.*, M2.

[29] *Discourse of Witchcraft*, v, 643. Perkins attacks not only the thatch burning test but the 'fleeting on the water' test which king James commends specifically.

[30] The source work, Goodcole's *Wonderful Discovery of Elizabeth Sawyer*, attributes the thatch burning test to the Justice himself, does not tell whether or not it was successful. See C. L'Estrange Ewen, *Witchcraft and Demonianism*, p. 237 ff., for a condensed account of the whole affair.

[31] Certainly many of the phenomena of *maleficium* were trivial and *The Witch of Edmonton* is not lacking in these, for example the withholding of butter for all the maid's churning. But even in this the evil is patent in Mother Sawyer's vindictive "Let 'em eat cheese and choke!" Heywood's play runs to trivialities for their own sake. Mrs. Generous once says:

> This night wee'l celebrate to sport:
> 'Tis all for mirth, we mean no hurt.

With her spirits she does indeed present a merry jape; but one quite foreign to the purpose of *maleficium*. This, it is true, is not without pneumatological authority —*Malleus Maleficarum* says (Pt. II, Q. 1, ch. iii, p. 105) that there are certain slightly sinful devils who merely trouble men with practical jokes—but it seems without any integral dramatic purpose.

[32] This is, of course, exceedingly inept. Robin, the servant, was indeed the author of the craft that turned Mrs. Generous to a horse—so far as any human craft was concerned—even as she had previously turned him, and she need not have confessed, but might easily have proclaimed herself a victim. But such ineptitude, of course, is in line with the play's obvious purpose: the simple exploitation of the late sensation from Lancashire. Perhaps it may be said, too, that Mrs. Generous' confession is as sequential as most witch confessions in actual life—statements which Elizabethans received in dead earnest.

[33] See *Malleus Maleficarum*, Pt. II, Q. 1, ch. vii, p. 121; Remy, *op. cit.*, II, v, 111, for the story of St. Macharius and how he recognized as a girl one whom all others, by the delusions of devils, thought a filly.

[34] See Remy, *loc. cit.;* Delrio, *op. cit.*, Bk. II, Q. 18, p. 209. *Malleus Maleficarum* says (Pt. II, Q. 2, ch. iv, p. 174) that the delusion of the subject extended to his bodily faculties, imaginative and perceptive, but not to his reason which yet knew

him for a man essentially. The victim of delusion could perform acts consonant with his illusory shape. Thus werewolves could bring down cattle (Remy, *op. cit.,* II, v, 112) and men shaped as horses carry burdens beyond the strength of men, the devil, of course, helping invisibly. (Le Loyer, *A Treatise of Spectres,* xii, 127.)

35 See Boguet, *op. cit.,* xlvii, 146 and Delrio, *op. cit.,* Bk. II, Q. 18, p. 209.

36 See *Malleus Maleficarum,* Pt. II, Q. 2, ch. iv, p. 174.

37 The witches' gathering, or Sabbat, was not so prominent in English witchcraft as in that of the continent. So far as I know this witches' feast in Act IV of *The Late Lancashire Witches* is the only instance of it in Elizabethan drama, though there are, of course, references to it, as in *The Witch* and *Macbeth.* Nor is the scene in Heywood's play by any means a replica of the picture as Remy *et al.* paint it. The witches indeed feast and dance according to prescription, but the Great Devil who was the central figure at continental Sabbats is missing as, of course, are the more obscene features of the ritual as described by the authorities. One minor characteristic, however, which is according to rule is the lack of salt and savor in the food, which the captive Boy puts aside as tasteless though the witches devour it. Salt, as the symbol of eternity, neither witches nor devils could abide (see Bodin *La Demonomanie,* II, ii, 183). On the unsatisfying quality of witches' banquets see Remy, *op. cit.,* I, xvi. In Middleton's *Witch* Almachides, waking after his banquet with Hecate, says:

> What a mad toy took me to sup with witches!
> Fie of all drunken humours! by this hand,
> I could beat myself when I think on't: and the rascals
> Made me good cheer too; and to my understanding then
> Eat some of every dish, and spoiled the rest:
> But coming to my lodging, I remember
> I was as hungry as a tired foot-post. (II, ii.)

In *The Late Lancashire Witches* there is a further interesting allusion to the Sabbat. Mrs. Generous inquires after the welfare of a companion witch and Mall answers:

> Of one leg
> Shee's growne lame.
> *Mrs. Gen.* Because the beast
> Did miss us last Goodfriday Feast,
> I gest as much.
> *Mall.* But All-Saints night
> She met though she did halt downe right. (IV, p. 235)

This is an obvious reference to the demon's custom of punishing those who dared to miss the nocturnal assembly. See Remy, *op. cit.,* I, xiii, 44.

38 See *Malleus Maleficarum,* Pt. I, Q. 7, 89; Pt. II, Q. 1, ch. vi, vii.

39 For a thorough orthodox treatment of all the ostensible instruments of *maleficium* see Delrio, *op. cit.,* Bk. III, Pt. I, Q. 1–4.

40 On Sycorax and the kind of power she wielded, see Curry, *op. cit.,* p. 166 ff., and p. 177 ff.

41 See *Malleus Maleficarum,* Bk. II, Q. 1, ch. iii, p. 104. Also Margaret A. Murray, *The Witch Cult in Western Europe,* Oxford, 1921, for a modern treatment (discounted by Mr. Summers) and *A Dialogue of Witches* (the 1575 English translation of Lambert Daneau's *Les Sorciers*), G v, for a Protestant mention. The hints in the Canon Episcopi and later writings may be traced in H. C. Lea's *Materials Toward a History of Witchcraft,* Philadelphia, 1939.

42 On these witches see chapter i of Rev. Montague Summers' *Geography of Witchcraft,* New York, 1927. They were not witches at all in the medieval sense of compact, a doctrine not formulated before the twelfth century (see *The Attitude of the Catholic Church toward Witchcraft and the Allied Practices of Sorcery and Magic* by Sister Antoinette Marie Pratt, Washington, 1913); but, as Mr. Summers shows, they had so many things in common with later witches that it is difficult not to identify the two sorts, and would be doubly so with the sixteenth century's two dimensional view of history.

43 *Vanitie of the Artes and Sciences,* xliv, 113.

44 See Summers, *loc. cit.*

[45] *Occult Philosophy,* I, xxxix, 77.

[46] Orthodox authorities were agreed that demons could not compel love, but that they might by application of their powers to the imagination and other parts of man's constitution, strongly incline one to it. See Delrio, *op. cit.,* Bk. III, Pt. I, Q. 3, p. 346; *Malleus Maleficarum,* Bk. I, Q. 7, p. 51; Vair, *Trois Livres des Charmes. . . .* III, ix, 513. For the St. Cyprian legend, which embodies the theme of a virgin resistant to sorcerer's assaults, see Palmer and More, *The Faust Tradition.*

[47] H. W. Herrington, "Witchcraft and Magic in Elizabethan Drama," *Journal of American Folklore,* xxxii, (1919), p. 484.

Notes on Chapter IX

[1] The principal exception, of course, is in the Good and Evil Angels of *Faustus.* On them see *ante,* p. 102 ff.

[2] See J. Dover Wilson, *What Happens in Hamlet,* or for an earlier statement of the same material see his Introduction to the Shakespeare Association reprint of Lavater's *Of Ghosts and Spirits.* Miss Campbell arrived independently at much the same conclusions, states them in her *Shakespeare's Tragic Heroes.*

[3] See W. C. Curry's *Shakespeare's Philosophical Patterns,* p. 84 ff.

[4] See Lily Bess Campbell, "Theories of Revenge in Elizabethan England," *Modern Philology,* xxviii, (1930–31), 281.

[5] Elmer Edgar Stoll, "The Objectivity of the Ghosts in Shakespeare," *PMLA,* xxii (1907), p. 205.

[6] Opposed views were expressed by W. W. Greg in his article, "Hamlet's Hallucination" in the *Modern Language Review,* Oct., 1917, xii. Mr. Greg is dealing specifically with *Hamlet* and does not mention Mr. Stoll's work. Mr. Stoll touches on *Hamlet* only incidentally, holding its ghost to be of a self-evident objectivity.

[7] This point is insisted upon by Miss Campbell in her chapter on "Those Who See Spirits" in her *Shakespeare's Tragic Heroes.*

[8] See his note to the ghost scene in Act II of his edition of Tourneur's play.

[9] I have translated this from the French (which is here appended) of the 1611 *Les Controverses et Recherches Magiques* which is a translation of the *Disquisitionum Magicarum.* I have checked the French against the Latin of the Lyons edition of 1608. The French from Bk. II, Q. 26, sect. ii, p. 250 of the *Controverses* is as follows: "Les anciens ont distingué la Vision du Fantosme. La Vision est, lors que nous pensons premierement voir ce qui puis apres auient ainsi qu'il nous estoit apparu. Le Fantosme, lors que pendant la veille or le sommeil certaines formes & figures se presentent aux yeux de celuy qui pense veiller ou dormir. Nous disputerons aux Liures suiuans de la Vision. Parlons maintenant icy du Fantosme que les Chrestiens ont mieux aimé nommer Apparition: & laquelle est de trois sortes selon sainct Isidore, Scauoir est intellectuelle, imaginaire, & corporelle. L'Apparition intellectuelle est, quand les substances separees viennent à s'insinuer en l'entendement non en forme estrangere, ains en la leur propre: ce qui artiue rarement, & est comme une certaine image de l'eternelle vision des bienheureux, fort eloignée de ce Traité. L'Imaginaire, dite aussi Spirituelle, est, lors que non les esprits corporels, qui seruent aux sens, ainsi que pense Cardan; mais les ames mesmes separées de leurs corps, font repasser certaines formes etrangeres par deuant nostre sentiment interne, au moyen desquelles nous soions conduits & menez à la cognoissance d'icelles. Finalement la Corporelle est, quand tels simulacres sont representez au sens exterieur. Et c'est de ces deux dernieres que nous disputons, & soutenons que ny l'une ny l'autre ne sont contraires aux Loix de la Nature."

The *Vision* here—which may be left out of account for our purposes—is the instrument of highest prophecy and is a foreshowing (rather than a foretelling through a mediary) direct from God of events to come.

[10] I do not intend criticism of Mr. Stoll's use of terms. My purpose is slightly different from his in that whereas he seeks simply to establish that the dramatist's usage was not metaphorical, I investigate just what, within the play world, the

stage figures stand for in the light of pneumatology. Though I prefer not to use for that purpose the terms *objective* and *subjective,* I borrow Mr. Stoll's term *substantive,* and even make of it a noun, *substantivity,* for which only my need, not the dictionary, gives warrant.

[11] See *A Discourse of Devils and Spirits,* xix, 435.

[12] For a brief, thorough analysis of the Aristotelian, medieval faculty psychology upon which all Renaissance pneumatologists depended, see *The Medieval Morality of Wisdom who is Christ* by Joseph C. Green, a doctor's thesis at Vanderbilt University for 1937. Miss Lily Bess Campbell, *op. cit.,* deals with the same material out of sixteenth and seventeenth century sources. Perhaps the most convenient contemporary summary is to be found in Burton's exposition of the anatomy of the soul. See particularly I, I, ii, 6 of *The Anatomy of Melancholy.* On the imagination as a motion of the soul and the genus of Specter and of phantasm, see note 13 *post.*

[13] My usage in these terms rests largely on Le Loyer's, which is not completely in agreement with Delrio's. Le Loyer introduces the term *spectre,* and limits *phantasm* (as Delrio does not) to the groundless apparition. In this, of course, I do not follow him. He says (*A Treatise of Spectres,* 1605, i, 1): "A Specter, or apparition, is an imagination of a substance without a Bodie, the which presenteth itselfe sensibly unto men, against the order and course of nature and maketh them afraid. And not without great reason do I make the Imagination to be the Genus unto a Specter: because the Imagination (according to the iudgment of Themistius) is no other thing, but a motion of the soul, which the sense (being in action) doth create and engender. And forasmuch, as the sight is of all other senses the most excellent, liuely, and actiue: therefore is it, that the Imagination hath sometimes taken the name of a Specter, or strange sight: of a Phantosme, & of a vision. And the Fantasie also, which is formed in the spirit or understanding, hath been called by the name of light: . . . So that the seuerall and speciall kindes of the imagination are, the Specter or strange sight, the Phantosme, the vision & the fantasie. . . . And first of all . . . a Phantosme . . . is an imagination of things which are not indeede, and doth proceede of the senses being corrupted: which Plutarch also doth seeme to confirme: Howbeit that some moderne Physitians doe goe further, and doe confound a Spectre and a Phantosme together, taking both the one and the other for a false vision. The which opinion for my part I cannot allow. . . . Specter is that which our Ciuil Lawyers haue cald and albeith many authors, and namely the holy Scriptures, do take a Phantosme for a Specter, truly appearing unto the sense not corrupt nor deceiued: yet, if we will soundly interpret them, we must say, that they must be understoode to speake according to the vulgar and common opinion, which doth confound the Specter and the Phantosme together: or else that they regarded the properties of spirits, the which do use to take a fantastique or imaginatiue bodie to appear unto us. And to show yet further, what difference there is betweene them both: certaine it is, that a Phantosme is a thing without life, and without substance: and the Specter hath a substance hidden and concealed, which seemeth to moue the fantastique body, the which it hath taken."

By *vision* Le Loyer seems to mean, like Delrio, a special prophetic visitation vouchsafed from God, and by *fantasie* simply the images of the uncorrupted fancy.

[14] See Charles Edward Whitmore, *The Supernatural in Tragedy,* Cambridge, 1915, p. 217, ff.

[15] I take this last title from the Malone reprint of the play.

[16] I do not attempt to name, much less to discuss, every ghost play in Elizabethan drama. For a list no doubt complete of ghost plays see Karl Ankenbrand, *Die Figur des Geistes im Drama die Englischen Renaissance,* Leipzig, 1906.

[17] My citations from this play are from the Mermaid edition.

[18] Le Loyer in his preliminary concessions to the rationalists confesses (*op. cit.,* vi, 56) that the sight may be abused when the air is overcast with storm and that the "darkness and obscuritie of the night, wherein both fear, & and the deception and dimnesse of the sight, and the obtusion of the other senses . . . do cause marvellous effects of false visions, of phantosms, & of fearfull terrours," is potent with the bravest.

[19] *A Treatise of Ghosts,* xvi, 113.

[20] The scene of the first two apparitions offers in its obvious play for suspense before the second and—to Charlemont—convincing apparition, a dramaturgical confirmation of the ghost. But this is, perhaps, not allowable as evidence here.

[21] The only other argument for the insubstantiality of the wraith in *The Atheist's Tragedy* is found in the speech of the scoundrelly Puritan chaplain, Langbeau Snuffe. He says that ghosts are "mere imaginary fables. There's no such thing in *rerum natura.*" (IV, iii.) But the play does not present him as a person to be credited. He is allied to the materialistic atheist, D'Amville, and he has earlier, in his fright at the appearance of Charlemont, supposed dead, given evidence of his belief in demonic, if not in ghostly, apparition.

[22] See note 8 *ante.*

[23] Save that Guendoline says (V, iv of the edition in Tucker Brooke's *Shakespeare Apocrypha*) that her father's ghost has haunted her for revenge.

[24] The stage figure represents, indeed, a phantasm, an object in the imagination, but of what nature is yet to prove. It may be, as Professor Stoll believes, that the stage figure signifies substantivity, that its presentation conforms to a stage convention for such signification. But the surmise of such a convention is itself a thing on trial here. Mr. Greg, at least, does not in his article on *Hamlet* (see *ante,* note 6) agree that the convention is such. Professor Stoll says that Elizabethan dramatists never make the audience "a prey to a delusion" (*op. cit.,* p. 200). This may be generally true, yet have no application here. Let the figure be taken as one will, it yet represents a phantasm limited to the inner senses. The Elizabethans would not, perhaps, consider themselves deluded simply because there remained an open question which no subsequent action answered as to whether the phantasm is natural or supernatural. It must be remembered that the contemporary idea on "delusion" was itself vague. The phantasm which represented a spirit was, in current usage, quite as much a "delusion" as that which was a groundless hallucination.

[25] *Op. cit.,* p. 221, footnote.

[26] I have used the Mermaid edition of this play.

[27] Le Loyer says (*op. cit.,* xi, 112) that such men as are "guilty of some notable and notorious crime," have "a biting and remorce of conscience within their breasts," are afflicted with "phantosmes" (in his meaning, self-induced hallucination—see *ante,* note 13); and he names tyrants and murderers so afflicted. Also: ". . . such persons as by some sodaine griefe, or by a burning and intollerable iealousie . . . do fall into frensie & madness . . . do see many false Specters, and do entertaine a thousand furious imaginations. . . ." (xi, 115.)

[28] *Ibid.,* p. 220.

[29] *Op. cit.,* Bk. II, Q. 26, sect. iii, p. 258.

[30] The rubric "ghost" does not by any means settle the matter, for the term was used loosely even by pneumatologists, and as a rubric it may be taken simply to signify an apparition in the image of the man named. The apparition of Banquo is labelled his "ghost"; yet Professor Curry demonstrates that it may be best taken as the work of the fiends who had beset Macbeth. (See Curry, *op. cit.,* p. 84 ff.) Phantasms that may be groundless are often labelled "ghosts."

[31] Le Loyer says (*Discours et Histoires des Spectres,* IV, i, 279) that it is the business of devils to give murderers a foretaste of hell. Mother Sawyer's dog is not behindhand.

[32] Bodin says (*La Demonomanie,* II, iii, 204) that when a murdered person dies without appetite for vengeance his soul does not pursue the murderer, though otherwise it may.

[33] See p. 121.

[34] "Objectivity of the Ghosts in Shakespeare," *PMLA,* xxii, (1907), 209, 210.

[35] *Ibid.,* pp. 229, 211.

[36] This idea of a feud after death was first presented to English audiences says Mr. Whitmore (*op. cit.,* p. 218) in *The Spanish Tragedy,* won instant favor. *Locrine* and *The Battle of Alcazar* are other plays I know of which have similar passages.

[37] *Op. cit.,* p. 244–5.

[38] "Theories of Revenge in Elizabethan England," *Modern Philology,* xxviii (1930–31), p. 296.

[39] *Occult Philosophy,* III, xli, 481.

[40] *Ibid.,* III, xxviii, 435.

[41] Apuleius in *The God of Socrates* makes a simple and clear statement of distinctions between the various classes of *daemons* according to the Greek conception. See the translation in *Bohn's Libraries* by Thomas White with notes by Thomas Taylor.

[42] *Op. cit.,* Bk. II, Q. 26, sect. iii, pp. 258–60. Taillepied, however, says (*op. cit.,* xviii, 123) that "These angels who are our Guardians, most certainly can and do appear, but in my opinion they never manifest themselves as though they were disembodied spirits, or to be taken for ghosts."

[43] *Op. cit.,* Bk. II, Q. 26, sect. ii, p. 251. He says he prefers to call *animas separatas* what the pagans denominate *umbras.* The French translation renders the Latin literally for both terms.

[44] See *ante,* pp. 75, 90, 122, 134.

[45] Whitmore says (*op. cit.,* pp. 240–3) that the *umbra* was an afterthought induced by the favor Marston's ghosts found with the public, and performed no function that the Friar might not have performed alive. Professor Parrott, however, finds artistic justification for at least the killing of the Friar in the effect of it on Tamyra, and lauds Chapman's fine touch here. However these things may be, the *umbra* seems in line with the rest of the supernatural in Chapman's plays: circumstantially presented, somewhat hollowly conceived so far as pneumatological background is concerned.

[46] These lines appear only in the quarto of 1607 and Professor Parrott relegates them to the notes in his edition. The Mermaid edition by Professor W. L. Phelps has them, but at an earlier place than the quarto does.

[47] *Op. cit.,* xxii, 148.

[48] *Op. cit.,* V, vi, 508 ff.

[49] *Ibid.,* V, vi, 516. See also Apuleius, *op. cit.,* on *manes, larvae* and other classes of separated spirits. For a modern summary: Lacy Collison-Morley, *Greek and Roman Ghost Stories,* London, 1912, p. 11 ff. The *Aeneid,* of course, is also illuminating.

[50] *Occult Philosophy,* III, xli, 475.

[51] The "spirit" here Agrippa seems to take as virtually synonymous with the guardian angel, always faultless and the conductor of the soul.

[52] *Ibid.,* III, xli, 476.

[53] Truly there exist so many discrepancies between *Bussy* and its sequel that one more is no great matter. And perhaps under my general method I am unjustified in treating the worlds of the two plays as though they were the same. But on the other hand, *The Revenge* does make the profession of continuity and for purposes of appreciation of it as fiction the profession ought to be accepted as far as possible.

I am aware, too, that the Friar's speech is figurative, poetic rather than reportorial. But as editors Parrott and Boas have cast light on it by proper classical references, I think it cannot be amiss to give a reference a little nearer contemporary by way of recalling how literal the Renaissance might sometimes be in its following of ancient doctrine.

[54] This resembles the Stoic doctrine—quite fitting in Clermont's mouth—that the passive principle in a man, the only part individual to him, persisted for a time as a diaphonous material form about the spot where the body lay, whereas the active principle, or reason, was re-absorbed into the universal, there to exist until the cosmic cycle had run its course and all things were recreated. (See C. H. Moore, *Ancient Beliefs in the Immortality of the Soul,* New York, 1931.) Professor Parrott compares *Phaedo,* 81, but notes that Plato is there "speaking only of the souls of the wicked, 'dragged down by the corporeal element.'" It resembles too, of course, in a general way many other kindred doctrines all the way from primitive animism to Buddhism. The idea of the sidereal body, the vestigial shape of the decayed elementary body, which either drifted of itself or was guided by some extraneous possessing power about the scenes of its vital existence was

widespread in the sixteenth century though not acceptable to the orthodox. Paracelsus, who held man constituted of seven principles (amazingly agreeable, say the authorities, to the seven principles according to Buddhism), explained that the sidereal body "carries about with it the thoughts and the heart of the dead man," hence automatically pursues for awhile those things in which his interest lay. (See Waite's translation of the *Hermetic and Alchemical Works of Paracelsus,* vol. II, pp. 303, 285. Hartman's *Paracelsus* gives extracts from the sage's works on anthropology and pneumatology. See p. 68 of the first edition for the constitution of man according to Paracelsus, and its correspondence to Buddhism. For the same thing from the point of view of the Buddhist see A. P. Sinnett, *Esoteric Buddhism,* sixth edition, p. 65.) An explanation of apparition similar to Paracelsus' and more prominently noticed by disputants on the matter in the sixteenth century was that of Pomponazzi, who in his eagerness to bring all phenomena under the aegis of Nature attributed apparitions and the works of magic wholly to the power of the stars. (See A. H. Douglas, *The Philosophy of Pomponazzi,* Cambridge, 1910.)

[55] Agrippa says (*op. cit.,* III, xliv, 496): "The minde (*mens*), because it is from God or from the intelligible world, is therefore immortal and eternal; but reason (*ratio*) is long lived by the benefit of its celestial original from the Heaven; but the sensitive [soul] (*idolum*) because it is from the bosome of the matter and dependeth on sublunary nature, is subject to destruction and corruption: therefore the soul by its minde is immortall, by its Reason long lived in its etherial vehicle, but resolvable unless it be restored in the circuit of its new body; therefore it is not immortal, unless it be united to an immortal mind; therefore the sensitiveness of the soul or the sensitive or animal soul (*ita idolum animae, siue ipsa sensibilis & animalis anima*), because it is produced out of the bosome of a corporeal matter, the body being resolved perisheth together with it, or the shadow thereof remaineth not long in the vapours of its resolved body, partaking nothing of immortality, unless it be also united to a more sublimed power . . ."

All of this, Agrippa seems in the next line or two to attribute to Trismegistos. Dr. W. C. Curry has pointed out to me a passage from Trismegistos that is almost identical with Clermont's speech: "And the soul of man is vehicled thus: The mind has for its vehicle the soul; the soul has for its vehicle the vital spirit; and the vital spirit, transversing the arteries together with the blood, moves the body, and carries it like a burden. Hence some have thought that the soul is the blood. But those who think this are mistaken as to its nature; they do not know that at death the soul must quit the body first and then, when the vital spirit has withdrawn into the atmosphere, the blood must coagulate along the course of the veins, and leave the arteries emptied. This is the death of the body . . ." (See *Hermetica,* edited and translated by Walter Scott, Oxford, 1924, *Libellus* X, 13. Dr. Curry cites also 16, 17, 18, and 11 of *Libellus* X.) It is quite possible that Chapman knew this very passage from Trismegistos, for Ficino's translation had been many times reprinted and was widely read in England. For my purposes the immediate source is less important than the general form and meaning of the doctrine and its place in a rationale of ghosts.

[56] I have used Bullen's edition of this play in *The Works of John Marston.*

[57] For a concise statement of such reasons see Delrio, *op. cit.,* Bk. II, Q. 26, sect. iii, pp. 254–6.

[58] In *Hamlet* Horatio, the learned sceptic, adjures the ghost:

> If there be any good thing to be done,
> That may to thee do ease and grace to me,
> Speak to me.

But the ghost, though he later professes to be from purgatory, does not ask either of Horatio or of Hamlet the help purgatorial ghosts were said by Catholics to seek. Horatio in his adjuration gives equal notice to the occult theory of ghost-motive:

> Or if thou hast uphoarded in thy life
> Extorted treasure in the womb of earth,
> For which, they say, you spirits oft walk in death,
> Speak of it . . . (I, ii)

On the treasure-guarding ghost, see Paracelsus, Waite's translation, *op. cit.,* vol. II, pp. 285, 303.

[59] *Op. cit.,* p. 203.

[60] On the reasons for ghosts according to Catholicism see Delrio as cited in note 57 *ante.* Only occasionally and reluctantly do Catholic writers mention the function of vengeance (see Taillepied, *op. cit.,* xvii, 117); but their examples contain instances of revenge ghosts. Bodin (*op. cit.,* II, iii, 204) even seems to state an explicit adherence to the doctrine cited in Plato's *Laws* that the souls of the murdered often pursue the murderers. Most other Catholic writers seem to cite this as but a pagan opinion on which they will not pronounce further than to say that it aids to establish the fact of return.

[61] Aquinas says that souls may return from hell (*Summa,* Pt. III, [supplement] Q. 69, A. 3) and Taillepied agrees (*op. cit.,* xii, 73), citing a story of a damned soul which returned to warn others. Le Loyer, however, says explicitly (*op. cit.,* VI, vii, 590) that the damned cannot leave hell, never appear to men. Delrio is of the same opinion, *op. cit.,* Bk. II, Q. 26, sect. iii, p. 257.

[62] *Op. cit.,* p. 203.

[63] *Op. cit.,* p. 4.

[64] Stoll, *op. cit.,* p. 204, traces two lines of dramatic tradition for ghosts. One, originating with *Locrine* and running "down through Massinger to the end of the drama," is of ghosts who appear to the offender; the other, beginning with Kyd and running down through *Hamlet, Antonio's Revenge, The Revenge of Bussy, The Atheist's Tragedy* to Webster's *White Devil* is of ghosts who appear to the revenger.

[65] See, for instance, Scot (*Discourse of Devils,* i, 411) on this. He quotes Cardan (*de. var. rer.* 16. cap. 93) that belief in spirits is corollary to that in immortality of the soul. Scot, of course, makes reservations, but only as to the appearing of spirits, not as to their existence.

[66] *Op. cit.,* III, xli, 476.

[67] The continued interest of the separated soul in its body was, of course, a widespread article of pagan belief and one adopted by sixteenth century occultists. Agrippa says (*op. cit.,* III, xlii, 488): ". . . it is manifest that souls after death do yet love their body which they left, as those souls do whose bodies want a due buriall. . . ." For another and perhaps more appropriate dramatic use of the idea of posthumous defilement, see Marston's *Sophonisba* V, i, 58, where Syphax threatens to vex Sophonisba's soul, if she kills herself, by the lustful use of her dead body.

[68] *Op. cit.,* III, xl, 475. See, too, Pictorius.

[69] *Op. cit.,* p. 274.

[70] The first appearance of Andrugio's ghost in Marston's *Antonio's Revenge* has certain elements of necromancy. Antonio has resorted to the tomb and has purefied the air "with odorous fume." In these two things his procedure meets with that of necromancy. Agrippa says (*op. cit.,* III, xlii, 489) that burial places are especially suited to necromancy and that vapors and perfumes, among other means, are useful to lure the spirits forth. But Agrippa's language seems to indicate that he means the common burying place of criminals or other unfortunates, would not have admitted the possibility of necromancy in a church.

[71] As Ward says (*History of English Dramatic Literature to the Death of Queen Anne,* vol. I, p. 394), *Alphonsus* "presents a noble confusion of the association of different religious systems, subjugated by a free use of allusions derived from Graeco-Roman mythology."

Index